As Good As It Gets

As Good As It Gets

What School Reform
Brought to Austin

Larry Cuban

Harvard University Press
Cambridge, Massachusetts
London, England
2010

Library of Congress Cataloging-in-Publication Data

Cuban, Larry

As good as it gets : what school reform brought to Austin / Larry Cuban.

p.   cm.

Includes bibliographical references and index.

ISBN 978-0-674-03554-6 (alk. paper)

1. School management and organization—Texas—Austin—History.
2. Educational change—Texas—Austin—History.   3. Educational leadership—Texas—Austin—History.   4. Educational achievement—Texas—Austin—History.   I. Title.

LB2802.A87 2010

371.2′0709764252—dc22   2009035218

For Barbara

1937–2009

The love of my life

Contents

As Good As It Gets

Introduction

In May 2007, forty firefighters and two helicopters, dumping water from the air, worked to put out a fire in a 5,000-plus-acre peat bog near Vancouver, Canada. A peat bog is wet spongy ground formed from centuries old-rotting moss and other plants. The soil is unfit for farming but can be cut, dried, and used for fuel. As compressed carbon—bogs can become coal if other factors come into play—peat can burn on the surface and underground as well. Peat bog fires are tough to fight because the fire can "smolder underground and pop up unexpectedly when one area is extinguished." Moreover, escaping methane gas and deep sinkholes are potential dangers to fire crews. Firefighters established a perimeter around the Vancouver fire within a few hours, and helicopters scooped water from a nearby lake to douse hot spots. Only one firefighter was injured.[1]

In addition to unexpected flare-ups, these bogs have yielded other surprises as well. In England and elsewhere, people have dug up thousand-year-old bronzed bodies preserved by the chemicals formed from the decomposing plants.[2]

These features illustrate a point I wish to make about school reform in large U.S. cities since the mid-twentieth century. In both bogs and cities, the past is too often ignored until fires and cadavers appear. In urban school systems, layers upon layers of historical events, including school reforms, are compressed into social, political, and organizational patterns that inescapably influence current actions—yet those effects may be unseen, like buried bodies and underground fires.

In the early 1900s, the nation's major cities found themselves dealing with an influx of hundreds of thousands of immigrants. This new population spoke scores of different languages and crowded the schools, which often had to cope with classes of more than fifty students. Minimally trained teachers struggled to deal with children who lived in poverty and who learned English on the streets.

By the 1920s, educational progressives had broadened the goals for schooling to include the intellectual, physical, emotional, and social development of children. Schools now had lunchrooms and gyms, and suites where doctors and dentists could examine the children. Progressive-minded school boards set standards for teachers and principals and created age-graded elementary schools and junior high schools with curricula aimed at preparing children for civic duties and a variety of careers. These reformers brought order, efficiency, new structures, and expanded roles for big-city schools in shaping children and society. Within a few decades, progressive ideas about school organization, curriculum, and classroom lessons had become established concepts among urban educators and the norm for how good schools assimilate immigrants while teaching the "whole child."[3]

In the 1920s and 1930s, large urban districts such as New York

City, Chicago, Boston, and Denver had become leaders of educational progressivism. Parents with children moved into urban neighborhoods, seeking the best schools. In these schools, staff made dollar-saving efficiencies while offering a rich array of medical, dental, recreational, and social services. In classrooms, teachers used the language of active learning, projects, field trips, real-world problem solving, and interdisciplinary concepts. Bulletin boards and curriculum guides overflowed with the vocabulary of progressivism. These urban schools became a mecca for visitors near and far.[4]

By the mid-1950s, however, poor rural migrants and another generation of immigrants had poured into cities just as World War II veterans took their middle-class families to seek homes in newly built suburbs. Businesses vacated downtowns for suburban malls. Churches and synagogues pulled up stakes and bought empty tracts of land for larger congregations near housing developments. City neighborhoods deteriorated as impoverished families, many displaced by "urban renewal" projects, also searched for a better life. Many schools became racially segregated and viewed learning as secondary to maintaining order. Those very same progressive urban schools that had attracted middle-class children were now being portrayed in films and newspapers as gang-infested places where little learning occurred. High dropout rates and increased juvenile delinquency captured headlines. By 1960, for example, 75 percent of the public elementary schools in Manhattan were black and Puerto Rican. The movement of people both into and out of cities altered the demography of urban schools for the next half-century.[5]

These changes in social geography occurred at the same time that Americans' vision of a good life shifted from living in densely packed neighborhoods to having one's own home, a lawn, backyard barbecues, and a new school down the street. In a few decades, suburban schools had become the model of excellence and urban schools had become a nightmare for parents and civic leaders.

In the South at this time, decades-old legal segregation and a tradition-crusted caste system kept blacks as second-class citizens and social inferiors in rural and urban areas. Largely white suburbanization was just beginning in northern Virginia, Louisville, Charlotte, and Atlanta. Further west, in Texas, a tripartite system of segregated schools and public facilities kept both blacks and increasing numbers of Mexican Americans separate from whites.[6]

As middle-class white families and poor minority families in public schools followed different trajectories, reform, beginning in the 1950s and continuing for the next half-century, swept across public schools every few years, often pushed by national policy leaders who saw fixing schools as part of the solution to urgent political, social, and economic problems.

Courses in driver education, sex education, and the dangers of substance abuse, for example, are not put into the curriculum by chance. All were developed because civic, business, and religious leaders asked schools in the 1950s and 1960s to deal with serious social problems, such as automobile accidents, drug addiction, and teenage pregnancy. They pressed schools to solve these problems, rather than acting through political channels to change the way cars were manufactured, to reduce illegal drug supply and demand, and to rein in movies and television programs that put a glossy sheen on premarital sex. Historians of education have often pointed to this "educationalizing" of societal problems.[7]

The educationalizing of social problems—the process of making it transparent that schools are, indeed, political institutions—also extended to national defense. Increasing discontent with progressive education became wrapped up in Cold War rhetoric and the U.S. response to the Soviets' launch of the Sputnik satellite in 1957. Attacks on low academic standards in schools and fear of Communist domination of space mutated into an education crisis: U.S. schools were seen as graduating insufficient scientists and engineers to compete with a resurgent Soviet empire. Reformers called for tougher math and science courses and better-trained teachers. Soon afterward, in 1958, President Dwight D. Eisenhower signed the landmark National Education Defense Act. It provided federal funds to attract college students to careers in engineering, science, and foreign languages and supported summer institutes training better math and science teachers.[8]

At about the same time, the civil rights movement, fueled by *Brown v. Board of Education*, drew attention to southern segregated public accommodations, biased criminal justice, housing discrimination, and widespread academic failure among blacks in both northern and southern schools. To expand equality of opportunity, President Lyndon Johnson signed the Civil Rights Act (1964) and the Elementary and Secondary Education Act (1965) in an effort to end racial discrimination and break the link between poverty and academic underachievement in schools.[9]

Urban school reform in the 1950s and 1960s—spurred by the inmigration of minorities and by civil rights actions in the North and South—aimed at "culturally deprived" children and youth (later called "disadvantaged" and "at-risk" students) and prompted curricular, instructional, organizational, and governance changes in big cities across the nation. These initiatives sought to promote equal opportunity and academic excellence among poor and minority children.[10]

Better schools not only became solutions to demographic, foreign, and social problems but also alleviated economic slumps. Recessions in the 1970s and accelerated global competition with Germany and

Japan led to fears in the early 1980s that schools had failed to produce graduates who could compete in a postindustrial society. Schools, reformers argued, had to be more in sync with the demands of a growing economy in a fiercely competitive world, especially when other nations were trouncing U.S. students on international science and math tests. Reformers then and reformers now sing from the same hymnbook: school critics in the early twenty-first century point to the way Chinese and Indian engineers and entrepreneurs are edging out U.S. companies in market competition.[11]

These attempts by policy elites[12] in Washington, state capitals, and city halls since the 1950s to solve such national problems by fixing broken public schools moved each generation of reformers to design educational initiatives that were soon replaced by another, equally fervent generation of leaders cocksure that their policy agendas would solve those problems. This piling up of hodgepodge reforms spurred by external political and social pressures is apparent especially in urban districts where demands for improved student academic performance in largely minority and poor schools date back decades.

The argument that U.S. public schooling is broken and in need of repair has been heard again and again but consistently since the *Nation at Risk* report appeared in 1983. With increased awareness among policy elites that the future workforce will be far more ethnically and racially diverse than existed in mid-twentieth-century America, deep concerns over high school graduates' skill levels for an information-based economy have ratcheted up demands on states and urban districts to reduce the test score achievement gap between minorities and whites, rescue minority and immigrant students from chronic low-performing schools, send more well-prepared high school graduates to college, and, afterward, have them smoothly enter an ever-changing labor market.[13]

Yet policy elites are split over how much schools can do by themselves to achieve what appear to be compatible values of equity and academic excellence.[14] For decades, many influential policy brokers, civic leaders, and academics—both political conservatives and liberals—have rejected the idea that the problems of schools are attributable to poverty, racially isolated neighborhoods, and disadvantaged families. They insist that underperforming schools occur because of district organizations' misplaced incentives for teachers and principals, mismanaged bureaucracies, unmotivated staff, and lack of accountability. Or, as one group of urban reformers recently put it, "The sad reality is that these systems are not broken. Rather, they are doing what we have designed them to do over time. The systems were not designed with the goal of student learning first." Instead, such reformers say, urban schools are adult-run preserves where privilege-protecting administrators and teachers' union contracts ensure that the status quo persists. If new structures and incentives were put in place, if parents had broader choices among schools, and if responsibility for students' performance clearly fell on those in authority, including teachers, staff would work harder and smarter to see that students learned and achievement gaps between minorities and whites would disappear.[15]

In short, reform rhetoric says that fixing the schools is a tough job but one that can achieve both equity and excellence if it has strong leaders who value efficiency. Staff members who treasure the status quo should be reassigned to no-nonsense schools that will direct students to learn more and better than they ordinarily would in undemanding settings. Michelle Rhee, chancellor of the Washington, D.C., school system, told teachers: "You have to be willing to take personal responsibility for ensuring your children are successful despite obstacles." No excuses accepted. "You cannot say, 'My students didn't get breakfast today' or 'Their electricity got cut off in the house so they couldn't do their homework.'"[16]

In the 1980s, efficiency-minded reformers pointed to high-achieving urban elementary schools that were then called Effective Schools; now these reformers single out high-flying public schools and charters such as the Knowledge Is Power Program (KIPP), the University Park Campus School in Worcester, Mass., Amistad Academy in New Haven, Conn., and private schools catering to the same population, such as East Side Prep in East Palo Alto, Calif., and the Christo Rey Jesuit high schools.[17]

The message these schools send is clear: Don't blame poverty or family background. Well-run and demanding schools can improve poor children's lives by focusing on academics and behavior. Current socioeconomic status is not destiny. If you imagine policy activists arrayed along an urban school reform continuum, this "Effective Schools and Districts" crowd will be at one end.

Other policy elite reformers, also fervently committed to reducing inequalities and boosting academic progress for urban children, view the problem of big-city schooling differently. These reformers—both political liberals and conservatives—are at the other end of the urban school reform continuum. Their rhetoric dwells on the half-century of research studies that have documented again and again the strong link between families' low socioeconomic status and children's low academic achievement: many five-year-olds enter school unprepared to learn. These reformers have argued for an expanded concept of education where both in-school improvement strategies and out-of-school connections with family and community institutions are jointly pursued. These reformers insist, "There is no evidence that school improvement strategies *by themselves* can close these gaps in a substantial, consistent, and sustainable manner. But there is solid evidence that

policies aimed directly at education-related social and economic disadvantages can improve school performance and student achievement."
Thus, such reformers claim that a dual-track strategy of strong school
improvement efforts wedded to high-quality early childhood and preschool programs, health-targeted services, parent education, and attention to how children and youth spend their time after school and
during summers is essential for the education of the whole child—
academic learning, character formation, good health, and civic development. Such a community-driven strategy, these reformers say, can
get at the roots of low academic performance and weaken the hereto-
fore strong link between socioeconomic status and achievement.[18]

A long history of community-based schools can be traced to urban
progressives working in big cities since the early twentieth century,
when the school became a center for medical attention, social services,
recreation, and adult education. The Mott Foundation in Michigan
began developing community centers in schools in the 1930s and remains active in supporting such ventures. Since the late 1960s, School
Development Program schools (also called Comer schools, after Yale
child psychiatrist James Comer) have reached out to parents and community members to foster academic achievement. More recently, the
president of the American Federation of Teachers and other community and school leaders have formed the Coalition for Community Schools (also supported by the Mott Foundation), which fur-
thers academic improvement by building strong links between schools
and community-based services. Call these reformers the "Improved
Schools and Community" crowd.[19]

No surprise, then, that each subsequent generation of reformers in
these coalitions lodged at either end of the continuum were joined by
individuals and groups of reformers who hugged the middle between
the two poles. These reformers, including those running for high po-

litical office with a school reform agenda in their portfolio, borrowed language and programs from different groups to create mixes of both approaches. In the 1980s and 1990s, however, reform-minded groups ranged back and forth along that continuum, uncertain of their agenda and what they wanted.

Frederick Hess's *Spinning Wheels*, a book on urban school reform, captures these decades of business-inspired reformers and superintendents in big cities as they innovated, reorganized, and restructured schools. The "policy churn" of reform after reform, Hess concludes, was largely symbolic and ultimately reinforced the status quo. He presents a damning indictment of the layers of reform laid down over many years, saying that such efforts were little more than political theater where the actors shouted their lines yet left little trace of their performance. They did, however, establish patterns for the strategies used to repair broken schools.

Since the 1980s, urban district leaders in concert with business and civic elites have hammered out generic reform strategies aimed at grasping the competing values of equity and academic excellence:

- Fix the system by changing the racial, ethnic, and socioeconomic mix of children;
- Fix the system by altering governance of schools, streamlining bureaucracies, installing whole-school reform models, improving principal and teacher performance, and holding staff and students accountable for achievement;
- Disrupt the system with market-driven competition from without and within through vouchers, charter schools, and similar ventures;
- Use various combinations of these strategies.

These different reform strategies and the inspired words that accompanied these plans have rallied business-oriented billionaires, networks of politically liberal and conservative policy entrepreneurs, state and federal officials, and street-wise reformers to overhaul broken public schools and prepare graduates for an ever-changing workplace while reducing social and economic inequalities. Working within these strategies, current "Effective Schools and Districts" and "Improved Schools and Community" reformers exert pressure on low-performing schools.[20]

Fixing urban schools by changing the mix of the students who attend them (transferring students from school to school) reached a peak in the 1960s and 1970s, with racial desegregation policies initially launched by the U.S. Supreme Court and pursued by federal officials who took districts to court in order to implement those judicial rulings. Segregated schools were closed; new structures (such as metropolitan districts composed of large attendance areas) were introduced; schools that were largely black were paired with those that were largely white; and busing was instituted in many places. By the 1980s, however, opposition to desegregation, particularly busing children from their neighborhoods to racially isolated schools, allied parents and politicians in the effort to end desegregation court orders in city after city. The success of Republicans in defeating busing and returning to neighborhood schools led to a sharp increase in racially and ethnically segregated schools in urban districts. In these years, new presidential appointments to the U.S. Supreme Court added up to a majority of justices increasingly hostile to the practice of using racial categories to create more balanced mixes of students in schools. They proclaimed the U.S. Constitution to be color-blind.[21]

Even though federal court decisions show a pronounced trend away from structural remedies for school inequity, research on the effects of racial desegregation has accumulated sufficiently to persuade many academics and some local decision makers that mixing children can yield academic excellence and equity.

Over time, many studies have demonstrated strong links between racial and socioeconomic integration of students and improved academic and nonacademic gains (for example, those adults who experienced desegregated schools developed positive attitudes toward differences in ethnicity, race, and class in the workplace, in church, in civic engagement, and in the choice of mates). Recent efforts to bring together students from different socioeconomic backgrounds in a few districts such as LaCrosse, Wisc., Raleigh, N.C., and Cambridge, Mass., are variants of racial and ethnic desegregation and further confirmation that who goes to school with whom indeed matters. However, the vast majority of urban districts now use (and have used) neighborhood schools to enroll children, a fact that has resulted in increases in school segregation because most cities have been residentially segregated. Few elected policy makers have been willing to push for racial or socioeconomic integration in the face of strong political support for neighborhood schools and judicial opposition to non–color blind remedies. So by 2009, the strategy of improving schools by changing the makeup of school populations was seldom advocated by policy elites in either the "Effective Schools and Districts" or the "Improved Schools and Community" group.[22]

A second strategy to mend big-city systems became popular with policy makers, especially those in the "Effective Schools and Districts" band. These reformers wanted to fix schools by changing school governance, picking better superintendents, jolting bureaucracies, inviting education entrepreneurs to work in districts, challenging unions, getting field-tested reform models into schools, and holding staff and students accountable for achievement. Change district politics, organizational structures, and key actors, advocates said.

Urban policy elites sought just the right CEO-type superintendent and copied "best practices" from the business world as they unrelentingly pursued better management and efficient operations. In various cities, reformers changed governance structures, instituting either mayoral control or ward election of school board members. They established standards-based curricula, accountability regulations, and achievement testing, while providing more parental choices among schools. They sought models that would change traditional high schools and age-graded schools. They welcomed business-minded entrepreneurs in the effort to recruit teachers and principals and innovate programs. And some urban district leaders cobbled together these various reforms into school improvement agendas.[23]

All of these efforts aimed at altering classroom instruction and lifting student achievement. Reform efforts would flare up in a city as new superintendents roared through the schools, leaving staff spent after a few years. Then another wave of reforms would burst on the scene with the arrival of yet another superintendent eager to apply a "code blue" to a dying patient.

Since the early 1990s, champions of the third strategy, "disrupt the schools"—including idealistic entrepreneurs who had Masters of Business Administration degrees but little experience in urban schools —sought to expand the menu of schools (magnets, charters, models run by for-profit companies, and so on) from which parents could choose.

These entrepreneurial-driven reformers brought in companies such as EdisonLearning, Inc., and charter management organizations such as Green Dot, KIPP, and Achievement First, to run schools. They wanted to create a competitive market within the district where parents-as-customers could choose among the best schools for their sons and daughters—schools that would be held to the same standards as every other public school. They also wanted to change the work rules and salary schedules that governed teachers' daily schedules and compensation. They pressed for changes in union contracts, to give managers more flexibility in dealing with mediocre staff and in paying teachers and principals on the basis of performance.[24]

The idea was that a public school system was a quasi-monopoly that squelched natural competition and strangled teacher and principal initiatives, leaving parents with few alternatives from which to choose. If parents had options within the system and if principals and staffs had more autonomy to run these schools, then competition among schools for better student performance would lead to innovations and academic gains, in turn attracting parents to higher-achieving schools. This political and organizational logic lay behind the strategy of disrupting the system.

Many business-oriented reformers bridged these strategies. They talked about overhauling district governance, picking smart leaders to better manage bureaucracies, and ensuring that rigorous curriculum standards were in place. They wanted noneducators, non–university-trained teachers, and principals to enliven classrooms and schools. They wanted to establish a broader choice of schools, introduce incentives and flexible work rules that would induce teachers and principals to focus on standards and performance, and, most significantly, hold political leaders and staff accountable for students' test performance.

For many ardent reformers, using these strategies to fix broken schools depended upon first shocking the system. For example, Ross Perot, a Texas school reformer and business executive, said in 1992: "We got to drop a bomb on them, we got to nuke them—that's the way to make changes in these organizations." And Alan Bersin, a former federal district attorney and San Diego city school superintendent, said in the late-1990s: "You've got to jolt a system, and if people don't understand you're serious about change in the first six months, the bureaucracy will own you. The bureaucracy will defeat you at every turn if you give it a chance."[25]

Whatever the metaphor, getting the attention of resistant bureaucrats and educators was the first order of business before extensive changes could be made inside the organization and then within schools and classrooms. Reformers used top-down strategies; they picked smart, politically savvy superintendents and gave them full authority—often calling them CEOs—to make wholesale changes. For example, Boston's mayor, Tom Menino, selected experienced superintendent Tom Payzant in 1995; Chicago's mayor appointed his budget director, Paul Vallas, to the post in 1995; Adrian Fenty, mayor of Washington, D.C., chose the entrepreneurial Michelle Rhee, a graduate of Teach for America, as chancellor in 2007. And some reformers combined strategies in particular districts, such as the "small high school" initiative funded by the Bill and Melinda Gates Foundation.[26]

These strategies, driven by policy elites and donors and adopted pell-mell by besieged educators, took it for granted that these lofty-sounding plans would produce organizational and political structures that would somehow transform how teachers teach and students learn in ways that would increase academic achievement, narrow the gap in test scores between minorities and whites, bring English-language learners into the academic mainstream, and produce suitably skilled graduates to enter college or the workplace.

These assumptions were so compelling that policy elites, drawing on principles that made market-driven firms successful, endowed them with the status of common sense and accepted them as self-evident truths. As one writer put it, "Good organizations, in schooling and elsewhere, are characterized by clear goals, careful measurements of performance, rewards based on outcomes, the elimination of unproductive employees, operational flexibility, the ready availability of detailed and useful information, personnel systems that recruit and promote talent, and attention to training and professional growth."[27]

Apart from citing CEOs who ran successful public and private organizations, neither experience nor scholarly studies justifying such "common sense" decisions were necessary, since very little research evidence was available to demonstrate that one strategy worked better in public schools than the other.

New York City chancellor Joel Klein observed in 2008: "We don't have . . . an entire urban school district—one that's predominantly made up of minority kids, with lots of English-language learners and lots of poverty—that really works, that works in a way that people say, 'OK, I want to replicate that district.' To get there, you're going to need a combination of circumstance and individuals. . . . Despite our progress, we haven't achieved yet in New York . . . a school district that people from other cities can come to and say: 'This works.'"[28] Of course, the lack of direct evidence has seldom stopped policy makers from trying out innovations and citing obscure research studies to support the "common sense" direction they had already chosen.[29]

After years of spinning their wheels without coming much closer to equalizing test scores between whites and minorities or to improving the academic performance of immigrant children learning English, big-city schools instituted a combination of organizational, political, and curricular structures with the "common sense" of fixing urban districts: pick a powerhouse superintendent and focus on standards-based testing and accountability, mixed with large doses of parental choice through charters, magnets, and small specialty schools.

This "Effective Schools and Districts" strategy of fixing the system from the top and building competition from within had gained solid footing in most big cities by the end of the 1990s. Presently, test-based accountability is the primary structure for reaching curriculum-based standards and changing what occurs in classrooms. Since 2002, test-based accountability has become federal policy with the passage of No Child Left Behind (NCLB). While market-based accountability comes into play where new structures for expanded parental choice become a substantial component in a district's improvement strategy (e.g., Dayton, Philadelphia, New Orleans, Washington, D.C.) and political accountability is a factor when mayors take over schools (e.g., Boston, Cleveland, Chicago), test-based accountability is central to district, state, and federal strategies for school success and repairing broken systems. For example, included among the 2008 signatories of the Education Equality Project—the "Effective Schools and Districts" group—were former state and federal officials, five current mayors of big cities, and nine sitting superintendents of large urban districts.[30]

But the vital, irreplaceable link between picking the right leaders, adopting the right policies, and implementing the right structures aimed at lifting student academic achievement consists of what happens daily between teachers and students—often invisible in the words spoken and dollars spent in pursuing grand strategies, but assumed as the desired policy outcome. The classroom connection is the Holy Grail of student learning, academic achievement, and moral behavior —everything else is secondary.

District leaders will often resort to bumper-sticker slogans and soaring rhetoric about the importance of the teacher to student learning, but ensuring that classroom connection occurs routinely remains elusive in practice. Researchers, for example, still cannot say with confidence which structures (such as parental choice, or state and district accountability programs) and which district policies (such as whole school reforms, converting principals into CEOs, small learning communities, advisories in high schools) can lead to both improved test scores and reductions in the achievement gap. Nor can researchers say with confidence which are the best ways to put these reforms into practice in a particular district (whether top-down with school board and superintendent mandates, or bottom-up through schools choosing their own reforms, or some blending of the two approaches), because local context is so powerful in shaping policy implementation.[31]

If context is important to improving urban schools, so is knowing how complicated it is to journey from the macro level (policy) to the micro level (classroom practices). Converting reformers' lofty rhetoric into policy, creating or renovating structures that bridge the distance separating mayors and school boards from principals and teachers, and determining whether adopted policies actually make it into teachers' lessons is but a slice of that complexity. Key questions, then, need to be asked about any strategy heralded as a cure-all for the ills of urban schools.

- Did reform structures aimed at improving student achievement (such as mayoral control, small high schools, pay-for-performance plans, parental choice) get fully implemented?
- When implemented fully, did they change the content and practice of teaching?
- Did changed classroom practices account for what students learned?
- Did what students learn achieve the goals set by policy makers?

These questions about urban reform strategies get at the long chain of policy-to-practice within districts (which becomes even longer when the federal government and state are active players). These questions distinguish policy talk and policy action from classroom practice, student learning, and the fulfillment of district goals. I answer these questions in subsequent chapters and, in doing so, uncover the common errors that urban districts commit in their determination to fix broken schools.

This brief trip through the history of urban school reform and current thought among policy elites reveals the bog-like strata of compressed changes piled atop one another. What gets buried in these layers of reform, including the most recent efforts focused on economic problems, are the abiding but conflicting purposes of tax-supported public schools in a democracy.

The goals for public schools have shifted over time. In the nineteenth century, students merely had to acquire enough literacy to read the Bible. Nowadays, the educational system must prepare students for civic duties, ensuring that they adopt the community's dominant social values, become independent decision makers, appreciate the arts and humanities, successfully enter college and career, and strive to reduce inequalities. Note that public goods, such as civic engagement, cultivating appropriate behaviors, preparing workers, and lessening the inequalities that children bring to school, compete with private goods, such as parents' desire for schools to award educational credentials that would boost their children a few rungs further up the ladder of success.[32]

Schools in a democracy, then, are governmental instruments for achieving specific public goals such as political participation, the socialization of children into community values, erasing economic inequalities, and smoothing entry into jobs. They also serve parents' desire for their sons and daughters to become sufficiently literate to acquire essential credentials that serve as passports into the middle and upper social classes. As a result, school boards have had to respond to different stakeholders (parents, taxpayers, policy elites) and to the local consequences of external events (economic recessions, war, global competition, demographic changes). Thus, emphasis on particular goals may shift as external events and lobbying from organized groups impinge upon public schools. The practice of "educationalizing" national problems continues. At present and for the past thirty years, among policy elites, both public and private aims converge around a dominant economic purpose for schools. Global rivalry for markets and a communication-driven shrinking world have narrowed these broad (and competing) goals: schools today are responsible simply for producing graduates armed with the knowledge and skills to complete college and enter an increasingly diversified workplace. "The source of America's prosperity has never been merely how ably we accumulate wealth, but how well we educate our people," President Barack Obama said. "In a twenty-first-century world where jobs can be shipped wherever there is an Internet connection, where a child born in Dallas is now competing with a child born in New Delhi, where your best job qualification is not what you do, but what you know—education is no longer just a pathway to opportunity and success, it's a prerequisite for success." And it is here in the primacy of an economic goal for public schooling that the "Effective Schools and Districts" reform ideology has gained ascendancy.[33]

Within this big picture of school purposes, there are various reform strategies, and myriad tension-filled conflicts embedded in the policy-to-practice journey being taken by urban districts with largely poor, minority, and immigrant enrollments. Austin, Texas, is a prime example. For a decade, the Austin Independent School District (AISD), under the leadership of its Board of Trustees and its superintendent, Pascal (Pat) Forgione Jr., has introduced initiatives aimed at reforming the district organization, curriculum, and instruction in order to improve academic achievement and reduce the gap in performance between white and minority students.[34]

The culminating reform of these efforts over the past decade is High School Redesign, launched in 2005. But we cannot fully understand High School Redesign as a district-wide effort to reinvent eleven high schools unless we examine AISD's previous efforts to solve a broad array of problems highlighted by local, state, and federal dissatisfactions with student performance over the previous fifty years.

Why pick Austin? The district is similar demographically to many big-city school systems. With a 2009 enrollment of just over 82,000 students, of whom 73 percent are minority (including a substantial number of English-language learners) and 60 percent are poor, the district has nearly 6,000 teachers, most of whom are white and work in both high-performing schools and chronically low-performing ones. Like every big-city school system in the nation, Austin has a history of reform laid down in layers over time. Its past has had an enormous influence on how the problems of schooling and their solutions have been defined, especially with regard to the chronic low academic performance of minority and poor students. Legacies of racial segregation and poverty have flared up time and again whenever Austin leaders set out to remedy academic failure.[35]

Austin is also located in a state that, in the late 1980s, embarked on efforts to mandate testing, establish a regulatory accountability system, and rate districts and schools. With almost two decades of these rules in place, Austin offers an example of an urban district in a state that is trying to meet the demands of test-based accountability rules similar to those of many other states, such as California, Florida, Massachusetts, and New York, with big-city systems. Austin's experience with state standards of performance and school ratings, then, speaks to the experience of other cities across the country grappling with similar challenges.

Moreover, as in other districts where turnstile superintendencies, policy churn, and half-baked implementation often stalled or aborted sustained improvement, Austin during the 1990s had a turbulent decade of entering and exiting superintendents working under micromanaging boards of education. Since then, there has been remarkable stability in Austin's leadership, similar to only a few other urban superintendencies, such as those of Boston, Long Beach, Calif., and New York City, where school chiefs found a good match with mayors and school boards and have served seven to ten years, compiling strong records of improving student achievement across their districts.

Finally, although many other cities have been examined and reexamined many times, Austin has escaped such scrutiny. Its experience with school reform over the past half-century offers a fresh example of the successes that can occur in urban districts and of the problems in student performance that continue to afflict Austin and so many other urban systems wrestling with how to reconcile the paradox of achieving equity and reaching academic excellence in largely segregated schools.

Thus, the title of this book: *As Good As It Gets.* The title can be interpreted in many ways. Joyfully, as on a sunny, 70-degree day, when you take a long bike ride followed by dinner at a fine restaurant with your family or a best friend. Ironically, as the actor Jack Nicholson, playing a man with obsessive-compulsive disorder, speaks the phrase when he looks around at the patients in his therapist's office. Pessimistically, as when you're caught in traffic gridlock with the radio tuned to your favorite station, knowing that you'll be stuck in for another two hours. Optimistically, as in an urban district that is improving schools far beyond what observers and critics would have predicted, yet still has serious unfinished work in high poverty, low-performing schools. It is the latter meaning that I intend.

In this case study of a half-century of reforms in AISD, with particular emphasis on the past decade, I first turn to the years since the 1950s. As William Faulkner wrote, the "past is never dead; it's not even past."[36] AISD's previous reform efforts and its struggle to deal with long-term problems color the present and illuminate the abiding issues of race, ethnicity, and social class. We can learn much from Forgione and other urban superintendents by looking at the obstacles they confronted in their quest to promote equity and academic excellence.

1

The Past Is Never Dead

Austin School Reform, 1950–2000

From 1950 to 1990, the Austin school system had only three superintendents. Irby Carruth reigned for twenty years (1950–1970), managing politically AISD's foot-dragging resistance to *Brown v. Board of Education* until he retired. Jack Davidson (1970–1980) presided over court-ordered desegregation. John Ellis (1980–1990) guided the district as it moved from desegregation to resegregated neighborhood schools, and contended with the breathtaking expansion of state authority in mandating curricular, organizational, and instructional policies for local districts. Yet in the single decade 1990–1999, there were three appointed school chiefs and three who served as pinch-hitter superintendents. They worked with micro-managing boards who hovered over administrators, making the 1990s at best turbulent and at worst chaotic, before a meltdown occurred in 1998–1999. Why such a wobbly decade after forty years of long-serving superintendents?

In the years 1950–1990, two powerful reforms coming from federal and state governments shaped AISD governance, curriculum, and organization: court-ordered desegregation and state-driven educational policies. These policies formed the compacted underground strata for the periodic peat bog fires that rattled AISD in these decades, as various boards and a string of superintendents tussled with local problems rooted in Austin's history as a previously segregated school system. To enable us to understand AISD's disordered 1990s and the subsequently stable Forgione years, I describe Austin's confrontation with race, ethnicity, and poverty in its legally segregated, then desegregated, and later resegregated schools, alongside the steady growth of state policy intervention in local districts.

Segregated Austin, 1900–1954

Apart from shopping for antiques, drawing family trees, and sighing nostalgically over Norman Rockwell paintings, few Americans like to dwell on the long ago. Even though they know that the past colors the present, history, as they remember it from school, is deadly dull and best forgotten.

So it is easy to forget that in 1860 one-third of Austin's white families owned slaves, and that those 1,000 slaves accounted for nearly 30 percent of the city's population. Also that the state capital's black community, freed and flourishing after the Civil War, was in a few decades trapped within a caste-like Jim Crow regime no different from the one endured by African Americans in Baton Rouge, La., and Jackson, Miss.

By World War I, nearly 80 percent of blacks lived in East Austin. Most black men and women left their homes early in the morning for white neighborhoods to clean homes, launder clothes, care for children, work in yards, build houses, fix machines, and collect garbage.

East Avenue (where Route I-35 now runs) and adjacent blocks had a full array of black-operated businesses, churches, schools, professional offices, and social institutions. St. John's Orphanage and the King's Daughters home for elderly women, for example, were located in East Austin. There were also black teachers, ministers, dentists, doctors, lawyers, and bookkeepers who served their own race, avoiding to some degree, but never completely, the pervasive slights that came with being labeled inferior by law and custom. Confirming the intent of the white community to keep separate from blacks while continuing to exploit cheap labor, the City Council in 1928 approved a formal city plan that designated East Austin as the "negro district" and recommended that "all facilities and conveniences be provided the negroes in the district, as an incentive to draw the negro population to this area."[1]

In the 1920s another color line emerged, this one for the Mexican Americans who lived in various parts of Austin. Until World War I, some Hispanics, who had been classified as white in earlier U.S. censuses, had escaped oppressive Jim Crow. With the surges of migration from Mexico in the 1920s, however, pressures from white leaders and the exclusionary practices of realtors drove many longtime Hispanic residents and newcomers to congregate in East Austin, in neighborhoods adjacent to black ones. As the *Austin American-Statesman* put it in 1922, "Mexicans are regarded as on a level with negroes." The decision by federal officials in the 1930 U.S. Census to switch racial categories and record Hispanics as "nonwhite" or "Mexican" only hastened the hardening of the city's color line and continued the economic subordination of darker Austinites.[2]

Austin's emerging barrios contained crowded housing mixed with small and large businesses (one of the major firms was Crescenario Segovia's Tortilla Manufacturing Company), private social services

(La Cruz Azul for women and La Comisión Honorifica for the poor), professional services (such as Roy Velasquez's taxi company), and Catholic churches and schools that catered to Spanish-speaking residents.[3]

By the 1940s, then, when Austin had 88,000 people, of whom 17 percent were black and 11 percent were Mexican, a three-way residential segregation and socioeconomic caste system anchored in law and social practice had become apparent in Austin and other southwestern cities.[4]

Blacks and Mexican Americans knew that in the white community only certain jobs were available to dark-skinned Austinites, most often in domestic service and unskilled labor, with a smattering of skilled artisans. Within the caste-like system of subservient labor, the possibility of genuine caring and respect across the color line existed, but so did the chances of personal humiliation. One black teacher recalled the jarring ache of the color line when he was a teenager doing yardwork in segregated Austin: "I worked in a lady's yard one day. . . . She was supposed to pay me a dollar for the entire day! And lunch. When lunchtime came, I was [sitting] on the back step and she put my lunch here and the dog's lunch next to mine on the same step! So I never cut another yard."[5]

Blacks and Mexican Americans knew where they could and could not rent and buy homes. During the Great Depression of the 1930s, federal officials made efforts to improve housing in segregated neighborhoods where both poor and middle-class people lived in uneasy proximity. Federally funded New Deal programs to clear slums and make room for public housing led city officials to accept federal funds, so long as the new housing was segregated. There were separate developments for blacks (Rosewood Court), for Mexican Americans (Santa Rita Court), and for whites (Chalmers Court).[6]

They knew which stores they could shop in. Black women knew that they could buy some products at Scarbrough's department store, but were not permitted to try on a dress. To try on a hat, black women would first have to cover their hair with paper.[7]

They knew where in the buses they had to sit. Even after blacks boycotted Austin's horse-drawn streetcars in 1906, city officials still refused to repeal the ordinance that required discriminatory seating. A year later, the state of Texas mandated segregated trolleys. In 1925 Willie May Cavaniss was fined $14.80 for sitting in a whites-only seat.[8]

They knew which parks they could go to. For blacks, it was Rosewood; for Mexican Americans, it was Zaragosa. Oswaldo "A.B." Cantu, a longtime activist for youth recreation, recalled that when he and other Mexican Americans would walk a few blocks to play softball at Palm Park, "the playground leader would come up to us and tell us to leave, we couldn't play there, we'd have to go to Zaragosa Park."[9]

They knew they could receive medical attention in downtown Brackenridge hospital only in the "Old Building" or "Annex," a building condemned by state fire insurance inspectors, who recommended it be demolished in 1917. In 1928, it was still in operation.[10]

They knew where they could go to the bathroom. In 1937, Dr. Connie Yerwood worked for the state health services located downtown and had to walk nearly ten blocks to her East Austin home to use the toilet.[11]

They knew which restaurants would serve them. They could go only to black-owned ones, until the Night Hawk chain opened their booths to blacks in 1963. Light-skinned Mexican Americans, however, patronized some restaurants serving whites. As business leader Roy Velasquez commented, "Them blacks was in helluva shape, you know? God Almighty, least we could eat in some of the restaurants."[12]

And, yes, after 1905, when Texas passed its school segregation law, they knew which schools they could attend. For black elementary school children, it was initially Gregory (later renamed Blackshear) and Olive Street; other schools were built as the black community grew. Anderson High School was the only black high school for decades. In 1928, Kealing Junior High School opened, and for the small percentage of students that finished Kealing and sought a high school diploma, it was Anderson. When it came to higher education, there was only Samuel Huston and Tillotson colleges; the University of Texas remained closed to blacks until 1956.[13]

Although Mexican Americans were not included in the 1905 law, Austin officials set up two schools for non-English-speaking children, the East Avenue School in 1916 and the Comal Street School in 1924, both adjacent to Mexican American neighborhoods. The schools were established to teach English to children in the first three grades before they could transfer to other schools in the district, but few learned to speak English fluently enough to transfer. Most students dropped out to earn money for their families. The handful of Mexican American students who remained in school could go to white Austin schools and, if they graduated and had the funds, could attend the University of Texas and other higher-education institutions.[14]

These segregated schools were indeed separate but hardly equal. They received less money per student and had larger classes than white schools. For example, in 1928–1929, each teacher in white schools had twenty-eight students; in black schools, forty students; in Mexican American schools, fifty-four students.[15]

Lest black, Hispanic, and white Austinites forget that Jim Crow was official policy, reminders appeared repeatedly in visible official actions, public signs, and daily speech. By 1917, for example, nearly three-quarters of white homes were connected to the public sewer system, but the City Council didn't authorize connections to black and Mexican American neighborhoods until 1930. There were "Whites Only" signs on restrooms and water fountains. At the entrance to Scholz Garden, a drinking and eating establishment, a placard trumpeted that "none but the best white society will be admitted."[16]

Mayor A. P. Wooldridge reminded a black audience in 1919 that the "white man outnumbers you 9 to 1 and is the stronger race. He knows his power and will not hesitate to use it if he must." That same year, when the national secretary of the NAACP visited Austin, a mob, including Travis County judge David Pickle and constable Charles Hamby, beat him and forced his exit from the city. For weeks, the police harassed local branch members of the NAACP so relentlessly that the Austin chapter remained underground during the 1920s.[17]

Shortly thereafter, the Ku Klux Klan came to Texas and openly operated in Austin and Travis County, enforcing white supremacy among blacks and Mexican Americans. City officials, police officers, and businessmen joined the Klan. By the end of 1921, the Austin branch of the Klan had carried out three whippings, one tar-and-feathering, and one murder. By the end of the 1920s, however, because of aggressive local action by the Travis County attorney, public Klan activity had largely disappeared from Austin. But not from Texas.[18]

In the years 1917–1929, Texas recorded seventy lynchings. The state capital's leading newspaper set itself apart from such activities by editorializing that Austin was a place "wherein the races are at peace," noting that the city "has never had a race riot and has never had a lynching."[19]

Thus, three-way segregation came to dominate Austin's social, economic, political, and institutional life between the early twentieth century and 1954, when the U.S. Supreme Court handed down its unanimous *Brown v. Board of Education* decision. At that time, Austin had just over 132,000 residents, of whom 13 percent were black (75 percent of these lived in East Austin) and 18 percent were Mexican American. In the district's forty schools, there were nearly 22,000 students, of whom 14 percent were black and 20 percent were Mexican American.[20]

For a half-century, the economic and social consequences of Austin's tri-ethnic caste-like system had settled into patterns of white and minority behavior that starkly revealed the negative effects of segregation and poverty. Surely, many blacks who had grown up in East Austin knew that legal segregation, unfair and humiliating as it was, had also created close-knit communities where businesses, teachers, ministers, and other professionals found opportunities for both service and profit while creating home ownership rates that rivaled the percentages in the white community.

Segregation also produced churches, schools, recreation, and social clubs that cared for both middle-class and poor families, generating pride in race and ethnicity and strengthening the ties of blacks and Mexican Americans to their neighbors within their separate communities. Yet the segregated services and institutions that provided social glue and uplift to these communities could not fully compensate for the high price blacks and Mexican Americans paid for the economically exploitative system that Jim Crow customs and laws had created for more than half-century in Texas' capital city.[21]

Consider the death rates among minority adults, compared to those among whites. In 1927, about nine whites per thousand died; the figure for blacks and Mexican Americans was fourteen per thousand. When it came to tuberculosis, Mexican Americans were thirteen times more likely and blacks four times more likely to die of the disease than whites. Access to city services was likewise unequal: there were fewer sidewalks, sewers, paved streets, and garbage collections in East Austin. And jobs that were open to blacks and Mexican Americans paid lower wages. Segregated jobs made cheap labor available to whites, while keeping hardworking black and brown Austinites mired in poverty. Moreover, the limited housing stock contributed to over-crowding and unhealthy living conditions in East Austin neighbor-hoods.[22]

Higher arrest rates and unequal penalties were routine for blacks and Mexican Americans who were picked up, indicted, and convicted of crimes in the criminal justice system. Minority Austinites knew that getting arrested on a serious charge and receiving a fair trial with all-white juries was nearly impossible. One 1930 study showed that of those charged with rape, 100 percent of Mexican Americans were found guilty, as were 75 percent of blacks and 58 percent of whites.[23]

All of these socioeconomic consequences of a Jim Crow system that treated minorities as inferior had strong effects on children—ef-fects that worsened when the children attended ill-equipped, crowded facilities where white school officials spent far less money per pupil and paid teachers less than in schools across town.

Even under these most difficult conditions, ones that black and Mexican American community leaders brought to white officials' at-tention time and again, black teachers at Anderson High School often secured advanced degrees. They helped many students go on to black colleges in Texas. The ethic of working hard, reaching beyond one's grasp, and being proud of one's race was part of the mentoring that went on between caring teachers and ambitious students.[24]

Still, even dedicated teachers could do only so much with students who spent most of their time working, playing, shopping, and simply living on the harsh side of an unforgiving color line enforced by cus-tom and white officials.

That color line extended into their futures. Darker-skinned Austinites were expected to be satisfied with menial labor. As the *Austin
American-Statesman* bluntly put it in 1927, "This is a white man's country. The Texas negro . . . knows where he is wanted and where he isn't
wanted. He is popular in his place—that of hewer of wood and
drawer of water." Most whites expected blacks and Mexican Americans to be maids, laundresses, cotton pickers, servants, cooks, laborers,
mechanics, and craftsmen rather than high school or college graduates
who sought posts as office clerks, letter carriers, bank tellers, doctors,
engineers, and lawyers. Such expectations mirrored a racial capitalism
that easily accommodated the reigning ideology of Tuskegee's Booker
T. Washington and other southern black leaders' preferences for man-
ual and vocational training at the turn of the twentieth century.[25]

So it should come as no surprise that illiteracy, school attendance,
and dropout rates varied greatly between whites and minorities. In
1920, nearly 3 percent of whites were illiterate while the figure was 14
percent for blacks (no data were available for Mexican Americans).
For 1929, average attendance among white students was 135 days
(Mexican Americans were included in that figure); for blacks, attendance was 122 days. Dropouts occurred throughout the eleven grades
of school that Austin offered in the 1920s and 1930s. Most poor
white and minority students lasted only a few grades in school, and
left to find work in Austin. In 1925, one-quarter of white students
were enrolled in high school compared to 13 percent for blacks (no
figures were available for Mexican Americans).[26]

And it is hardly surprising that attendance and dropout rates were
connected to test scores. From the 1920s through the 1950s, when
school officials gave psychologist-designed intelligence and academic
achievement tests to both white and minority students in Austin
schools, scores for black and Mexican American students were much

lower than those for whites. Two scholars in 1925, for example, studied children in Austin, El Paso, San Antonio, and six rural districts. Results from intelligence tests showed that "scores made by whites surpassed those made by negroes in all comparisons," including by age and grade.[27]

Although some scholars in those decades attributed differences in test scores to such factors as Jim Crow practices, poverty, language differences, and dreadful school conditions, the dominant belief among white elites, academics, and parents continued to be that disparities in achievement were due to inherited traits. Analysis of test results in these years began with that hard-core bias, and test scores merely confirmed what most whites already assumed.[28]

By 1954, then, large gaps between Austin whites and minorities in health, family income, and contact with the criminal justice system mirrored gaps between white and minority students in academic performance, attendance, graduation, and dropout rates. These disparities were evident to most Austinites by the time the U.S. Supreme Court announced its decision in *Brown v. Board of Education*. Banning segregation in schools and society, however, hardly erased the disparities in social and economic effects that had accumulated over decades of Jim Crow practices.

National Patterns of Desegregation, 1954–2007

The U.S. Supreme Court's unanimous reversal of separate but equal education—the policy embedded in the 1896 *Plessy v. Ferguson* decision—sought to alter the institutional and practical social relations among the races in American schools. Changing who goes to school with whom is a fundamental reform. Yet the court decision that jarred the nation and dominated the media for months did not lead to swift changes in Jim Crow laws, which had officially determined school attendance for more than a half-century.[29]

The story of what occurred in Austin, and in Texas generally, is a familiar one that can be summed up crisply: in the years 1954–1968, most southern civic and school officials resisted *Brown* by taking tiny piecemeal steps such as "freedom of choice" plans that allowed a few black students to attend white schools, or desegregating faculty by assigning a few black teachers to teach in white schools—or prescribing a range of incremental moves in various combinations.[30]

Note that these measures were voluntary and depended on the good will of well-intentioned whites and blacks. In 1964, for example, a decade after the *Brown* decision, 98 percent of black children in Austin still attended segregated schools. Even with the spread of the Civil Rights movement through the South, President Lyndon B. Johnson's Civil Rights Act (1964), the War on Poverty (1964–1968), and passage of the Voting Rights Act (1965), desegregating schools for blacks and Mexican Americans occurred haltingly.[31]

The pace picked up, however, in the years 1968–1975. The Civil Rights Act gave federal officials in different agencies the authority to sue local officials and business owners, forcing them not only to dismantle Jim Crow in parks, courthouses, voter registries, libraries, public conveyances, courts, housing, and restaurants, but also to integrate blacks and Mexican Americans in classrooms. Even with this litigation, 40 percent of Texas school-age Mexican Americans in 1968 attended schools where 80 percent of the students were of the same ethnicity. Surely an improvement over the mid-1950s but still a long distance to go, especially as challenges to these reform-driven legislative and judicial decisions went to federal appellate judges, and key cases ended up on the docket of the U.S. Supreme Court.[32]

When clear evidence was presented to the Supreme Court in these years that districts had intentionally segregated blacks and whites prior to *Brown v. Board of Education*, the Court ordered these districts to abolish those vestiges of *de jure* segregation and to promote integration in the schools. For example, in *Green v. County Board* (1968), the Court ruled that offering "freedom of choice" to black students as a means of encouraging transfers to white schools was insufficient to uproot the segregated system of schooling in most southern districts. Such districts had to be more aggressive in becoming a unitary, nonracially based system. Districts could adopt policies that paired white and black schools, bused students, and closed previously segregated schools. Many districts underwent major organizational reforms to eliminate policies and practices rooted in *de jure* segregation.[33]

As these court-mandated reforms spread, however, public opinion in favor of desegregation ebbed. Hostility to busing, fueled by media coverage, mounted. Southern suburbanization and grassroots political organizing intersected with burgeoning affection for Republican candidates across the South, as metropolitan areas grew in population and white parents sought mostly white districts where students were not bused for desegregation.[34]

At the national level, in 1968 Republican presidential candidate Richard Nixon attracted white Southerners to the GOP as opposition to busing stiffened and reports of "white flight" from cities to suburbs, amplified in the media, led to antibusing legislation. By the early 1970s, President Nixon's policy of "benign neglect" toward civil rights—including affirmative action, set-asides for minority businesses, and desegregated schooling—had become more apparent. Also, his appointees to the Supreme Court (Warren Burger was made chief justice in 1969) became increasingly allergic to upholding laws that had racial classifications favoring minorities. An emerging majority of justices favored a color-blind approach to decisions. Yet lower-level federal officials in the Office of Civil Rights and the Department of Justice, using prior court decisions made while Earl Warren was chief justice of an integrationist court, slowly (and ironically) enforced previous judicial mandates that sent higher percentages of children to desegregated schools in the South than in the North and Midwest, particularly in those districts that included metropolitan areas such as Charlotte / Mecklenburg County (N.C.), Jacksonville / Duval County (Fla.), and Nashville / Davidson County (Tenn.).[35]

Soon, however, federal court decisions mirrored the popular discontent with busing. In *Milliken v. Detroit* (1974), for example, the Supreme Court closed the door to a metropolitan solution to racial isolation by prohibiting the largely minority Detroit school district from merging with districts in adjacent white suburbs. Justice Thurgood Marshall, in his dissent, spoke directly from the bench: "Our nation, I fear, will be ill-served by the Court's refusal to remedy separate and unequal education, for unless our children begin to learn together, there is little hope that our people will ever learn to live together."[36]

In the years 1975–1990, there was a decided shift in the Court's interpretation of *Brown*. Republican presidents filled nearly all vacancies on the Court in those years. From the late 1950s to the early 1970s, judicial ardor for interpreting *Brown* as integrationist faded considerably and the counter-interpretation of *Brown*—judges and federal and state officials had to be color-blind in applying court decisions and legislation—gained strength. Affirmative-action plans that gave preference to minorities in employment, college admission, and special school programs came under attack as discriminating against whites.

Whereas in past decades federal officials and courts had looked favorably upon busing and other mechanisms to achieve integration, more and more judges, pursuing a "color-blind conservatism," granted relief to districts that requested freedom from court-mandated desegregation plans after local officials had gotten rid of racial classifications and previous discriminatory practices. Federal courts permitted districts to end busing and return to neighborhood schools, even if this meant that those schools would become either predominantly white or predominantly black.[37]

Since 1990, the Supreme Court has continued to advance the position (usually in 5-to-4 votes) that the Constitution is color-blind and that using racial classifications to advance integrationist policies was impermissible. In *Parents v. Seattle School District* and *Meredith v. Jefferson County School District* (2007), the Supreme Court voted 5-to-4 disallowing the policies that the Seattle and Louisville school districts employed to promote integration. As Chief Justice John Roberts wrote, "Simply because the school districts may seek a worthy goal does not mean they are free to discriminate on the basis of race to achieve it." Color-blind conservatism had triumphed.[38]

The story of AISD's efforts to desegregate a Jim Crow system fits neatly within this national picture.

"With All Deliberate Slowness": Desegregation in Austin, 1954–1986

For the first decade of desegregation, the Board of Trustees and superintendent Irby Carruth adopted "freedom of choice," starting with high school and applying the policy to one grade at a time each year.[39] Black students were permitted to transfer to white schools in their neighborhood rather than go to all-black Anderson High School and Kealing Junior High School. Only a few blacks parents, however, chose to transfer their children. In 1964, the district began transferring black teachers to white schools and white teachers to black schools. For the next seven years, thirty-three African Americans and fifty-two whites served as "cross-over" teachers in high schools. By 1968, none of these incremental reforms had done much to alter school enrollments. Wilhelmina Delco, who in 1968 became the first African American elected to the Board of Trustees, recalled that her colleagues on the board "said they would do what the courts ordered and not one thing more." The previously black schools segregated by law remained all-black, even with "freedom of choice" and "cross-over" teachers.[40]

The strategy pursued by the Board of Trustees mirrored the path taken by the liberal City Council's newly formed Human Relations Commission when it sought an open-housing ordinance. A close observer said the commission's multiracial members were developing "an ordinance that would end discrimination against minorities without offending the larger white public"—a task that would have discouraged even Sisyphus.[41]

Using the authority of the Civil Rights Act (1964), officials from the U.S. Department of Health, Education, and Welfare (HEW) identified districts that had failed to dismantle their systems of segregation. In 1968, a team from HEW came to Austin and found the district out of compliance with the Civil Rights Act, since AISD's "freedom of choice" sustained rather than ended segregated schools. After protracted negotiations between HEW and AISD officials and after federal officials repeatedly rejected AISD's plans to desegregate, HEW asked the U.S. Department of Justice to prosecute AISD for failing to integrate its schools.[42]

In 1970, Department of Justice officials filed suit against AISD in federal district court. At this time, East Austin had eighteen schools with a student population that was more than 90 percent black and

Mexican American, accounting for nearly 80 percent of Austin's black students and almost 60 percent of its Hispanic students. The judge ordered the district to close one elementary school, transfer its black students to nearby white schools, and change the boundaries of all-black Anderson High School to include white neighborhoods. No white students, however, showed up at Anderson when school opened that fall.[43]

By this time, the desegregation struggles and court-ordered reforms had taken their toll on Superintendent Carruth, who retired in 1970 after serving twenty years. The Board of Trustees appointed Jack Davidson, whose decade-long tenure in AISD was marked by constant litigation with the federal district court and sharp public confrontations over busing.

In 1971, the Board of Trustees (with Wilhelmina Delco the only black member) closed Anderson High and Kealing Junior High, the only black secondary schools in Austin. Their students were bused to white schools and their teachers were transferred to other district schools. Serious disturbances initially flared at schools receiving bused students, but soon simmered down. Black parents, upset over troubles at the receiving schools, often brought their complaints to Davidson and the Board of Trustees in these years.[44]

Superintendent Davidson weathered many pitched battles over desegregation after assuming the post in 1970. According to AISD administrators who served as teachers while Davidson was superintendent, the school chief "stood his ground." One said "he was a man of courage, caught up in emotional conflicts" that few educators at the time could withstand. He was "a superintendent who believed in desegregation in his heart and soul."[45]

Yet reform-minded Davidson also saw the white community's deep reluctance to move forward with desegregation, which meant that many schools in East Austin (also known as Eastside) would remain segregated and fall even further behind in both resources and achievement. Like many Eastside parents and staff members, he saw that these mostly minority and poor schools would be around for a long time and that something must be done to reduce the gap between Eastside schools and those in the rest of the district. In 1978, Davidson chose three elementary schools (Metz, Blackshear, and Sims) to receive new "educationally designed programs" that focused on basic academics.

The reform-driven program reduced class size to twenty-two students, recruited teachers who pledged to stay for three years, increased teacher schedules by twenty days (paying them for the extra time), and added librarians as well as art, music, physical education, and special education teachers. AISD officials gave the three schools freedom to develop their own curricula. The Blackshear principal said the special project "looked like a blessing from heaven." Such reforms, however, were not at the top of the superintendent's agenda. Far more important was the need to respond to and negotiate with federal officials over the numerous details of court-ordered school desegregation.[46]

From 1971 to 1979, the AISD court case meandered through the federal judicial system. The federal district court judge was of the opinion that Hispanics were a separate ethnic minority and that AISD had not discriminated against the group. The Department of Justice appealed the judge's decision. The NAACP Legal Defense Fund and the Mexican American Legal Defense and Educational Fund (MALDEF) joined the Department of Justice's suit and it went to the Fifth Circuit Appeals Court, which reversed the district judge's decision. After seven more years of court battles, the same judge finally ordered AISD to submit a tri-ethnic desegregation plan.

In 1979, nearly a decade after the Department of Justice sued

AISD and a quarter-century after the *Brown* decision, the district judge approved a plan worked out by AISD, the Department of Justice, the NAACP Legal Defense Fund, and MALDEF. It established new schools in East Austin and mandated bilingual programs, affirmative action in hiring minority staff, and—for the first time—the busing of both white and black students. If implemented fully and faithfully, the Consent Order (basically a court-ordered reform) stipulated that after three years the federal district court would end its jurisdiction and would declare AISD a "unitary" system free of any further federal intervention.[47]

After the court order, Davidson declared: "We have moved from the stage where our principal concerns were dealing with physical confrontation" to a "greater concentration on the academic and extracurricular participation of all students in all phases of the school program." He spoke prematurely.[48]

When schools opened following the federal judge's Consent Order, nasty conflicts erupted over its busing requirement. White parents opposed to busing mounted organized protests, as other groups had done elsewhere in the South. Antibusing rallies drew large crowds that heaped scorn on Superintendent Davidson and the Board of Trustees. About 300 white students and parents rallied at the Carruth Administration Building, waving antibusing signs and chanting, "Hell no, we won't go!" Shortly afterward, a spent Davidson left AISD for another superintendency and the Board of Trustees appointed John Ellis, an experienced Ohio superintendent who had also served in the U.S. Office of Education.[49]

Ellis arrived in 1980 to face the anger of both the white community and the black community. Since newspaper photos, television reports, and first-hand accounts of white parents hostile to busing had been a staple of news programs for years, it is easy to visualize their ire. It's much harder, however, to recapture the feelings of Eastside blacks, whose stories were seldom told in white-owned newspapers or television.

Try to imagine the indignation of black parents and residents who had to bear the burden of busing because Anderson and Kealing secondary schools had been closed. Resentment and anger seethed in homes, street conversations, barber shops, beauty salons, church gatherings, and social club meetings. These schools had been sources of community identity and racial pride during decades of Jim Crow humiliations. Parents, grandparents, uncles and aunts remembered the slights and the pain, and how these segregated schools, impoverished and neglected as they were, still created opportunities for children while remaining beacons of pride in their communities. Except for athletic trophy cases sitting in warehouses, fading Anderson and Kealing banners with school colors (black and red; black and gold), and dust-covered yearbooks in basements, they were gone forever. It was a loss to individuals and the community. Such losses seldom afflicted the white community, further underscoring the disparate perspectives on racial experience in the United States.[50]

For ten years, John Ellis strove to mend the tattered relations between blacks, whites, and Mexican Americans. He was a careful superintendent whose reserved temperament and businesslike demeanor—he was not a chitchat kind of administrator—served him well during the heightened tensions arising from busing. "It's immoral," he said, "for society to request its children to do something and then withhold its support. . . . These children didn't ask to be reassigned. We're asking the children to do something the adults should have done and didn't." Ellis made massive efforts to bring the community into compliance with the Consent Order. He hired parents and activists to work with staff and schools over busing, provided human relations training, set up hotlines to defuse rumors, and sparked dozens of other initiatives to redirect attention to teaching and learning, rather than continually reacting to rallies and fearmongering.[51]

In 1983, after three years of implementing the Consent Order, AISD went to district court and filed for release from the judicial mandate. As that request worked its way through the docket, the Board of Trustees approved Ellis' proposal to attract white students to largely minority schools by establishing magnets (Science, Mathematics, and Computers) within East Austin's newly built and largely black Kealing Junior High and another Science Academy within LBJ High School. These magnets were schools-within-a-school that had all the usual strengths of magnets, attracting white middle- and upper-middle class students, yet also had serious flaws, in that they were separate operations within the largely minority student bodies in each school.[52]

In 1986, AISD finally became a unitary district. In plain language: it was free of any legal traces of discrimination. Busing for desegregation ended, although parents who provided their own transportation could transfer their children to any schools they wished.[53]

With the formal end of court-ordered desegregation and a return to neighborhood schools, the number of schools with largely poor and minority students rose sharply as the city's patterns of residential segregation took hold anew. Under the original Consent Order, only six of sixty-four elementary schools had been racially and ethnically isolated. Now there were twenty. The Board of Trustees (which now included three minority members), concerned about offering equal schooling to all Austin children, approved a five-year program to begin in 1987. Called the "Plan for Educational Excellence," the new program covered twenty elementary schools, each of which had 80 percent minority enrollment. Sixteen of these twenty high-poverty schools, however, had no possibility of ever attracting white students as the two magnets were doing. So the white and minority members of the Board of Trustees, who still wanted racial and ethnic diversity *and* neighborhood schools—contradictory values in a city historically segregated by neighborhoods—struck a political bargain: they would give additional money and programs to these sixteen schools—now called "Priority Schools"—but not to other largely minority schools.[54]

Similar to Jack Davidson's small "educationally designed program" developed for three Eastside low-performing elementary schools nearly a decade earlier, Priority Schools (they included the three from the earlier program) established full-day pre-kindergartens, reduced class size to fifteen in the lower grades and twenty in the upper grades, added funds and support staff (full-time helping teachers, parent-training specialists, counselors, and clerks), and central-office curriculum support for language arts. Aimed at basic academics, these schools required the principal to be an instructional leader, offered direct instruction in classrooms for mastering basic skills, hired teachers sensitive to students' cultural backgrounds, had teachers prepare students for state tests, and frequently monitored students' performance.[55]

Thus, after thirty-two years of "freedom of choice," "cross-over teachers," court battles, antibusing rallies, and street confrontations, concluding that desegregation in Austin occurred "with all deliberate slowness" is neither snide nor cute; it is an accurate one-liner. True, more white, black, and Mexican American students sat together in AISD classrooms than had been the case in 1954. Reform-driven court-ordered busing and enforcement of the Consent Order had indeed reduced the number of segregated schools—as it also had increased the departure of whites to other parts of Austin and nearby suburbs. That reduction of segregated schools, however, reversed itself in the years after 1986.[56]

Another observation is just as accurate: those Austinites who had dreamed of desegregation as a reform that could achieve academic excellence and equity, by enabling white and minority children to attend school together, now saw political power shift to those reform-minded educators and parents who believed that excellent schools—now redefined as meeting high academic standards and scoring well on achievements tests—could occur in predominately brown and black neighborhood schools with rising numbers of poor children, so long as those schools received extra dollars and programs. Facing raw racism over busing and in schools, both black and white supporters of desegregation pulled back. Such a retreat from desegregation led Sam Biscoe, the NAACP attorney in Austin who litigated the case against AISD (and who is now a Travis County judge), to say: "When I look back on the Austin desegregation case, the African American and Mexican American students won in the legal sense but lost in education. The average black parent gave up on desegregation because the experience was harmful to black students. Even at the end of the [bus] trip, black students were treated as though they were inferior. That's hard to get over."[57]

In the years following the district court's release of AISD from federal jurisdiction and the reestablishment of neighborhood attendance zones, AISD embraced the reform strategy of making largely minority and poor schools equal in quality to mostly white schools through more resources and staff hard work. In 1990, for example, of ninety-one schools in AISD, forty-five had student enrollments either 75 percent minority or more than 75 percent white. A decade later, sixty-one schools were either more than 70 percent white or 70 percent minority. The consequence of reestablishing attendance zones for neighborhood schools and creating Priority Schools as the primary reform engine for seeking equity and academic excellence in chronically low-performing minority schools meant that AISD had drifted into a post-*Brown* separate-but-equal schooling for many Austin children.[58]

After 1986, boards and superintendents continued to make rhetorical commitments to ethnic and racial diversity in schools as the best way to prepare children and youth for citizenship, college, and the job market. AISD officials remained committed to magnet schools. They sought federal and state funds to foster special programs where students from different backgrounds would learn together. And AISD officials were just as committed to maintaining neighborhood schools with mostly black and Mexican American students or mostly white segregated schools. In the search for equity and academic excellence, district officials—seldom publicly acknowledging the contradiction in which they were stuck, like flies on flypaper—fastened on those reforms geared to increase academic achievement within black and brown segregated schools.

So, for example, the "Plan for Educational Excellence" components operating in sixteen Priority Schools were consistent with the popular national reform called "Effective Schools," aimed at urban minority and poor students in largely segregated schools. In 1988, John Ellis imported consultants to further train these principals and staffs in Effective Schools concepts and practices. This was the separate-but-equal road that Priority Schools were to travel in reaching academic excellence.

Consultants taught staffs that Effective Schools have principal-leaders who know the curriculum and closely monitor classroom instruction. Such schools have teachers with high expectations, teachers who believe that all children, regardless of background, can learn.

Staff members at Effective Schools create a structured environment that is safe and orderly and where learning is prized. Teachers use direct instruction to help students master basic skills. They test students frequently and use the results to improve teaching. The concepts and practices of Effective Schools, consultants promised, would increase student attendance, reduce teacher and principal turnover, and lead to higher scores on state tests. Although the head of a national group advocating Effective Schools spoke to all administrators, the consultants were not asked to work with largely white schools. They were sent only to Priority Schools.[59]

In effect, after 1986 a three-tiered system of schooling reemerged in the district. Mostly white and middle-class high-achieving schools occupied the top tier. In the middle were schools that made satisfactory academic progress, sometimes ascending into the top tier, sometimes slipping into the bottom one. The third tier consisted mostly of Eastside high-poverty, high-minority schools. The district sent extra resources to these bottom-tier schools in the name of equity, but district administrators expected that these principals and teachers would no longer blame poverty, race, or immigrant families for poor student performance. Instead, achieving academic excellence and reducing the gap in achievement between whites and minorities would now become the staff's primary responsibility. When bottom-tier schools' academic performance fell short year in and year out, top district officials pressed principals and teachers to explain the unsatisfactory results.

At roughly the same time that this significant shift in reform strategy was occurring in a steadily resegregating district, John Ellis and the Board of Trustees also had to deal with increasing state efforts to mandate reform policies that touched AISD's daily operations and reached into classrooms.

Expanding State Policies into
Local Schools, 1984–2008

The story of why and how Texas governors and legislatures began in the early 1980s to put education high on their reform agenda, and what happened to districts, schools, and children as a result, has been told often.[60]

The "why" has to do with the consequences of a decades-long change in the Texas economy—a shift from farming, ranching, and oil to financial services, high tech, and other post-agrarian enterprises. Shrewd business leaders, like their peers in other southern states, saw that a different economy was emerging globally and reaching into Texas—from Dallas, Austin, and Houston to San Antonio and El Paso—and that employers would need both white and minority skilled high school and college graduates (if they were bilingual, even better) to staff and run these new companies.[61]

The existing state system of education, however, was deeply mired in Friday-night football, laissez-faire academic standards, and clogged bureaucracies that left too many white and minority students either drifting through school ignored by teachers or dropping out to take dead-end jobs. The result, reformers argued, was a workforce divided by color and ethnicity, even by language, and largely unprepared for a changing economy. Something had to be done, since Texas employers responding to global competition needed highly skilled graduates to negotiate an increasingly information- and service-based economy.

The "how" is the story of Texas business leaders who lobbied legislatures and governors to reform public schools to make them more nimble in responding to labor market changes. In the early 1980s, state governor Mark White appointed Ross Perot, founder of Electronic Data Systems (EDS), to head the Select Committee on Public

Education. The committee's report to the legislature became House Bill 72 in 1984. The law assumed that Texas schools were lousy because of overemphasis on sports, poor management, low teacher salaries, and insulation from market competition; the cure was efficient, top-down control through state policies such as "no pass, no play," rigorous testing, increased district funding, charter schools, and strong accountability measures that would provide incentives to students for higher academic performance and sanctions for unsatisfactory results.[62]

Shrewd political maneuvering from a series of conservative and liberal governors and legislatures, continually prodded by business leaders, thoroughly transformed the role of the Commissioner of Education and the Texas Education Agency (TEA). The TEA went from a hands-off agency to an iron-fisted managerially driven, bureaucratic arm of reform-minded governors and legislators focused on lifting academic standards, expanding testing, and imposing tough accountability as a means of spurring economic growth.

Yet those shrewd, determined (and tax-averse) state officials and their business allies kept stumbling repeatedly as they tried to implement heaps of reform initiatives. Governors and legislators ignored their policies' negative consequences on teachers and students; they thrashed about to find dollars to underwrite these top-down initiatives, while endlessly squeezing inadequate funding formulas in an effort to equalize spending among the thousand-plus low- to high-wealth districts in the state.[63]

Looking back a quarter-century from the vantage point of 2009, we see that state-mandated policies and TEA efforts have indeed influenced local district governance, school organization, curriculum, and instruction. Of central importance have been the higher academic standards (Texas Essential Knowledge and Skills, or TEKS) legislated by the state, and the increasingly tough tests that determine whether those standards are being met. In the beginning, there was a test called the Texas Assessment of Basic Skills (TABS), which in the mid-1980s begat the Texas Educational Assessment of Minimum Skills (TEAMS), which in turn begat the Texas Assessment of Academic Skills (TAAS), which in 2002 begat the current Texas Assessment of Knowledge and Skills (TAKS).[64]

The legislature also ensured that public accountability for test scores would follow, since districts and schools would be rated as Exemplary, Recognized, Academically Acceptable, and Academically Unacceptable or Low Performing. Schools receiving a rating of Academically Unacceptable for more than one year would be subjected to escalating penalties. By 2003, the state Commissioner of Education had the authority to change the staff and the principal and to close those schools receiving three consecutive Unacceptable ratings. Critics called this the "naming, shaming, and blaming" part of holding educators responsible.[65]

Mandating educational policies, however, was contagious. In Texas, they have ranged from requiring that students pass academic subjects before they can participate in football and band to cultivating patriotism (all students must now salute the flag of Texas after reciting the pledge to the U.S. flag); from fighting obesity (all students must have 135 minutes of physical activity per week) to preventing violence (students who fight in school get sent to an alternative facility, receive police-issued tickets for misdemeanors, and must appear in court); from improving instruction (school districts can spend no more than 10 percent of class time on standardized tests and preparation for tests) to dozens of other school practices.[66]

If the view from the state capitol, the governor's office, and TEA is clear about making new rules to improve schooling in 1,000-plus districts, then the view from AISD offices at 1111 West 6th Street, barely two miles from these state officials, is equally clear. Here is John Ellis writing to AISD staff in 1990, a few months before he departed for New Jersey, where he would become state commissioner of education: "Frankly, I'm tired of the flood of top-down dictates flowing from the Legislature, State Board, or local board. You would probably add 'superintendent,' and possibly 'principal,' to the list of people who contribute unwanted requirements to your life. Despite the heavy-handed prescriptive approach already in place in Texas, some legislators are calling for even more requirements that will 'reform our schools.'"[67] Ellis' complaints about the state's prescriptive rules flowing downward into districts echoed what many of his peers were saying across Texas. The unspoken message in these reforms was that local school boards and superintendents (as well as principals and teachers) could no longer be trusted to do the right thing for students and the future state economy.[68]

Austin's history as a community with a racial caste system anchored in tri-ethnic segregated neighborhoods shaped the character of the city and its school district and the lives of its residents until the 1950s. Then, for the next half-century, a series of major federal and state policies pushing local districts to change their ways had enormous influence on daily life in schools and on city/district politics.

Federal legislation and court decisions, at first fostering desegregation by dissolving attendance zones and expanding parental choice through magnets, busing, pairing of schools, and other tools, soon gave way to color-blind court decisions in the 1970s and 1980s. Eventually, jurisdiction over Austin schools reverted to district leaders, who swiftly restored neighborhood schools—as did other large

Texas districts. In doing so, these districts—like many across the nation—faced the conundrum of wanting schools that were academically strong as well as racially and ethnically diverse, even though they were located in residentially segregated neighborhoods.

AISD officials' strategy of managing the contradiction mirrored that of many other urban districts across the nation (such as Seattle, Boston, Denver) with sizable percentages of whites and minorities living in segregated neighborhoods. Officials made public statements about the importance of school diversity and support for parental transfers to magnet schools and other programs encouraging mixes of students; at the same time, they tried hard to improve poor racially and ethnically segregated neighborhood schools through special efforts combining federal Title I dollars, state grants, and local funds.[69]

Around the same time that AISD implemented its major shift in desegregation policy, state decision makers were pushing reform-driven policies that would prod schools to produce graduates who could adjust to changing labor markets as the state moved from farming, ranching, and mining to a metropolitan service-driven, information-based knowledge economy. Both federally driven desegregation and business-inspired state educational policies shaped AISD's direction in the 1990s. Unfortunately, the Board of Trustees, often with active cooperation from local business leaders, contributed to the instability of leadership in the decade after John Ellis' departure by making poor choices of superintendents. Their appointees would move on after only a few years, barely leaving a mark on the district. These superintendents and boards, locked in noisy battles over district management and various reform directions, were unable to raise low-performing minority and poor schools out of the bottom tier.[70]

2

Turning Chaos into Stability, 1990–2009

The Board of Trustees appointed two superintendents in the 1990s. One left after two years; the other after three. Neither was a good fit for AISD. In the remaining years, two veteran AISD officials served as interim chiefs. These were years when academic achievement meandered up and down, public confidence in Austin schools plummeted, and staff morale declined. In 1998–1999, a cascade of events swept over the district, including the exit of yet another superintendent, a test-fixing scandal, a first-time state rating of a district's performance as Unacceptable, and a downgrading of the district's bond rating. This decade was a disaster for the district.

John Ellis departed from AISD in 1990. The Board of Trustees waited well over a year before appointing Jim Hensley, the former school superintendent of Waco, Texas. Hensley served just two years, leaving hardly a trace on the district. Administrators I interviewed had trouble remembering who succeeded Ellis as superintendent.[1] Following Hensley's hasty departure, the Board of Trustees appointed an interim superintendent who served nearly two years, allowing some board members to engage in serious micro-managing of the system, before the board chose James Fox, a well-regarded chief of schools in suburban Atlanta.

Austin's business leaders spearheaded the campaign to appoint Fox, even traveling to Georgia to interview the candidate.[2] They were concerned about AISD's poor management, the board's meddling into administration, the slow adoption of technology for instruction, and district leaders' inability to look around the corner before things got worse. They were also very concerned that a high school diploma was no guarantee a student had the skills to succeed in college or enter the job market. They sought an experienced school chief who would grab hold of district management, plan ahead, and keep academic improvement at the top of the district agenda. Acting on their advice, the Board of Trustees appointed Fox in 1995.

At first, the match between leader, AISD, and the times seemed to be a nice fit. The board wanted their newly appointed superintendent to shake up the system, so as to improve achievement in low-performing schools and produce better-prepared high school graduates. Called the "technology messiah" by some, Fox often said that "technology is at the point where children who do not interact with [it] all the way through their public school career will be crippled as citizens later on."[3]

Fox prided himself on being businesslike in his approach, and agreed with critics who said he was more interested in managerial effectiveness than in charming parents and staff. "Not everybody here," he said, "will like all the decisions I make. I will tell you that up front. I like to get things done." He told AISD staff that when he went into a district, "I like to mix [insider and outsider] personnel. There is talent in this district and I will find it. Combining local talent with people who have experience in other parts of the country provides creativity and eclectic possibilities. . . . The combination of the two makes things sing."[4]

Yelling, rather than singing, was closer to the mark. Fox moved central-office and school principals who had been in their posts for years. Less than two years after he arrived, thirty out of ninety-six principals had retired, had been reassigned, or had been transferred, including the heads of all but two high schools. One administrator remembered Fox telling principals to move to another school or resign. Another administrator called him "Attila the Hun" for driving "many of the best people out." As one candidate running for the Board of Trustees put it: "Dr. Fox was asked [in 1995] to pull a few weeds and in the beginning he did, but by the end he was mowing down everything in sight, including the flowers." The board brought the ill-suited marriage to an end. After Fox's departure in mid-1998, the board appointed another interim superintendent, who served until Forgione was appointed in 1999.[5]

In those Hensley-Fox-interim years, the Board of Trustees and the school chiefs responded to state-mandated reforms and low academic performance in largely minority and poor schools by seizing upon one innovation after another when each superintendent entered (site-based management, new math and reading programs, the Madeline Hunter method of direct instruction), only to dump them when the superintendents exited. Board members intervened in administrative matters weekly, seeking supporters for their innovations. Here were the spinning wheels of reform with a vengeance. Few reforms lasted longer than the applause for the departing superintendent.[6]

As bad as those years were for Austin, events in 1998–1999 left the district staggering from one blow after another as its reputation was torn to shreds. For parents, staff, and community leaders, that year and a half was midway between farce and tragedy.

During the prior years of desegregation, sure, there had been dislocation, frustration, and much anger among whites, blacks, and Hispanics; but the litigation, beginning in 1954, had caromed like a billiard ball between AISD, federal courts and the U.S. Department of Education for more than three decades. And, yes, the Texas legislature and courts had stumbled through different financing formulas, wreaking havoc on AISD budgets; but that, too, had stretched out over many years.

And, yes, there had been embarrassments over the frequent squabbles among the board's nine elected members and accusations of micro-managing a succession of superintendents. Two school chiefs had been forced out by the board, and interim ones had served only a year or so in the period 1990–1998.[7] None of these events, however, matched the flood of troubles that inundated the Texas capital, the fourth largest school district in the state, during 1998–1999.

Consider the following:

March 1998. Board of Trustees negotiates the departure of superintendent James Fox after only three years in office. Although supporters have praised Fox for raising test scores and lowering dropout rates, critics have blasted his imperious style. Many experienced principals and teachers have left the district. He has often ignored parents and seldom sought community involvement in decisions.[8]

Summer 1998. Board of Trustees begins search for new superintendent.

September 1998. Interim superintendent announces that two top administrators have been reprimanded for fudging results of the Texas Assessment of Academic Skills (TAAS). They wanted to boost scores in three low-performing elementary schools, so as to get higher ratings from the Texas Education Agency (TEA).[9]

January 1999. Citywide Parent-Teacher Association declares, for the first time, a lack of confidence in the AISD Board of Trustees. "Parents see a discontinuity," one member says, "between officials reports at meetings and what they see in schools on a day-to-day basis."[10]

April 1999. The Travis County Attorney indicts the Austin Independent School District and two top administrators for tampering with state test scores. No grand jury has ever indicted a school district in Texas for cheating. AISD officials are charged with changing the identification numbers of sixteen low-scoring students so that their scores would be tossed out and state ratings of the three schools would be raised.[11]

June 1999. The finalist for AISD superintendent visits the district. Board members are entranced by candidate's educational vision and seeming openness to parents and community. Trustee Olga Garza says: "For the last twenty-four hours I've had two songs going through my head. One is James Brown's 'I Feel Good' and the other is that old camp classic, 'I've Got Joy, Joy, Joy, Joy.'"[12]

Shortly after the visit, finalist withdraws from consideration.

Travis County attorney offers deal to Board of Trustees: all fines against AISD for manipulating test scores will be dropped if the district agrees to take responsibility for the cheating scandal. School board rejects offer. The county attorney continues an investigation into allegations that AISD officials fiddled with high school dropout figures. The aim is to find out whether low dropout rates reported to the TEA are a result of sloppy bookkeeping or intentional falsification.[13]

July 1999. Board of Trustees hires search firm to recruit candidates for superintendency. President of the board, in an unusual move, meets with mayor, who seeks involvement in selecting next school chief.[14]

August 1999. Texas comptroller Carole Rylander announces that she will conduct an "uninvited" audit of AISD. The Texas School Performance Review will investigate alleged illegalities (cheating on state tests and reports of falsified dropout rates) and inefficiencies in the district. "I am not going to wait for an engraved invitation when 78,000 of our kiddos are at stake."[15]

National bond-rating companies place AISD on a "negative watch" because of test-tampering scandal and confusion over dropout data, causing loss of public confidence in district's financial integrity.[16]

Four finalists for AISD superintendency meet parents and community leaders. Mayor and small group of business leaders also interview finalists, one of whom, Pascal (Pat) Forgione Jr., applied the first time but was not the board's choice.[17]

Board of Trustees unanimously appoints Pat Forgione as AISD superintendent. The day Forgione arrives in Austin, the Texas Education Agency rates AISD Unacceptable because the dropout data submitted months earlier is deemed unreliable.[18]

Forgione is a former commissioner of the National Center for Educational Statistics (1996–1999) and has served as superintendent of public instruction for the State of Delaware (1991–1996). Soon after moving into the superintendent's suite, he puts up a placard in his office: "Children First: Better Data, Better Collaboration, Better Student Achievement."[19]

The Forgione Reforms

After such a dreadful year and a half, a rudderless school system with its reputation in tatters needed a superintendent who could restore community trust in the Board of Trustees and district educators. The Board of Trustees needed a leader with enough smarts to hire people who could manage data, and with sufficient instructional savvy to reassure a skeptical community that 5,000-plus teachers could raise the academic performance of nearly 80,000 students, many of whom came from minority and poor homes. The Board of Trustees, with a history of micro-managing a series of superintendents in the 1990s, entered into a marriage with a superintendent who had never led a big-city district; and this union took place at a time when stable leadership, trust building, and initiatives to improve chronic low achievement in high-poverty, high-minority schools were high on the agenda. No fortune teller could predict whether the match would be as ill-fated as the earlier ones or whether it would last long enough to achieve the board's immediate goals.

Within a few months, Forgione created top posts in finance, student data reporting, operations, and accountability—bringing in outsiders and promoting insiders—all of whom reported directly to him. He admitted the mistakes AISD had made. As one journalist put it, "Reporters are actually reading AISD releases again." The brand-new superintendent reached out to business and civic leaders for advice. He held "Ask the Superintendent" forums in various schools across

Austin, inviting parents and community activists to question district policies and air their concerns. Even riskier was Forgione's request that the board recommend raising property taxes 10 percent over the previous year to pay for technological improvements in antiquated data systems and ensure the integrity of any data AISD reported. The board approved the superintendent's recommendation, and at the next election city voters approved the tax increase.[20]

Supported strongly by the board, and having made shrewd appointments of key staff in instruction and data assessment, the new school chief found various pots of money in the budget by reorganizing the central office, carefully monitoring expenditures, and tapping new money raised from property taxes. He instituted new management systems to restore public trust in its schools, and set out to improve the academic performance of those who did poorly on state tests. Local media that had been highly critical of Forgione's predecessors largely supported the superintendent's initiatives in their editorials, except for occasional slaps on the wrist after what they felt were mistakes or missed opportunities.[21]

In 2002, a contentious board president departed after ten years. Her replacement, Doyle Valdez, the first president elected by other trustees rather than by Austin voters, worked to give the superintendent running room to make more decisions without constantly looking over his shoulder at the trustees. During the years he served, Valdez often restrained the board from second-guessing staff decisions. He shortened long meetings, except during budget season. Valdez's calm, deliberate style of working through differences between the superintendent and the trustees gave Forgione more flexibility and support in implementing policies. The superintendent's widened zone of decision making also gave community activists and some board members the distinct impression that Forgione made far too many top-down, unilateral decisions. The trustees, they felt, were no more than a "rubber stamp" for the superintendent's decisions.[22]

Even with these changes, unexpected events quickly segued into crises requiring immediate board and superintendent attention. Within six months of Forgione's appointment, the state notified AISD that it would be classified as a "high-wealth" district, meaning that the district would lose $55 million in revenue in 2000–2001 and would be forced to make budget cuts. Among many money-saving measures, Forgione ordered the end of block scheduling (that is, rather than fifty-minute periods, classes were sixty to ninety minutes long) in all middle and high schools—a sudden decision that caught teachers and administrators by surprise and thoroughly antagonized them. Then, a few months later, with a new instructional team and data systems in place for reporting to the state, Forgione announced that the TEA had given the Austin school district a rating of Acceptable, erasing what he called "the scarlet *U*" (the rating of Unacceptable) that the district had received in 1999. Furthermore, he praised the staffs of nineteen schools (out of the ninety-seven tested) that earned TEA's ratings of Exemplary or Recognized, especially schools with large percentages of poor and minority students. "Are we satisfied?" the superintendent asked. "No—we won't be satisfied until not one of our schools is on the low-performing list." Nine were listed.[23]

Three years into Forgione's tenure, one school board member praised the superintendent's boundless optimism, passion, and energetic leadership, likening him to a new coach who'd been hired in 1999 to create a winning team after a really bad season. "Dr. Forgione has gotten us up to a 9–7 record," he said. "He has us heading toward being a playoff team. We're not a championship team yet, but we have the right coach."[24]

In subsequent years, the Board of Trustees approved Forgione's efforts to align AISD curriculum with state standards, reorganize the district office by eliminating regional superintendents, and forge links with business and civic leaders. The trustees and their superintendent tap-danced through budget squeezes triggered by state finance reform, responded year after year to new state policy mandates, engineered successful bond referenda for new and renovated schools ($500 million for 2004), and made occasional stumbles that a grateful community was willing to forgive. The superintendent's political finesse (compromised at times by impulsive decisions), seemingly inexhaustible drive, and capacity to endure public rancor when parents and teachers railed at board decisions slowly won him respect among those inside and outside the district for his ability to be a "heat shield" for the Board of Trustees and district administrators. He did this by working one-on-one with high-profile influential people in local chambers of commerce and key business groups, and with individual Hispanic and African American leaders.

By being a buffer and absorbing criticism, the superintendent learned that Austin had a feisty mix of politically liberal and conservative sentiments where neighborhood groups and key stakeholders needed to be consulted and stroked—a task that Forgione welcomed but occasionally mishandled. The city had been nicknamed the "People's Republic of Austin" for its liberal attitudes, yet its progressive activists operated within a state capital housing conservative legislators who read the daily paper about AISD schools, made educational policy, and appropriated funds to all Texas districts. Under the microscope of a largely conservative legislature, Superintendent Forgione characterized Austin—using a baseball metaphor—as his "home field disadvantage."[25]

Once solidly Democratic, Texas elected its first Republican to statewide office in 1978. In subsequent years, the GOP captured nearly all statewide posts. Republican perspectives on teachers and education became policy. Consider unions. Currently, Texas law allows unions, but collective bargaining is banned. Texas is a "right to work" state. So Education Austin, the largest teachers' union, monitors the Board of Trustees and the superintendent closely to protect the interests of its membership. It offers advice to AISD officials on salaries, working conditions, and other policies but cannot do more than meet and confer with the superintendent's representatives and try to persuade parents and civic leaders to support its positions.[26]

Over the years Forgione and his staff, knowing this blend of Texas-style liberal and conservative opinions in Austin, introduced programs that would appeal to both sides. "Character education" was imported into the curriculum ("We've got to counteract MTV, folks," Forgione said), dress codes were instituted for students and teachers ("I would go into a classroom, and a teacher would bend over, and I would see things I don't want to see"), sugary soft drinks were banned from school vending machines even before the state mandated their removal, and a new small secondary school called the Ann Richards School for Young Women Leaders (named after a former Democratic governor) was established. These initiatives pleased both sides of the political spectrum.[27]

Forgione's whirlwind actions—he once said, "I don't know what fourth gear is like"—and a strong, committed staff slowly restored the community's confidence in the data published by the district and set a clear direction for improving low-performing schools amid ever-rising accountability standards.[28] Year after year, AISD officials wrestled with competing state and federal rating systems. McCallum High School could be on the *Newsweek*'s list of the nation's "Best High Schools," yet would be labeled Needs Improvement under the federal

No Child Left Behind act (NCLB), and in the Texas system of ratings it would be called Academically Acceptable.[29]

These ratings, using different criteria yet fully reported in the media, created, in Forgione's words, "an oppressive and mechanistic accountability that allows no credit for progress" made in schools with high percentages of poor and minority students and English-language learners (ELL students). Under NCLB, proficiency levels had to be reached each year. Strong gains in test scores were not even considered if the level—the set percentage—was not reached for an entire group or any of the subgroups. Although the Texas Education Agency raised the bar on test scores that students had to meet each year, it did at least recognize increases in test scores. But NCLB did not recognize those schools where students raised their scores far higher than those of the previous year; if they fell short of the standard set for the current year, they were judged as failures. Still, that "oppressive and mechanistic accountability" impeded neither the pace nor the reach of district reforms that the superintendent and his staff proposed and the Board of Trustees adopted.[30]

Three Phases of Reform, 1999–2008

Being candid even about occasional slip-ups was a trademark feature of the Forgione superintendency. From admitting receipt of a traffic ticket to describing the reforms undertaken in these years, Forgione seldom dressed up the facts. For example, the superintendent told a newspaper reporter that he had paid a fine of $116 for speeding in a school zone (he'd been traveling at twenty-seven miles per hour in a twenty-mph zone). Forgione, returning from a pep rally at a middle school, said: "I was still pumped up from all the . . . enthusiasm and was, frankly, not paying attention to the posted speed limit." The school chief also couldn't resist teaching a lesson: "I believe this occurrence is an appropriate time to urge all motorists to pay special attention to the marked school zones."[31]

In another display of candor, Forgione, speaking to researchers in 2006, described the various reforms that he and his team had designed and phased in over nearly a decade. This talk was clearly Forgione's version of his tenure as superintendent. He skipped over occasional impulsive decisions, omitted lapses in judgment, and often avoided mention of neighborhood input. Still his frankness about the flow of the changes he and his staff had recommended and the board had approved followed the documentary record reasonably well. Forgione divided those initiatives into three stages.[32]

Restore Public Trust in AISD's Data and Build an Instructional Infrastructure, 1999–2002

"From that first day [in office]," Forgione declared, "I decided the best approach was to drill down until we got to the bottom of our bad news. We shared everything we learned with the Austin community. In that way, we developed public trust, which we would need as we rebuilt the district from the ground up. . . . We set up a new accountability department to scrupulously oversee our use of data. These were the relatively easy reforms. I knew our greatest challenge would be to reform teaching and learning in our more than 5,000 classrooms."[33]

To reach into classrooms to improve academic work, Forgione had to get the entire staff to focus on curriculum and instruction. He saw AISD as "all *e pluribus* and no *unum.* Our schools were peacocks on the prairie, strutting off in different directions because they'd had no district leadership for so long."[34]

To direct attention to a core curriculum that all students would take, the new superintendent ordered that AISD content standards would henceforth be those established by the Texas Essential Knowledge and Skills (TEKS). "These standards," Forgione said, "became our first nonnegotiable—the *unum*." It didn't matter whether you were going to school in predominantly minority East Austin or in affluent Northwest Austin—"we'll have the same expectations and high standards for you in every classroom." What counted was teacher and student effort, not the location of the school. "We believe that effort creates ability. You become smarter by working harder in a system set up for high achievement."[35]

To help teachers and administrators address these standards and develop common principles and vocabulary about classroom teaching and student learning, AISD contracted with the University of Pittsburgh's Institute for Learning to help teachers and administrators. With a great deal of work by district instructional staff in creating an infrastructure and actual materials to help principals and teachers, linkages between state standards and classroom lessons were slowly forged.

One top administrator recalled the new superintendent's focus on curriculum, teaching, and learning:

Before Dr. Forgione came, everybody did their own thing, and if they worked great, no one bothered you. . . . I remember being a principal . . . and one of the first things he [Forgione] asked us to do, . . . something we'd never been asked to do by anybody, was to write up and send in to him [a memo] that really got at what our philosophy of learning was. That sent a clear message to us at the beginning there here is somebody who is really interested in how teaching and learning is going on at our campus. He's asking us questions which typically [previous] superintendents never got involved [with] at our level.[36]

With data systems, accountability procedures, curriculum standards, and staff development programs in place, AISD entered the second phase of Forgione's plan.

Strengthening Classroom Teaching and Learning, 2002–2006

Under the leadership of Darlene Westbrook—AISD's chief academic officer and a well-respected insider who had climbed the career ladder of teacher, principal, and district administrator to her current post—experienced teachers and curriculum specialists developed Instructional Planning Guides in academic subjects closely aligned with the upgraded state standards and a new state test (Texas Assessment of Knowledge and Skills, or TAKS) that demanded far more from both teachers and students than had the previous test (Texas Assessment of Academic Skills, or TAAS). Because AISD, like most urban districts, was losing teachers every year for various reasons (nearly 15 percent, with greater percentages at high-poverty, high-minority schools), having these planning guides available for both newcomers and experienced teachers, Westbrook believed, was essential for providing students a common framework in reading, math, science, and social studies. For more difficult academic courses, Westbrook's team developed guides for pre–Advanced Placement courses. These actions coupled district practices more tightly to state standards and tests—a process that other urban districts called "curriculum alignment."[37]

With tougher tests facing students and with unforgiving state rating systems for schools' academic performance, Forgione, Westbrook,

and their team decided not to wait until end-of-school-year test results were published to find out how well Austin students were meeting state content standards. They developed beginning and midyear
tests, called "benchmark assessments," to monitor the academic
growth of students and identify those needing help. For the large
number of English-language learners, teachers were expected to be
rigorous and consistent in their instruction so that students could
learn the vocabulary and concepts of different academic subjects.
Thus, data-driven interventions would help students during school,
after school, and in the summer. Furthermore, professional development for both teachers and principals would become anchored in the
rich yet often overwhelming data pool available to them on individual
student performance.[38]

To Westbrook and her team, creating these planning guides, benchmark assessments, and staff development goals were essential parts of
a district-wide infrastructure that would prevent children from slipping through the cracks. These veteran Austin educators remembered
that in the late 1980s, after the end of court-ordered busing to desegregate schools, sixteen East Austin schools enrolling mostly poor and
minority children had been designated Priority Schools. For five years
these schools, unlike other elementary schools in AISD, had had lower
student-teacher ratios, more staffing, and full-day pre-kindergarten.
They'd received twice as much money as other district schools. Yet by
1992, academic achievement, as measured by state tests, showed only
slight improvement in reading and no improvement in math. Westbrook also knew that in 2002 Forgione had established Blueprint
Schools (four elementary and two middle schools), after East Austin
community activists had criticized the superintendent and the Board
of Trustees for neglecting mostly minority and poor Eastside schools.
Blueprint Schools got new principals, more resources, and on-site help

for teachers. Westbrook knew well that all of this was insufficient without a district-wide system of close instructional monitoring, benchmarks, and development of the staff's knowledge and skills.[39]

As these new systems were put into practice, the superintendent could report to the Board of Trustees that in the years 2002–2005, more and more Austin minority students had increased their scores on the TAKS test to reduce somewhat the large achievement gap between whites and minorities. High school graduation rates had increased from 72 percent to 80 percent, although rates for students from low-income families (72 percent) and English-language learners (53 percent) were significantly lower.[40]

Even though overall test scores and graduation rates were improving, much work remained to be done in high schools. And that is where churning AISD reforms entered the third phase of district improvement.

High School Redesign, 2004–2006

With community trust in AISD data and top leadership restored and an instructional infrastructure of standards, planning guides, benchmark tests, and professional development in place, the superintendent, whose contract a supportive Board of Trustees had repeatedly extended, tackled the toughest problem facing urban districts: improving high school students' academic achievement, especially for those coming from minority poor families and immigrant families with English-language learners.

Raising elementary school scores on the TAAS and then the TAKS exams took much hard work by principals and teachers that had paid off in higher state ratings and a gradual closing of the gap between white and minority test scores. But raising secondary school performance on state tests, especially in predominantly minority and poor comprehensive high schools, was a far harder nut to crack not only in Austin but in big cities across the nation. Why was that the case?[41]

High schools are larger than elementary schools. High school teachers are trained as subject-matter specialists and, more often than not, stress that they teach academic content, while elementary school teachers are generalists and, more often than not, focus on teaching children several subjects and skills. High school teachers see their 130-plus students for about an hour a day, while lower-grade teachers spend nearly five hours a day with their students. Finally, high schools with substantial percentages of minority and poor students have larger numbers of students who passed through middle school with reading and math deficits and now need to deal with even tougher material. For English-language learners, high schools had insufficient staff, many of whom were neither bilingual nor bicultural. All of these factors combined to make boosting the scores of high school students far harder than raising those of elementary school students.

So it comes as little surprise that TEA rated two to four high schools as Academically Unacceptable each year. "We recognized that we needed to make major changes," Superintendent Forgione said, "which would require us to be brave enough to look squarely at the problem of redesigning our traditional American public high school."[42]

In 2004, AISD officials asked the Southern Regional Education Board (SREB) and the University of Texas to assess the strengths and weaknesses of the district's eleven comprehensive high schools. Both reports laid out the problems facing students and teachers in these schools—problems that ranged from uneven instructional quality and low classroom expectations for minority and poor youth, to weak principal leadership and lack of supports for struggling students.[43]

Using this report and other data, the superintendent drew up a plan to overhaul the district's eleven high schools. He kept the board informed of the plan, but it was his initiative—a fact that board members in 2008 recalled with criticism rather than praise. The entrepreneurial superintendent then approached the Bill and Melinda Gates Foundation, which had been funding efforts across the country to create small high schools.[44]

The Gates Foundation awarded AISD an initial $1.5 million planning grant in 2005, and a four-year $15 million grant in 2006. The Michael and Susan Dell Foundation also funded parts of the high school reform. AISD contracted with Stanford's School Redesign Network to work with each of the high schools in designing programs aligned with its context, to help teachers and administrators draft proposals, and to involve the larger community in the overall effort.[45]

In smartly parlaying private and public funds into a reform-driven package for redesigning AISD high schools, Forgione, with the approval of the Board of Trustees, embraced a core reform strategy of building a portfolio of high school options, as had other big-city districts such as Boston, New York, and Chicago. But AISD, in contrast, decided to revamp all of its comprehensive high schools at the same time. The goals of High School Redesign were to close the achievement gap between white and minority students and increase the numbers of high school graduates, especially black and Hispanic students, ensuring that these graduates would be well prepared for college and the job market.[46]

I need to point out that the three-step AISD strategy (and policy logic) I have described thus far, taken from a talk that Forgione gave to researchers in 2006, appears planned and sequential. Yet as Forgione pointed out then and since, this strategy was vulnerable to random events that made even the best-planned reforms go awry. And unpredictable events did occur that forced AISD leaders to defer and even set aside initiatives.[47]

Bumps along the Path to Reform

Unexpected crises blindsided both the Board of Trustees and the superintendent during these years. Such events sucked up enormous time and energy from Forgione and his staff, as they set aside other priorities to work on the emergency at hand. From late 2000 to early 2002, for example, much time was spent in responding to demands for better schools for Austin's minority children—demands that came from Reverend Sterling Lands, minister of the Greater Calvary Baptist Church, and fiery head of the Eastside Social Action Coalition.[48]

In an October 2000 letter to board president Kathy Rider, Lands said that forty-six years after *Brown v. Board of Education,* "our schools are still separate and unequal." Pointing to minority students' lower achievement, high dropout rates, and high percentages identified for special education, Lands wrote: "Unless you believe that children of color are inferior in their ability to learn, you must conclude with us that we have an emergency of horrible magnitude, and immediate and deliberate action is required to reverse the trend."[49]

The 600-member Eastside Social Action Coalition (ESAC) had originally formed in reaction to police brutality in 1998. In the spring of 2000, Forgione's sudden and heavy-handed firing of the black principal of LBJ High School in what Lands called "a very cavalier and inhumane way"—the principal was escorted off campus by security officials at the end of the school day—triggered protests. The issue leading to the principal's removal was the unremitting tension between the staff of the magnet program (Science Academy) and the principal. The firing brought out 500 ESAC parents, students, and activists to a Board of Trustees meeting to protest the principal's removal. The board backed the superintendent. Over the summer, ESAC meetings that included Austin's Mexican American community groups also induced Lands to write his October 2000 letter to the Board of Trustees.[50]

The board did not respond to him formally, so Lands threatened to withdraw minority students from Eastside schools and educate them elsewhere. Whether the threat was serious or not, the loss of students would have jeopardized state funding and wreaked havoc on the district budget. Eventually discussions between Lands and the board president produced a thirty-two-page staff report that accepted some of the demands and rejected others.[51]

Lands lambasted the board and the superintendent for dragging their feet for six months. He then ratcheted up the pressure by proposing that Eastside schools split from AISD and form their own district. Legal obstacles and strong reaction from the board, the superintendent, and business and civic elites persuaded Lands to negotiate with the private, for-profit Edison Schools Inc. to take over East Austin schools and run them as the company had run some schools in Dallas. Edison presented a proposal to the Board of Trustees in January 2002.[52]

After much discussion of the Edison proposal and the entry of a proposed new Eastside school run by the Knowledge Is Power Program (KIPP), which operated schools in Houston and New York City, Forgione recommended rejecting the Edison plan but accepting the KIPP proposal. The Board of Trustees, however, rejected both the Edison and the KIPP applications. As one board member said, "I find it offensive to have folks come into our school district and say, 'Well, your kids are deficient, and this is how we're going to fix that deficiency.'" After the vote, the board asked Forgione to come up with a plan to improve low-performing schools. One month later, Forgione, who publicly accepted blame for not doing something sooner, presented his "Austin Blueprint to Leave No Child Behind."[53]

The Blueprint, as it became known, drew a great deal from the Effective Schools literature.[54] The plan called for transforming the six lowest-performing schools (four elementary and two middle schools, all located on the Eastside) by placing new principals in five of the six schools. Principals would hire certified teachers who had at least two years of experience and who agreed to stay three years. Blueprint Schools would add math and reading coaches, introduce Open Court Reading curriculum in the elementary schools, and hold mandatory staff training programs during the summer prior to implementation and each subsequent year.[55]

While the daily newspaper endorsed the Blueprint, Sterling Lands asked: "Why only focus on six schools when there are children of color suffering in mediocre schools across the Eastside? This is a political, not an honest effort to raise standards across the board."[56]

Lands was correct. The superintendent's recommendation and the Board of Trustees approval of the Blueprint was a band-aid political solution to a long-simmering problem (namely, the question of how much money and effort should go toward achieving school equity and academic excellence in a residentially segregated city) that had suddenly flared into a crisis. Lands, the Board of Trustees, and minority staff in district headquarters knew that this crisis was a legacy arising from the history of a segregated school district and would arise again, Blueprint or not.

After eighteen months of protests, discussions, and reports, AISD officials presented a program for six Eastside schools (adding Johnston and Reagan in 2004) that drew liberally from the earlier AISD

Priority Schools program and the Edison and KIPP proposals. Lands and ESAC grumbled at the smallness of the Blueprint, but those eighteen months trained a powerful searchlight on schools that had been neglected and did get the large district to respond to their concerns. Yet no AISD official had seen this issue coming in late 2000. Once it was being covered in the newspapers and on television, elaborate plans for other initiatives were pushed to the sidelines as this crisis unfolded. It persisted for a year and a half.

Neither did anyone foresee the financial roller-coaster ride that the legislature and courts forced on Texas districts in the previous decade, causing severe budget cuts in AISD. When the state altered its funding formula in 1993—called Chapter 41 of the Texas Education Code —to equalize funding between "property-rich" and "property-poor" districts, they required "high-wealth" districts like Austin, nearby Eanes, Lake Travis, and Manor to give up funds raised from local property taxes to "low-wealth" districts such as San Antonio's Edgewood Independent School District and the Laredo Independent School District, whose property taxes yielded very little. Thus, the ordinance was labeled the "Robin Hood law." In addition, the state capped the local district's property tax at $1.50 per $100 of assessed value.[57]

In 2000, the state required Austin to give up $55 million, or close to 10 percent of its budget. Three years later, AISD gave up $158 million (more than 20 percent of its budget) and had to cut 650 positions including one-third of its elementary school art, music, and physical education teachers. The board and the superintendent could offer only a 1.2 percent salary raise to teachers, which meant that when other state cuts to health benefits were taken into account, Austin teachers were earning less than they had the previous year. Even worse for AISD, in the throes of raising academic standards for Eastside schools, was the fact that poor families and English-language learners were becoming more numerous in the district and needed additional resources.[58]

In 2003, because the Texas governor and legislature had been re-ducing the total amount of money it spent on districts while requiring high-wealth districts to share their funds, Austin joined Dallas, Hous-ton, and 350 other districts, both high-wealth and low-wealth (repre-senting more than two million students), in suing the state to increase the amount of money it sent to both wealthy and poor districts; the lawsuit, however, did not challenge the "Robin Hood" sharing of wealth. A year later, after the state legislature failed to reform school finance in both a regular and a special session, a state judge ruled in favor of the property-rich districts, calling the current state funding unconstitutional. The state appealed the judge's decision to the Texas Supreme Court.[59]

In 2005, after repeated failed efforts by the state legislature to en-act finance reform, the Texas Supreme Court ruled 7–I that using lo-cal property taxes to pay for public schools was an unconstitutional statewide tax (low-wealth districts were taxing at the state-imposed cap of $1.50) and ordered the legislature to fix the financing of pub-lic schools. The governor and the legislature worked out a compro-mise, fueled by an $8.2 billion surplus, easing considerably the burden of budget cuts that AISD and other high- and low-wealth districts had to absorb. Few knew how long the governor and the legislature would keep dodging the finance reform bullet, or whether the courts would eventually intervene and force state authorities to catch that bullet in their teeth and bite it. As the situation played out from 2000 to 2005, the state financing burden placed districts squarely in the pincers of ever-escalating accountability standards, changing demographics, and budget cuts that inevitably touched schools and classrooms.[60]

The trouble-free rendition of reform that Forgione offered the audience of researchers in 2006 moved easily from one stage to another, yet skipped over some impulsive decisions and errors in judgment. A few weeks before he gave his talk, for example, Forgione had to withdraw a recommendation to close some schools.

To save money and more efficiently run the district, the superintendent made two proposals. In early 2006, he surprised the staffs of two minority schools (Becker and Oak Springs) by recommending that these small schools become pre-kindergarten centers. And a few weeks later, he suddenly recommended that both schools be closed, a move that would save AISD $400,000. Shocked parents went to board meetings and lobbied trustees. Neighborhood activists showered board members and staff with plans to keep the schools open. Seeing that the community was up in arms and that his recommendations would not gain a board majority, Forgione dropped the proposals.[61]

A similar rushed decision occurred six months after Forgione gave his talk to researchers. In January 2007 he sent a letter to Webb Middle School parents, saying that he would recommend closing the school because students had failed to pass the state test three years in a row. Webb students would transfer to two nearby middle schools, which were also performing poorly on the state test. The letter surprised and upset parents.[62]

More than one-third of Webb's 669 students moved in or out of the neighborhood every year; more than 90 percent of the students came from low-income families; more than 80 percent of the students were Hispanic; half of them had limited English skills; and teacher turnover was high (40 percent of Webb teachers left in 2006). In view of these circumstances, it is no surprise that the school had struggled again and again to pass the test. The commissioner of education had told AISD officials that if students failed the state test in 2007, the school would be closed or the commissioner would ask that an outside firm take over the school. Since the TAKS tests were taken in March, April, and May, scores would not be known until the end of the school year. If Webb students again failed to pass all portions of the test, the superintendent did not want to be in the position of scrambling to reassign teachers and students just before school opened in August. Thus, the superintendent's recommendation and letter were reasonable—from his perspective—except that parents and neighborhood activists didn't have a clue that the school would be closed.[63]

About 200 outraged parents, students, and community activists rallied at a community forum to discuss Forgione's recommendation. A parent told him: "You are sending our kids to two of the worst schools in the district." Another told the superintendent that he was treating "our children like merchandise." Rancor translated into harsh words, hand-printed signs, and angry outbursts. In the following weeks, as complaints poured into school board offices from neighborhood activists and negative newspaper editorials castigated the superintendent for top-down decisions made without parental consultation, Forgione back-pedaled by delaying the closing of the school and hastily drawing up improvement plans. Within four weeks of his proposal to close the middle school, the school board rejected the superintendent's recommendation to disperse Webb students to other schools.[64]

Finally, what is missing from Forgione's smooth description of sequential stages is reform overload: too many changes by too many people at too fast a pace for teachers and principals to absorb. High School Redesign, Advanced Placement Strategies, and district-wide professional learning communities (PLCs) are just a few of the board-approved system-wide initiatives that were expected to appear in schools and classrooms. Also consider that AISD officials had to juggle the competing agendas of numerous outside partners such as Austin's business leaders, the "First Things First" program of the Institute for Research and Reform in Education, the University of Pittsburgh's Institute for Learning (IFL) work in "Disciplinary Literacy," the Dana Center for Mathematics at the University of Texas, the Gates and Dell foundations, and other organizations.[65]

Such cross-cutting agendas caused wheels to spin when these organizations sent out their staff to work with teachers who may not have been fully informed about the initiative. As one upset veteran high school teacher put it: "We're getting this academy, and then . . . we're gonna do this and that. . . . When did that happen? It's like 'we're the last to know' kind of thing. You're not asking—you're telling us this is gonna happen. . . . So that people [teachers] are just saying, . . . 'Go ahead and sit on all of those committees. We told you it wasn't gonna work, told you it was gonna be crap.' . . . I hate that. You have no idea how I hate that."[66] A school administrator impatiently put it to an interviewer: "There are just too many initiatives. Too many consultants. Too much on our plate. No coherence. Everyone is vying to be *the* consultant. It is competitive. Who will be the lead dog? IFL? . . . AP Strategies? Dana Center? You cannot marshal that many initiatives. Especially when we have to justify for each group how we are doing it."[67]

Forgione recognized these dangers and saw that they could swamp the reform. On the fast pace of change, Forgione said: "It's important that you have the time to sequence and stage your reform efforts, so you don't overwhelm your campuses and your central [office] support capacity. You can't outrun your principals and teachers. No matter how good your ideas may be, nothing will change if you don't have the support of your administrators and teachers."[68]

Forgione also worried that too many reforms would whirl off in different directions, forcing staff to lose sight of the purpose for reinventing comprehensive high schools. Such worries about diverging reforms and overload led the superintendent—prodded by Gates Foundation officials—to hire Parthenon, a private consulting company, to study the central office's managing of redesign. The company's recommendations led to a strengthening of the already functioning High School Redesign Steering Committee (informally named the "Can Do Committee") to coordinate and vet proposed initiatives (for example, synchronize the late-morning start of high schools in 2007–2008 to provide time for professional development), to see if they ran counter to or enhanced existing programs. Even here, of course, better coordination in the district office often failed to translate into clear communication with principals and teachers.[69]

The superintendent acknowledged that his pell-mell style of rushing to acquire new funds and implement many initiatives, enterprising as such activities were, could confuse subordinates about the direction of High School Redesign. When teachers at five high schools involved in Disciplinary Literacy told researchers that they felt overwhelmed by the long menu of AISD reforms, state tests, and transformations of district high schools, Forgione agreed with the teachers that the pace of reforms and internal consistency among initiatives were a problem—telling an interviewer that "what I'm trying to do this year [2007] is have more coherence at the district level."[70]

By 2008, then, Forgione and his team had crafted a district reform strategy and implemented it sufficiently and flexibly, while being acutely aware of the dangers of having too many reforms churning simultaneously. By that time, he could point with pride to rising test scores, higher graduation rates, more Austin schools recognized by state ratings and national rankings, and strong links to Austin civic and business leaders committed to sustaining the reforms.

On test scores, Forgione cited the National Assessment of Educational Progress (NAEP), which had trial-tested urban students in eleven districts in 2005 and 2007. Austin had scored first or second in the rankings both times (Charlotte-Mecklenburg was the other high scorer). National media reports of these test results confirmed the superintendent's assessment of AISD progress and gave further legitimacy to the district's gains in student achievement. In spite of that progress, however, Forgione reminded others that four of the eleven high schools "need a big push and three others [are] on the critical list [under state and federal ratings]."[71]

In pointing out Austin's high ranking in the NAEP results, Forgione also announced that ninety-four campuses had been rated Exemplary, Recognized, or Academically Acceptable. Yet ten schools —the highest number since 2000—had been rated Academically Unacceptable. He offered a mixed picture of progress and regress. He cast the district as an urban school system moving in the right direction but still having a number of high-poverty, high-minority, low-performing middle and high schools.[72]

Although Forgione's 2006 speech outlining the three phases of reform skipped over the inevitable unpredictability, sudden crises, and errors involved in building a district-wide improvement strategy, Forgione, like other big-city superintendents and CEOs of large corporations, gave a rational patina to actions that he and his team took in solving district problems.

Readers need no reminder that urban school systems like AISD are large bureaucratic organizations whose leaders, through coercion, incentives, and persuasion, try to steer hundreds of administrators and thousands of teachers toward improved practices aimed at achieving district goals. Yet as independent and powerful as these boards and superintendents seem to groups in the community, they are totally dependent upon the political and financial support of parents, community leaders, and state officials. When organized groups of citizens demand changes in policy, school boards and superintendents often respond (as we've seen with Forgione's Blueprint and his recommendations for Webb Middle School). Or when the state alters its funding formulas to give low-wealth districts more money, wealthier districts suffer from leaner budgets and reduced programs (as when AISD cut art and music teachers in 2003).

Moreover, economic recessions, demographic changes, and unexpected events (the terrorist attacks of September 11, 2001; hurricanes Katrina and Rita in 2005) can shatter the shell of control and rational action that district leaders project to the community as they scramble to accommodate reduced revenues, a sudden influx of refugee families, or tragedies that affect schools. Nor is it a surprise that school districts mirror the larger socioeconomic structures and social beliefs that shape the expectations of parents and society at large about what should occur within its schools (everyone should graduate and go to college; students should follow mandatory dress codes) and classrooms (the atmosphere should be orderly; everyone should meet the academic standards). District leaders, then, while appearing as rational actors in charge of organizations governed by rules and bureaucrats, often act in political and nonrational ways.

Even if one acknowledges the nonrational features of district reform, the pride felt by Forgione and the board in the district's academic accomplishments is clear. Also clear is the superintendent's awareness of the zigzag path of reform, as it moves from the state capital to board meetings and from there to his suite at 1111 West

6th Street, and to each school, and, within schools, from the principal's office to classrooms. Not only is it a meandering path filled with potholes and dead-ends; it is a road with turnouts, where policy adaptations often occur as they wend their uncertain way into teachers' lessons. That classroom destination, however, remains a possibility, not a probability, since board members and the superintendent's staff know that what they proclaim, even demand, may not be what principals and teachers hear and do.

An understanding of the crooked policy-to-practice journey of district reforms and of the fact that boards of education and superintendents take political and nonrational actions is crucial, because High School Redesign in Austin is a huge undertaking. The conversion of comprehensive high schools into small learning communities is the subject of the next chapter.

3

Reinventing the High School, 2005–2008

Austin is very similar to other urban districts in its demography, its patterns of constant reform mixed with leadership instability, and its primary strategy of district improvement through standards-based testing and accountability. Austin is also similar to most districts in embracing small high schools as the vehicle for reforming the traditional comprehensive high school and reversing the familiar pattern of anemic academic achievement in high-minority, high-poverty schools. Where Austin differs from other districts is in its decision to convert all eleven of its high schools into small high schools at the same time.

In 2005, the superintendent informed the Board of Trustees of his five-year Strategic Plan. Forgione pledged that AISD would be a "world-class school district by 2010," with students achieving at higher levels in all subjects and "achievement gaps . . . eliminated." Further, "no campuses will be Academically Unacceptable." All high schools would "provide smaller, more intimate learning communities." One goal specifically called for ensuring that the "district meet the needs of all student groups," with priority given to "African American adolescents and recent immigrant English-Language Learners." The primary strategy to achieve these goals would be to "develop and implement a sustainable high school redesign program that is based on best practices, . . . that includes a strong focus on academic rigor, relevance, and relationships, [and] which results in college/career preparation and college entry."[1]

Of course, the superintendent and the Board of Trustees knew that substantial gains in elementary schools' academic achievement across the district had not yet shown up in largely minority and poor middle and high schools. The board also knew that at least four of the eleven high schools had been rated Academically Unacceptable in these years. Moreover, state pressure on high schools to meet annual escalating standards of test performance on the TAKS exam would be unrelenting. The Strategic Plan became a publicly available tool for Forgione to use in reinventing AISD comprehensive high schools—including high-performing ones such as Austin and Bowie, since low-income minorities in those schools (as NCLB revealed) were doing poorly.[2]

These goals and plan were well within the national pattern, in which urban district reformers saw high schools as broken and in need of wholesale, not retail, repair. As a means of transforming high schools, the "Effective Schools and Districts" strategy was pervasive among urban district leaders, and Austin was no exception.

Forgione was well aware that high school reform was popular among national civic and business leaders fretful over pressures from global competitors and inadequately skilled graduates. He certainly had heard that message often from Texas leaders when he testified before legislative committees. In Austin, Forgione's networks included contacts with the city's Chamber of Commerce (which sponsored partnerships with AISD schools), the Greater Austin Hispanic Chamber of Commerce, the E3 Alliance ("Education Equals Economics"), and Austin Area Research Organizations (a group of educational and business leaders). He shared their concerns for skilled high school graduates and often spoke publicly about the link between diplomas and economic success. At one High School Redesign meeting, he told the audience: "If you don't have some kind of post-secondary degree or certification today, you might as well kiss the middle class goodbye."[3]

Because money for high school reform flowed generously from national foundations and state agencies, getting dollars to plan and implement any redesign was relatively easy, so long as district leadership was stable, determined to alter the traditional comprehensive high school, accommodated donors' agendas, and had data to support the case for reform. All of those factors were present in AISD by 2004.

To obtain independent data, district officials contracted with the Southern Regional Education Board and the University of Texas to audit the eleven high schools. Their reports gave Forgione the data he needed. He knew what the Gates Foundation wanted: personalized schooling in small learning communities (SLCs). Because he, too, wanted those features and was willing to mandate them, he assured foundation officials those elements would be prominent in the reform of Austin's traditional high schools.[4]

With these grants and local funds, AISD rounded up external groups (including Stanford University's School Redesign Network, the University of Pittsburgh's Institute for Learning, and the University of Texas' Dana Center) to help district staff reconceptualize the traditional comprehensive high school while negotiating with whole-school reform developers such as James P. Connell at First Things First.

How similar was AISD's pursuit of high school reform to that of other urban districts? Most big-city districts had employed two different approaches within the Effective Schools and Districts strategy to fix broken systems: one was top-down, and the other was a mix of bottom-up and top-down. No large urban system that I know of had committed itself to a bottom-up strategy of relying upon teachers and parents to transform the district. Many, including AISD, opted for a mixed strategy.

Top-down mandates, along with rigorous (and sometimes hard-hitting) monitoring of subordinates to get desired outcomes, were implemented in the San Diego Unified School District when Alan Bersin, a former federal district attorney, served as superintendent (bringing in New York ex-superintendent Anthony Alvarado as his deputy), and were also implemented in New York City in the years 1998–2005 under Rudy Crew, school chancellor in the administration of Rudy Giuliani from 1995 to 1999.

Bersin and Crew both reorganized their bureaucracies, fired principals, and ordered massive district and school procedural changes that stressed instructional improvement. Both created professional development structures for helping new appointees and veteran staff gain necessary skills to operate within a reorganized system. And both exited from their respective districts after persistent fights with, in San Diego's case, a split school board and, in New York City, Mayor Giuliani. Whether or not schools had altered teaching practices sufficiently to help students improve their test scores, champions and critics of the departed school chiefs contested the results.[5]

An example of a blended strategy would be the one used in the 1990s in New York City's Community District 2, which contained lower Manhattan and a sliver of the wealthy East Side (community districts were abolished in 2002).[6] In those years, District 2 superintendent Anthony Alvarado presided over 22,000 elementary and middle school students, half of whom were poor. He cut his headquarters staff drastically and reassigned them to schools. He worked closely with teachers (including union leaders), while pushing principals to become instructional leaders. He encouraged schools to design innovations sharply focused on teaching and learning, and to create small learning communities. Teacher and principal leaders brokered strong ties with parents as dozens of choices flourished across District 2. Coaches from successful programs elsewhere were imported to work with school staffs. An entire infrastructure of professional development helped teachers, administrators, and parents share ideas across the district. And Alvarado ensured accountability by having district officials closely monitor test scores, surveys of parent satisfaction, teacher and principal turnover, and student attendance.[7]

Well aware of the literature on district change and the strategies used in other big cities such as Boston, where superintendent Thomas Payzant (appointed by the mayor) had been serving as superintendent since 1995, Forgione crafted a hybrid of both top-down and bottom-up strategies that would fit the broad variation in Austin's eleven high schools, where academic high fliers mixed with failure-prone schools.[8]

Based on the eleven schools' academic performance, AISD officials divided them into three levels: "urgent priority," "high priority," and "deliberate priority." The three levels mirrored the historical configuration of AISD; schools that had largely minority and poor enrollments were placed in the "urgent priority" category (Johnston, Reagan, LBJ, Travis, and Lanier).[9] These schools had received TEA's lowest rating of Academically Unacceptable or NCLB's rating Needs Improvement—both of which were euphemisms for failure, and possible closure if performance continued to lag. These chronically low-performing schools had predominantly enrolled minority and poor students for decades. Besides falling short of TEA's standards for passing the state test, these schools commonly had poor attendance, low graduation rates, and, worst of all, high dropout rates.

"High priority" schools (Akins, Crockett) skirted low performance ratings from time to time, yet were not immediately threatened by closure. Those schools labeled "deliberate priority" (Bowie, Anderson, Austin, and McCallum) were ones where staff, parents, and alumni of the high-performing schools (with majorities or substantial numbers of middle-class whites) were given more time to plan and implement changes. Stakeholders in these high-achieving schools were largely satisfied with their college preparation and sports programs. Yet although there were National Merit Scholarship finalists and trophies for academic excellence, minority students' low achievement and the staff's inadequacy in dealing with English-language learners worried officials and some parents. These schools were given more time to redesign.[10]

In these different high schools, a blend of district-office mandates with school-by-school redesigns emerged. For example, Forgione directed all high schools to introduce "advisories"—periods during the week when teachers would meet with small groups of students to discuss academic and nonacademic issues. All schools had to create small learning communities—sometimes called "academies" or "schools-within-a-school"—for students and teachers. Also, high schools had to choose whether they were going to be involved in Disciplinary Literacy, an instructional approach to classroom lessons that was imported from the University of Pittsburgh's Institute for Learning; whether they would adopt the whole-school reform model "First Things First" designed by the Institute for Research and Reform in Education and tested in Kansas City (Kans.) and Houston; or whether they would design their own model. Finally, from these SLCs and models, each school had to create professional learning communities

(PLCs) of teachers and administrators, to help them expand their expertise in school activities and classroom lessons.[11]

In pursuing this blended strategy of reinventing AISD comprehensive high schools, the Board of Trustees and the superintendent assumed that the following chain of actions would occur. Creating small high schools focusing on state curriculum standards using advisories and small learning communities would bring students closer to staff and thereby personalize instruction on existing campuses. Teachers and administrators forming professional learning communities would, in turn, move toward nontraditional school and classroom practices that would engage students in learning. This process would lead to improved scores on state and national tests, lower dropout rates, increased graduation rates, and larger numbers of Austin graduates entering college. This chain of linked assumptions is similar to those embraced in other districts pursuing small high schools.[12]

By 2006, the Austin Board of Trustees had approved each school's redesign and implementation plan. Within two years, all of the "urgent," "high," and "deliberate" priority high schools, working closely with Office of School Redesign staff, were engaged in the very complicated work of converting their high schools to SLCs, PLCs, and advisories. Block scheduling for SLCs—eliminated in an earlier budget cut—also spread quickly among "urgent" and "high" priority schools.[13]

Under great pressure to redesign their chronically low-performing schools, Reagan, LBJ, and Travis high school administrators, teachers, and parents visited Kansas City and Houston high schools that had adopted First Things First (FTF). After much arm-twisting by district administrators, school staffs adopted the comprehensive whole-school reform model.[14]

Policy Logic of High School Redesign

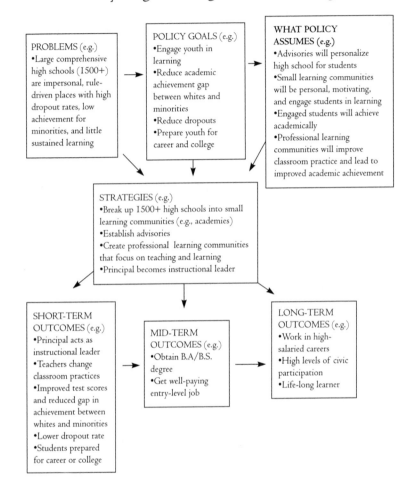

PROBLEMS (e.g.)
•Large comprehensive high schools (1500+) are impersonal, rule-driven places with high dropout rates, low achievement for minorities, and little sustained learning

POLICY GOALS (e.g.)
•Engage youth in learning
•Reduce academic achievement gap between whites and minorities
•Reduce dropouts
•Prepare youth for career and college

WHAT POLICY ASSUMES (e.g.)
•Advisories will personalize high school for students
•Small learning communities will be personal, motivating, and engage students in learning
•Engaged students will achieve academically
•Professional learning communities will improve classroom practice and lead to improved academic achievement

STRATEGIES (e.g.)
•Break up 1500+ high schools into small learning communities (e.g., academies)
•Establish advisories
•Create professional learning communities that focus on teaching and learning
•Principal becomes instructional leader

SHORT-TERM OUTCOMES (e.g.)
•Principal acts as instructional leader
•Teachers change classroom practices
•Improved test scores and reduced gap in achievement between whites and minorities
•Lower dropout rate
•Students prepared for career or college

MID-TERM OUTCOMES (e.g.)
•Obtain B.A/B.S. degree
•Get well-paying entry-level job

LONG-TERM OUTCOMES (e.g.)
•Work in high-salaried careers
•High levels of civic participation
•Life-long learner

Developed by Institute for Research and Reform in Education (IRRE) the model promises to increase attendance, reduce dropout rates, and improve students' scores on state tests. To achieve these outcomes, every FTF high school had to create:

1. Small learning communities of about 300 students centered on a theme (law and government, business and technology, performing arts, and so on) that would be pursued in core and elective subjects. The students would stay together for four years, taking core classes from the same cadre of teachers, who also have common planning time. In the students' senior year, internships relevant to each SLC's theme would become available.

2. A family advocate system that would meet weekly with fifteen students and one teacher. The teacher would monitor, advise, and celebrate students' achievements, and would meet regularly with students' families. Thus, each student and family would come to know (and count on) at least one teacher in ways that are uncommon in most large high schools.

3. Professional development for teachers, training them to design rigorous and varied lessons that both engage students and meet state standards. Available coaches and extensive data gathering in classrooms would establish the degree of rigor, variation, and student engagement in lessons. Professional learning communities would find homes in SLC academies and academic departments where teachers would discuss students, plan lessons, and work with coaches.[15]

Independent evaluations of First Things First in Kansas City supported IRRE's claims of success, permitting Forgione to sell FTF to the board and high school communities not as an experiment but as a tested model that did what it said it would do. As a result of intensive negotiations with Jim Connell and IRRE staff aimed at tailoring FTF to Austin's high schools, IRRE promised to provide coaches and technical assistance for Reagan, LBJ, and Travis. The three schools are currently in the early stages of putting this model into practice.[16]

Reagan High School, for example, has an enrollment of just under a thousand students, of whom 67 percent are Mexican American (nearly one out of three of these are English-language learners), 30 percent are African American, 2 percent are white, and 85 percent are poor.[17] Daily attendance averages 85 percent (the state average is 95; the AISD average, 94). Like the daily attendance rate, Reagan's graduation rate is dismal: only 60 percent of the students graduated in 2006 (the state's average percentage is 80; AISD's is 77). Scores on TAKS failed to meet any of the state's standards.[18]

In 2003, a male student at Reagan stabbed his ex-girlfriend to death during the school day. The murder sent waves of fear and anger through the Eastside community and led to the swift appointment of a Community Safety Task Force that examined school violence and security measures to prevent student attacks on other students and teachers. Neither the task force report nor added school security made Reagan any more attractive to new students or teachers. And state and federal Unsatisfactory ratings for low test scores in subsequent years hardly boosted confidence in Reagan's leadership or staff.

By 2006, TEA was monitoring Reagan with a "Campus Intervention Team Leader" because of a previous Unacceptable rating. Furthermore, under No Child Left Behind sanctions for substandard performance, the high schools also had a "Technical Assistance Provider" and offered parents transfers to other schools. In 2007, transfers to other high schools escalated.[19]

Frequent turnover in leadership has hurt the school. In the decade 1997–2008, the school had six principals. When I visited in 2007,

Ismael Villafane, a veteran of Texas and New York high schools that had undergone reform, had been at Reagan for a year. The majority of the seventy-five teachers had less than five years of experience (21 percent came to Reagan with no experience).[20]

With a growing sense of desperation at the school and in the Eastside community, top AISD administrators used High School Redesign to throw the life preserver of First Things First. After a full year of planning in 2006–2007, Villafane and his staff organized three small learning communities called Art of Learning (AOL), Leadership, Engineering, Architecture, Design (LEAD), and Medical, Science, Health (MASH), scheduled to begin in the fall of 2007. I visited the school for two mornings in December 2007.[21]

A few students were wearing T-shirts with their SLC's color and logo; most were not. Security aides patrolled the Old Mall and New Mall corridors, shooing students into classes. Some students had ID badges with their name, photo, and SLC on it. Motivational signs ("Hard Work Pays Off") dotted the walls of both classroom buildings. In the atrium of the Old Mall, a very large wooden sign posted the attendance goal: "95% and Better!!" with space for a number to be inserted next to each class, freshman through senior. A nearby wooden sign said, "TAKS Countdown!!!!" Below it were the words "Days Left" and, below that, "Raiders Preparing to 'Rock' the Test!!!"

Scheduling SLCs, Family Advocacy groups, electives, and sufficient in-class time for engaging and content-rich lessons remained difficult, according to teachers and students. Common planning time for teachers, for example, encompassed just two of the three SLCs. The school used a varied schedule during the week I visited. One day was block scheduled for ninety-minute periods and the other day was divided into forty-one-minute periods.

I observed two Family Advocacy meetings. One group of eleven students and a teacher was fertilizing the flowers and shrubs in the atrium with coffee grounds from a local Starbucks. The other advisory group of thirteen students were discussing with the teacher their course grades and an upcoming money-raising effort for AOL.

Of the fourteen classes I visited, many were small (one had only eight students; the largest had twenty-one; the average had fifteen). Most students were attentive to the teacher and worked on assigned tasks. In half of the classes, at least one or two students had their head down on their desk with their eyes closed. Some teachers said nothing to these students; other teachers asked them to pay attention, or to go to the nurse if they were feeling ill. In none of the classes I observed did I see any open conflict between teacher and students.

Teachers collected homework from some but not many students. When students read aloud in class, it was obvious that many had trouble with the text or worksheet passage. In one class, a late-term pregnant student helped the teacher set up the math class for group work; in another class, the teacher worked individually with a gang member (according to the teacher) who was trying hard to pass algebra.

I saw lessons where the teacher wrote the daily objective on the whiteboard, reviewed homework, distributed worksheets, and had question-and-answer exchanges with students. Nearly all of the lessons were geared to the state test. In one class, for example, the chemistry teacher reviewed with students how to write formulas, since such items appeared on TAKS.

Three of the fourteen teachers conducted lessons different from the norm: one social studies teacher had a thirty-minute discussion based on text and supplementary readings about the use of gross domestic product as an economic indicator; a geometry teacher used six learning centers, where students in groups moved from one station to another to complete tasks that would be on TAKS; students used graphing calculators for some of the station tasks. In another class, the teacher had students teach each other concepts of genes and alleles—items on the state test.

None of the above classroom observations struck me as being uncommon in largely minority and poor urban high schools. Nor did I see anything unusual in a school in the early stages of converting into small learning communities with advisories and block scheduling while under great pressure from district administrators and TEA to raise test scores or get shut down. Nor did I find strange the obvious home and neighborhood effects spilling over school and classroom. Sleepy students, gang tattoos, much absenteeism, and security concerns (evident in highly visible adults patrolling the halls) are also common in big-city high schools elsewhere in the nation. In short, what I observed briefly at Reagan is what one would reasonably expect to see in the first year of implementation of small learning communities in a school largely attended by mostly poor, minority students, including a large segment of English-language learners.[22]

Whether these determined efforts and FTF would prevent Reagan from being closed has yet to be seen. Reagan is in Stage 4 of NCLB, and after 2008 TAKS scores showed that the school would be again rated Academically Unacceptable, it moved into a "Reconstitution" phase mandated by the state. The restructuring plan that the district submitted to TEA calls FTF the school's "fundamental reforms" to improve academic achievement. But after the school was rated Unacceptable for a second straight year, district officials removed the principal and made further program shifts. This plan buys Reagan more time.[23]

For Johnston High School, however, the future has arrived. Johnston was closed by the state commissioner in 2008 after being rated Academically Unacceptable five years in a row (and eight out of the previous nine years).

In 2007 Johnston had around 700 students (more than 80 percent Hispanic; 17 percent black; more than 80 percent poor). It had eleven principals in fifteen years—the last one, Celina Estrada-Thomas, served three years, the longest tenure in nearly two decades. With only 80 percent of the students coming to school daily and just under 60 percent graduating, the label "urgent priority" barely captured the burning necessity for improvement. In 2005, Estrada-Thomas and her staff converted the comprehensive high school into three academies, using a Texas High School Redesign and Restructuring grant. In 2007, after the school received two more Unacceptable ratings, the decision to close the school rested on the desk of the state commissioner.[24]

Superintendent Forgione pleaded with the commissioner to keep the school open, because it was about to adopt the First Things First model and receive instructional help from IRRE. The commissioner agreed. Midway through the school year, however, Estrada-Thomas withdrew Johnston from FTF. No miraculous spike in test scores occurred—such bolts of lightning seldom happen outside of Hollywood. Johnston again missed the mark set by the state, and the commissioner ordered the school to close its doors.[25]

Within two weeks, the Board of Trustees had approved Forgione's plan for a new high school that basically followed state rules for reconstituting a closed school. For 2008–2009, the school was renamed Eastside Memorial High School—a name suggested by parents and alumni of Johnston. An interim principal was appointed; and upwards of 75 percent new staff, with substantial stipends and bonuses designed to attract experienced teachers, started work at Eastside Memorial. Half of the former Johnston students were assigned to other high schools, so half of the students at Eastside Memorial came from other attendance zones. Master teachers were hired to coach the faculty. In 2009–2010, Eastside will have schools-within-the-school, including New Tech High, a small school focused on science and engineering, and Global Tech, an international studies school.[26]

Reagan and Johnston illustrate the way schools with "urgent priority" labels have implemented the First Things First model or other approaches. Lanier, another high school in the same category, has assembled its own version of a redesigned high school.

In 1997 Lanier had been a blue-ribbon school, federally recognized for its improvement and its high performance. But demographic changes altered it so greatly over the next decade that it became "urgent priority." In 2006 it had nearly 1,600 students: 70 percent Hispanic (of whom 28 percent were ELL), 18 percent African American, and 8 percent white. Three out of every four students came from poor families. Daily attendance (88 percent) fell below both district and state averages. Ditto for the graduation rate (71 percent). Contributing to the grim list of statistics were low achievement on state tests and growing gang conflicts that spilled over onto the school. Lanier was a tough school needing strong leadership to ensure, first, students' safety, and, second, a strong academic program that met district standards and received satisfactory state and federal ratings.

AISD had appointed Edmund Oropez as principal in 2004–2005. By the end of the school year, he had hired new staff (many had departed for easier assignments), had banned gang colors from the school building, and had turned his attention toward redesigning the comprehensive high school.[27]

Seeking quick action, Oropez and a cadre of enthusiastic teachers were determined to reinvent Lanier in ways they wanted, with as little direction from the AISD district office as possible. He made it clear to the staff that they had to share his commitment to a Lanier they could be proud of; if they did not want to work toward that goal, they should look for positions elsewhere. Oropez extracted from his AISD superiors the latitude to use budgeted funds to trade allocated teaching positions for nonteaching staff, a waiver that gave him flexibility to hire people for key posts in the school. With high teacher turnover the first three years and the superintendent's use of this waiver, nearly two of three Lanier teachers and other staff in 2007 were new to the school and were willing to stay with Oropez. The staff had become "Lanier-a-sized."[28]

The initial task was to develop a ninth-grade academy as an SLC, in which teams of teachers across four academic subjects would share students. Faculty and administrators invented their version of an advisory, which had a common curriculum for all students in grades 9–12 and which met four days a week for thirty minutes (2007–2008). After much bargaining with district officials, Oropez and the Lanier staff came up with a block schedule that met the needs of department chairs, ninth-grade academy teachers, advisory leaders, and teachers of elective subjects (such as band and sports). Staff actually lengthened the school day by seventeen minutes without getting permission from district office administrators.[29]

Professional learning communities grew out of the ninth-grade academy, in which core-subject teachers shared the same students and met weekly to discuss their students' progress or lack thereof. Lanier staff pushed even further and developed their own lesson-planning cycle, as well as teacher-made Instructional Planning Guides to steer PLCs in math, science, social studies, and English / language arts. Again, Oropez had received permission from AISD to ignore district planning guides.[30]

Oropez and his staff also revised the traditional summer school sessions—calling them "camps"—and ran two of them, one for students who needed makeup credits to stay with their class and the other for targeted eighth-grade students entering Lanier who had failed middle school courses. Mornings were spent in long subject-centered periods to get students used to a block schedule, and afternoons were spent in clubs taught by elective teachers and coaches.[31]

These Lanier initiatives bent and occasionally ignored AISD directives, while carving out a large chunk of autonomy. The freedom also meant that when the principal and staff wanted to work more intensely with ELL students, they could reach out to another organization such as WestEd second-language experts to develop an improvement plan for these students. Staff members joked that Lanier had seceded from the district or that the district office, in the words of one teacher, let "us do our thing"—different ways of saying that a strong principal and committed staff had redesigned the school from the bottom up.[32]

By 2009, however, the situation had changed. Lanier received a rating of Academically Acceptable from the state, but under NCLB it failed to meet Adequate Yearly Progress (AYP) requirements (for example, the standard established for the graduation rate was 70 percent, but Lanier's rate was only 67 percent). With a new principal at the helm, the school was in stage 4 of NCLB's Needs Improvement category. In this stage, the state requires the district to submit a plan for restructuring the school—recall that Johnston High School was in the same boat earlier. District officials recommended to the school board that Lanier, like Johnston, be restructured into small learning communities.[33]

Even "urgent priority" high schools, then, showed variation in actual redesign and in the way each school went about restructuring.

Was there similar variation among "high priority" and "deliberate priority" schools?

Consider Akins High School. Named after a popular black AISD administrator who, in the 1960s, was one of the first "cross-over" teachers to integrate a white faculty, Akins opened as a brand-new school in 2000. Within six years, the 2,300-student school (65 percent Hispanic, 20 percent white, 12 percent African American, 34 percent poor) had exceeded its capacity. Even before High School Redesign was launched, Mary Alice Deike, a newly appointed entrepreneurial principal, believed that Akins was in trouble. Although the school's attendance, dropout, and graduation rates were very close to district averages and although Akins had been rated Academically Acceptable, gaps between minorities and whites on tests and in Advanced Placement enrollment had become obvious to the new principal.[34]

Impressed with the report on AISD high schools prepared by the Southern Regional Education Board, the hard-driving Deike snared a state grant to partner with SREB's "High Schools That Work" reform model. She wanted to transform the comprehensive high school into a group of high-achieving small learning communities with weekly thirty-minute advisories, block scheduling, and PLCs for teachers.[35]

In 2005, the work began. All ninth-graders became one academy. In the spring before starting tenth grade, students would choose to enroll in one of four career academies: Business and Legal Enterprise; Agriculture, Computers, and Engineering Sciences; Arts and Humanities; and Social Services. In 2007, another academy, New Tech High, joined the other four.[36]

As academies came online, PLCs involving academic departments and cross-subject teams appeared. Teachers of math, science, English, and social studies worked with Institute for Learning (IFL) staff in the Disciplinary Literacy program on subject-driven instructional issues and classroom lessons, to sharpen their skills and broaden their knowledge. These PLCs made up of cross-subject academy teams focused on sharing student information and on finding the best ways to reach those who needed help.[37]

In redesigning Akins to fit the "High Schools That Work" model, Deike also wanted to see assistant principals and teachers playing a larger role in school-wide decisions and leading academies, rather than waiting to hear from the principal. "Teachers are the sleeping giants of education," she told an interviewer. "We need to empower them. . . . It's what happens in the classroom that counts. All the redesign plans in the world won't matter if you don't change what happens in the classroom."[38]

This view about the signal importance of classroom teaching helps to explain Deike's abiding commitment to a pedagogy anchored in progressive practices and Disciplinary Literacy, where teachers lead students to question, investigate, and solve real-world problems through engaging projects and other activities. Teachers could see one another teach a lesson (through a technique called "learning walks," developed by the University of Pittsburgh's Institute for Learning but adapted by Akins staff and renamed "ghost walks" or "buddy walks") and then discuss what was observed. This helped to advance Deike's agenda of active student learning and ambitious teaching.[39]

All of these major structural changes and plans for pedagogical shifts occurred without disruption, despite teacher turnover and Deike's departure in 2007. Unlike other AISD high schools with similar student demographics and ongoing redesign, Akins maintained an average of 20 to 25 percent turnover in these years—equal to the district average but higher than the state figure. The exit of the entrepreneurial principal (who left to complete her doctorate) could have wreaked havoc with the redesign, but thus far it has not. The new principal, Daniel Girard, was a veteran administrator who had headed a school using the SREB model in El Paso and had been urged to apply by Deike. Once he was appointed, Deike deftly handed the redesign baton to Girard.[40]

The swift implementation of new structures such as five academies, advisories, PLCs, and block scheduling in less than three years, and hopes for dramatic changes in classroom instruction put Akins at the frontier of redesign in AISD. A principal who had snared state money and implemented a high school reform model had forged well ahead of what the district office expected and what sister schools in the "urgent priority" and "high priority" categories had done.

Finally, consider "deliberate priority" Austin High School, the oldest in the city, which celebrated its 125th anniversary in 2008. For decades, Austin's civic and business elite had considered Austin High a suitable school for its sons and daughters, including state governors and former president George W. Bush. In 2007 it had 2,200 students: 57 percent white, 36 percent Hispanic (5 percent of whom were ELL), 6 percent black, and 26 percent poor.[41]

Proud of its National Merit Scholarship semifinalists, its range of Advanced Placement courses, and the large numbers of students taking the AP test, Austin High is notable for its academic performance, on both the city and state levels. Yet TAKS scores reveal a tale of two schools in one: minority students score lower than whites in all academic subjects; fewer minorities than whites graduate from school; more minorities than whites drop out. As one staff member said, "For obvious reasons, the attitude is that if it's not broke . . . don't fix it. Well, that's not true. It *is* broke for a large segment of our kids."[42]

The recognition that Austin High is two schools in one mirrors talk of two Americas, rich and poor, inhabiting the same land but riven by inequities that undermine people's faith in meritocracy and fairness. A strong shove from the superintendent convinced principal Barbara Spelman and Austin High staff to participate fully in redesigning their seemingly successful school, but at a deliberate and carefully considered pace. Spelman, who had been there five years in 2005, appointed a "Big Picture" team of teachers and administrators to come up with a redesign plan.

The staff proposed a Freshman Academy of five teacher teams for core subjects, along with common planning time, an advisory program, a senior capstone project, and PLCs. Shortly after this plan was made public, however, Spelman resigned. Everything was put on hold until AISD appointed another principal, in the summer of 2006.[43]

New principal John Hudson, the sixth since 1990, had acquired rich experience heading high schools in Arizona and Connecticut. Within months, however, messy problems arose in the Freshman Academy over scheduling, the absence of common planning time for teachers, and larger than usual classes.[44]

In 2007–2008, Hudson worked closely with the veteran staff, many of whom had taught for more than twenty years at Austin. Together they reconfigured the Freshman Academy and solved the problems that had unfolded the previous year. Next, Hudson and his staff agreed to launch a twice-weekly advisory (twenty-five minutes each meeting) called the "community seminar," where all teachers and administrators, including the principal, would work with fifteen to twenty students. Advisory leaders received training and curriculum materials from an external provider called Educators for Social Responsibility.[45]

Hudson also wanted PLCs. At Austin High in 2007–2008, PLCs operated within departments. Hudson felt that if there were going to be any changes in classroom practice, PLCs and the school's leadership team would need to add depth and bite to daily teaching (when he visited classes, he noted that teachers tended to rely far too much on lecturing). As Hudson put it: "If we cannot recognize good instruction, we will reinforce poor practice." One veteran teacher at Austin High said: "[Instruction] . . . that's where [Hudson] is really right on. In the very first semester when he came in, he told me that just in, like, the first six weeks he knew that . . . we had this great reputation [but] we are in the trap of doing the same old, same old. We come up with the same excuses of why we do the same old, same old. . . . We need to be trained on inquiry, on Disciplinary Literacy." Through PLCs, teachers could observe their peers and discuss the observations. Hudson hired two on-site coaches for teachers in the Social Studies and Science departments, and expanded the work with Disciplinary Literacy.[46]

The engine for Austin High's PLCs was Disciplinary Literacy. In the summer of 2007, the school sent twenty subject-matter teachers to a workshop in Pittsburgh to improve their writing of daily objectives and creating common templates for lessons. With PLCs focusing on classroom instruction in academic subjects, with one SLC in operation, and with advisories meeting weekly, Austin High has slowly incorporated some pieces of High School Redesign.[47]

Although the description of Austin High's redesign ends here, I would like to say a few more words about Disciplinary Literacy (DL), for two reasons. First, five Westside high schools (Akins, Anderson, Austin, Crockett, and McCallum)—schools that have higher proportions of white, middle-, and upper-middle-class students than Eastside schools—have made it central to their PLCs. Second, district leaders assume that DL's work with principals and teachers will stretch their instructional knowledge and skills sufficiently to drive changes in daily classroom practice, and that these improvements will, in turn, lead to fewer dropouts, more graduates, and higher student scores on the state test. DL, then, is a strategy aimed at improving teaching practices—in contrast to First Things First, which is a school-wide reform.[48]

Principles of Learning and Disciplinary Literacy

Shortly after Forgione arrived in 1999, he told anyone who would listen that he had seen too much *pluribus* and too little *unum* in AISD curriculum and schools. The entire AISD staff needed a common framework and instructional language to help students measure up to Texas Essential Knowledge and Skills (TEKS) standards—which Forgione had mandated as AISD curriculum standards. After decades of innovative reading, writing, and math programs that tumbled over one another and sent staff off in different directions, Forgione, Darlene Westbrook, and top staff pressed for fewer and clearer concepts to drive instructional practice. In 2000, Superintendent Forgione hired Lauren Resnick, director of the Institute for Learning (IFL) at the University of Pittsburgh, to work with AISD teachers and administrators on IFL's Principles of Learning.[49]

With multi-year funding, IFL staff worked on selected "principles" such as "Academic Rigor in a Thinking Curriculum" and "Clear Expectations." IFL consultants ran workshops, provided on-site assistance, and trained principals to be instructional heads who worked closely with teacher leaders to put those "principles" into practice. They used methods such as "learning walks," in which administrators and teachers observed classroom lessons to determine if "clear expectations" were being practiced.[50]

AISD and IFL continued their partnership through 2003–2004. When High School Redesign started up a year later, Forgione and

Westbrook knew that IFL's prior work in the district, anchored in the belief that effort—not inherited abilities—made the difference in academic performance, had established common concepts and language directed toward instructional practice. AISD signed a contract with IFL. The program called Principles of Learning was renamed Disciplinary Literacy, and five high schools voluntarily signed up to work with IFL staff.[51]

Beginning in 2006, IFL staff trained lead teachers in English, math, social studies, and science (site and district administrators and curriculum specialists also attended sessions) to design rigorous lessons in each subject that would engage students. These teachers learned how to analyze lessons through videos and observations. They learned how to lead "learning walks" and guide PLC discussions in their academies and departments. Recall the way Akins High School had adapted IFL's "learning walk" into shorter and different forms, to take advantage of limited teacher time.[52]

In 2008, two outside evaluators reported the views of teachers and administrators in the five high schools and the district office. Many of them had been involved in the earlier IFL venture. Staff responses to DL were generally positive among the lead teachers, who had used it in designing and leading their PLCs. Even with two-thirds of the teachers reporting they attended PLC sessions, evaluators found much variation across school groups and within each school's PLCs. Although most teachers commented favorably on the sharing of ideas and practices that occurred in the five high school PLCs, only about half of them reported that their colleagues observed each other's classrooms.[53]

Still, the comments of lead teachers after two years in the program were highly positive. The evaluators were able to identify tensions that had existed before DL arrived and that continued to affect DL implementation. Lack of time bothered teachers a great deal. One lead teacher said: "There are not enough hours in my day to complete all the things mandated. I believe in DL principles, and I believe in strong AP [Advanced Placement] strategies, and I believe in PLCs—but I cannot [do all this] at the same time. The district knows how to ruin a good thing! My teachers don't want to be heroes—they just want to be able to teach and teach well . . . and they want the time to process information at a deep level without being bombarded with 'the next thing.'"[54]

The risk that too many initiatives will overwhelm teachers and principals and the potential danger posed by rambling confusion (do all of these programs move in the same direction?) have for decades been persistent issues in AISD. They constitute the "spinning wheels" syndrome that has afflicted other big-city districts. DL lead teachers, however, expressed to the researchers a "growing sense that DL professional learning communities and High School Redesign are on a collision course" over competition for scheduling meetings and over the frustration felt by teachers, who are torn between the demands from subject-matter departments and the demands for interdisciplinary lessons in their small learning communities.[55]

Also persistent is the tension between DL's pursuit of deep understanding of content and state testing for breadth of factual knowledge. Should teachers, for example, devote an entire week of lessons to the role of the Robber Barons in industrializing the United States? Or should they cover industrialization, the Progressive movement, and World War I in three days because TAKS has included items on those topics? And what about time taken for test preparation in January, February, and March? These issues, of course, predated Disciplinary Literacy, professional development, and small learning communities, but they are brought to the fore by the accountability squeeze and by state ratings that pack a wallop when a school slips into the category of Academically Unacceptable. These issues of potential incoherence and tension between DL's view of classroom practice and the demands of TAKS were painfully present during the early years of reconfiguring the eleven high schools.[56]

With All Deliberate Speed: Implementing High School Redesign

This discussion of AISD's policy strategy to transform high schools makes it clear that planning and implementation varied a great deal among the eleven schools. Disciplinary Literacy has been used in five high schools in the "high priority" and "deliberate priority" categories, while First Things First has been implemented in three "urgent priority" high schools. Two "deliberate priority" schools (Bowie and Anderson) have moved unhurriedly to initiate advisories and small learning communities. Lanier (an "urgent priority" school) has borrowed liberally from DL, FTF, and other models to fashion its own design from the ground up, further adapting it as practice dictated.[57]

In view of all of this district-office planning and school action, it is too soon to determine whether the complexity of High School Redesign, which has so many working parts (SLCs, advisories, PLCs), will fit together smoothly, rather than causing the entire reform machine to fly off in different directions. District officials might heap too many demands and other initiatives on these schools, even though the Office of Redesign is carefully monitoring activities. In that case, there would be a risk of stripping the gears of this ambitious attempt to reinvent eleven comprehensive high schools, alter teaching practices, and improve student achievement. Hardworking teachers and principals would continue to struggle with competing district and state demands upon their limited time. Yet the sought-after effects of the reform—ambitious teaching and engaged student learning—may get drowned out in the clatter of competing initiatives.

Surely, the district decision to adjust the pace of implementation among three levels of priority was a smart move, reducing harmful noise while creating a semblance of coherence. Establishing an Office of Redesign to coordinate key activities was another shrewd action. Within three years, varied components of the redesign were emerging in all eleven high schools, albeit at different speeds. Just as surely, Forgione displayed political and organizational moxie in using both the fist—pressing Eastside principals of schools rated Academically Unacceptable to adopt First Things First, or else—and the velvet glove, allowing some staffs latitude in putting their designs into practice and giving them permission to tailor their design and the pace of implementation to the unique contours of their schools.

The hybrid strategy mixing top-down and bottom-up is a reasonable fit for the Austin schools, which are in the early years of redesign yet are still prone to overloading teachers and principals with competing initiatives. But in 2009, no one—not the Board of Trustees, the superintendent, external evaluators, or AISD officials—could say with any confidence, beyond occasional stories heard from teachers, parents, and principals, what exactly had changed and what had remained the same in the eleven high schools' classrooms since High School Redesign was launched. The ultimate test of redesign will be how well it achieves its goals: improve the quality of teaching and learning in chronically low-performing high schools so as to raise test scores, reduce the achievement gap, increase graduation rates for minorities and English-language learners, and sharply reduce dropouts among the same groups. AISD has not yet passed that test.

Even without clear knowledge of the way High School Redesign affects the classroom, state and federal accountability pressures continue to be as unrelenting as Austin's summer heat. Every year, state and federal ratings squeeze AISD's discretion in its efforts to help low-performing secondary schools. Local crises arise each time the commissioner of education writes to Forgione, saying that Johnston High School or Webb and Pearce Middle Schools will have to be closed, reconstituted, chartered, or contracted out to for-profit companies.

What is likely to happen is that one or two of these "urgent priority" schools may dodge the bullet of closure if they show some improvement within a year (according to TEA rules, though not NCLB regulations), but the staff will still have to worry about the following year could bring. Fretting about what is around the corner is miserable business for a school. Constant agonizing over the future saps the vitality of staff, students, and parents. Often it leads to a downward spiral in which students, teachers, and administrators depart for less dramatic settings.

Why is it that schools not only in Austin but across the nation now shoulder complete responsibility for student failure, when as recently as the 1970s policy elites and educators blamed children and their families for poor academic performance? The answer to this question sheds light on how AISD approached implementation of High School Redesign and how most big-city districts now view their secondary school reform agenda.

How Blame for Academic Failure Shifted from Children and Families to Schools

The shame that staff members feel at being made responsible for a school's low academic performance is a recent phenomenon. Historically, policy elites and educators explained poor academic performance of groups and individual students by pointing to ethnic and racial discrimination, poverty, immigrants' cultures, family deficits, and students' lack of effort. School leaders would say that they could hardly be blamed for reversing conditions over which they had little control. Until the late twentieth century, demography as destiny was the dominant explanation for unequal school outcomes.[58]

Things began to change in the late 1970s. Other explanations for low academic performance among different groups of students gained traction: the school—not racism, poverty, family, culture, or even language differences—caused disadvantages in students. This explanation grew from research studies of urban elementary schools with high percentages of poor and minority students that did far better on national tests than researchers would have predicted from their racial and socioeconomic status.

These high-flying ghetto and barrio schools had common features. The staff believed that all urban children could learn; the principal of each school was an instructional leader; and the staff established high academic standards, with demanding classroom lessons and frequent testing; and each school had an orderly and well-regulated atmosphere. These "effective schools" proved to many skeptics that high-poverty urban schools could be successful, as measured by tests. Students' race, ethnicity, and social class did not doom a school to failure. And most important, a committed and experienced staff who worked closely together could make a decided academic difference in the lives of impoverished children of color. No longer could teachers and administrators blame students and their families for failing. Now it was the responsibility of school staff to ensure student success.[59]

Whereas policy elites and educators formerly said that students and families were to blame for poor performance, reform rhetoric has shifted: today policy elites and educators say that the school or the district is at fault. This fundamental change in perspective on the causes of inequities in outcomes is captured in the words of national leaders, who often repeat the phrase "all children can learn" and admonish teachers and administrators to avoid the "soft bigotry of low expectations." This reversal of responsibility for inequitable outcomes has shifted the burden for academic success almost completely from students' shoulders to those of their teachers, principals, and superintendents. It is as if professionals could take any student and make him or her a success regardless of background.[60]

While most of us cherish egalitarian beliefs—enshrined in the NCLB goal that all students will test proficient by 2014—research studies and the facts of daily experience should give us pause before we nod in agreement. This total equality in results may perhaps occur in heaven, but will never materialize on earth, where variability in families' behaviors and students' talents, motivation, interests, and skills remains a stubborn fact.

Thus, within a few decades, we've seen a 180-degree shift in responsibility for chronic academic failure. Neither extreme, however, squares with the facts. Responsibility rests with both community and district, both school and family, both teachers and students.

Blaming others may be momentarily satisfying but is unhelpful in either improving schools or motivating students to do their best. On the one hand, expecting a school staff to bear full responsibility for students' academic results neglects the long history of research and teachers' daily experience of students who come to school unprepared to learn. Family income, parental education and interest, health issues, neighborhood conditions, and other factors influence what happens to growing children even before they enter kindergarten. If there is one fact researchers have established over and over, it is that family income and education play a large role in children's behavioral and academic performance in schools.[61]

Striking a balance between the documented facts of inequities among students when they appear at the schoolhouse door and the documented facts of some educators' shabby inaction while other educators turn basket-case schools into high-fliers is essential. But it is hard to strike this balance in the current unforgiving climate of state and federal accountability rules that name, blame, and shame districts and schools for gaps in achievement, high dropout rates, and low graduation numbers.[62]

In the current frenzied climate of state and federal penalties for low performance, what students bring to school, both their strengths and weaknesses, are seldom mentioned publicly because policy makers and educators fear being called racist, making excuses, or having low expectations. The dominant one-liner repeated again and again is that efficient, well-managed schools and districts are accountable for students' academic success.[63]

This situation pains those federal, state, and local policy makers and reformers who want to address the socioeconomic structures in the larger society that contribute to economic inequalities and students' disadvantages—structures such as tax policies favoring the wealthy, residential segregation, lack of health insurance, immigration policies, and discriminatory employment practices—but who find it difficult to do so politically. Recall the reformers mentioned earlier who were described as pursuing a strategy of "Community and Schools." But for other state and federal policy makers and philanthropists—the "Effective Schools and Districts" crowd—who are either unaware of or ignore these taken-for-granted powerful structures, directing attention solely to fixing schools is both politically attractive and economically inexpensive, compared to the uproar that would occur if those who enjoy privileges were attacked for leaving those policies and structures untouched.

Austin's Board of Trustees and its superintendent are stuck in the middle of this dilemma as they pursue their ambitious High School Redesign, and have been caught in it ever since *Brown v. Board of Education* made headlines in Austin a half-century ago. Austin's history of segregated schools (Eastside and Westside), foot-dragging desegregation, and subsequent resegregation after 1986 colors the present. This is a reality that African American and Mexican American Austinites acknowledged when, for example, they responded to my questions about closures of Eastside schools with far more awareness of the checkered history of Austin minorities than white interviewees.

High School Redesign policy seeks to eliminate the historical achievement gap between minorities and whites, while rescuing chronically low-performing high schools from a trajectory of failure. In the current climate of putting full responsibility on schools for improving low performance, this reform-driven policy places substantial, nearly impossible demands on district administrators, principals, and teachers.[64]

As surely as Austin's past shaped its policy, other factors came into play. Muscular state intervention into district operations, beginning in the early 1980s, and expansive federal intervention through No Child Left Behind—both of which pressed test-driven accountability rules onto local districts—also influenced how AISD officials and school staffs viewed High School Redesign policies.

Here, then, is the larger context for the implementation of High School Redesign. Strong external factors (such as historical segregation, poverty, immigration from Mexico, economic inequities, strong state policy direction and financing, federal intervention) and the recent striking shift in responsibility for academic improvement often go unnoticed in public debates, yet are insistently present in shaping what schools do (and have done). In AISD's persistent reform efforts to improve low-performing schools, these factors, like underground peat bogs occasionally erupting into flames, have come into play in the continual dramas arising from efforts to close selected high schools.[65]

Even as these past and present conditions create both variations among high schools and complex implementation, the same theory of action still drives AISD redesign policy, as we saw in the figure on page 92. AISD policy makers have assumed that once SLC, advisory, and PLC structures were fully implemented, students would become sufficiently attached to individual teachers within a small learning community that they would be able to take on academically rigorous lessons. Teachers, as part of intellectually active professional communities, would have broadened their repertoire of lessons and altered their traditional teaching practices. Student engagement, personal relationship with teachers, and shifts in teaching practices would yield rising test scores that would narrow the achievement gap, reduce dropout rates, produce more high school graduates, and send more and more minority students to college, which would open doors to well-paying jobs. That policy logic driving High School Redesign remained in place in 2009.

Yet how much time is needed for these fully implemented structures to work as intended at, say, Reagan, Austin, Akins, and Travis? Five years? Ten years? Experts claim that five to seven years are the minimum required for implementing model programs and seeing results in student outcomes. Joel Klein, New York City chancellor, said that "eight years would be a minimal amount of time" to overhaul an urban district. No one really knows, especially when it comes to reshaping daily classroom lessons. But pressures from school board members, foundation donors, editorial writers, and school critics for swift test score gains make such time commitments seem like an eternity.[66]

Consider First Things First in Kansas City. IRRE began working with a couple of high schools in 1997, and expanded to all district high schools in 2001. Student outcomes had improved considerably by 2005 in a number of areas, yet, when city schools were compared with those in suburban districts, much work remained to be done. When the same program was implemented in Houston's three pilot high schools, student results after two years were disappointing.[67]

If district and school leadership remains committed to this theory of change after Forgione's departure, if AISD schools in jeopardy of being closed garner ratings of at least Academically Acceptable, and if sufficient resources continue to be available in times of state and local fiscal retrenchment, these schools would have the time and resources to determine whether the theory indeed accounts for classroom practice, student academic performance, graduation rates, and college matriculation. Yet those schools with scores that fail to meet state standards year after year may not have that luxury.

The test of the assumptions and policy logic of the entire reform, of course, would be to investigate what happened in schools and classrooms after complete implementation of SLCs, advisories, and PLCs. As the director of High School Redesign has said: "It all boils down to increasing the quality of teaching and learning, and improving rigor and relationships in the classroom." But after only two years of implementation in some schools and three years in others, no study can predict whether school and classroom outcomes assumed in High School Redesign policy will materialize. Can you tell if carrots and onions are growing well without pulling them up? No, but if you ask the right questions about fundamental assumptions, core strategies, and desired results of High School Redesign and AISD reform in general, you might find out.[68]

4

Assessing Austin Leadership and Reforms

Louis B. Mayer, a Russian immigrant who went into the film business, founded Metro-Goldwyn-Mayer (MGM) in 1924. He produced the blockbuster film of its day, *Ben Hur*, and wanted to join high-class society. Friends told him that upper-class men played golf. In his gruff, imperious way, he began playing golf but he never got the hang of the sport, failing to understand that you scored the game in strokes. He thought golf was a race and that finishing in a shorter time meant you were getting better. He hired two caddies and would post the first one down the fairway to find the ball after he hit it. Then, the second caddy would run ahead and put himself in position for Mayer's second shot. This would continue for eighteen holes. After the game was over, Mayer would look at his watch: "We made it in an hour and seven minutes! Three minutes better than yesterday!"[1]

Judging success often depends upon whether those playing the game understand the basic logic of the game and whether the metric used to determine success fits that logic. Mayer's beliefs about golf and the metric he used were, quite simply, wrong. It is equally tempting to use wrong measures to assess school reform. Metrics that have little to do conceptually with the "game" of education, especially when the reforms at issue concern such complex issues as mayoral control, parental choice, and High School Redesign, may appeal to policy makers and even satisfy parents and taxpayers but are unconnected to the reform policy's assumptions.

Judging the record of such initiatives requires, at a minimum, getting the basic idea of the reform right—realizing that it's the golf strokes that matter, not the speed. The aims of High School Redesign —what policy makers would call its "policy logic"—are focused on the creation of small learning communities and advisories within large comprehensive high schools. These subunits are designed to transform and personalize teaching and learning in such a way that graduating seniors are ready for college or have the knowledge-based skills to enter the workforce in a rapidly developing information-based economy.

The metrics most often used in big-city districts are test scores, achievement gaps between minorities and whites, dropout rates, high school graduation rates, and college admissions. These are the desired student outcomes that states and districts collect and display in great detail. Yet because research designs to evaluate policies (such as charter schools, mayoral control, small high schools, accountability ratings) that seek to achieve these outcomes are limited and because existing studies are, at best, unclear as to whether these policies produce the desired results, it is extremely difficult for policy makers to conclude that their reform-driven initiatives, even when put into practice, raised test scores, reduced achievement gaps, boosted graduation rates, reduced the dropout rate, and increased attendance in higher education.[2]

Judging the fit between policy logic and policy outcomes also depends on when the results are assessed. Often, reforms are judged too early and the evaluation yields inconclusive data—showing who's ahead at the end of nine holes of golf rather than after eighteen.

Assessing Reform: Four Questions

The success of an evaluation thus depends crucially on whether the assumptions contained in the reform's policy logic have indeed been put into practice, on whether the metrics used to measure the outcomes fit the policy's assumptions, and on whether the reforms are well timed. Few big cities judge their reforms in this manner—yet when test scores go up, school boards and superintendents are quick to take credit for the gains, even though it is unclear which aspects of the implemented reforms caused the gains. When test scores dip, people offer numerous reasons for the disappointing results and blame gets dispersed. Few, however, can go beyond guesses as to why scores declined.[3]

So to avert premature judgments, I propose using the four questions I raised in the Introduction to get at the issues involved in assessing current Austin reforms.

1. Did reform structures aimed at improving student achievement (such as Blueprint Schools, High School Redesign, small learning communities, advisories) get fully implemented? Without complete implementation of these structures in elementary and secondary schools, no determination of policy success or its validity as a theory of change can be made. In the case of Blueprint Schools, new curriculum structures (known as Open Court), math and reading coaches, and required professional development of teachers were all operating within two years. In 2005, an evaluation of the Blueprint elementary schools pointed out significant gains in test scores but could not attribute those gains to any one factor, including the astute leadership of the ex-principal overseeing the Blueprint. In the Blueprint middle schools, however, a mixed record of gains and losses made it impossible to draw any conclusions about which factors accounted for the ups and downs in scores.[4]

As of 2009, High School Redesign has been partially to completely implemented in the eleven high schools. The district office has managed redesign by reorganizing some of its headquarters' operations to ensure and monitor that key structures are either in the planning or the implementation phase.[5]

Akins, Lanier, and three First Things First schools (Reagan, LBJ, Travis) are clearly in the vanguard, since their versions of advisories, small learning communities, and professional communities have been in play for at least a few years. Those high schools using Disciplinary Literacy as an instructional strategy, advisories, or cobbled-together designs are also putting into practice these structures essential to High School Redesign's policy logic.

Unless these essential structures have been in place for a few years, the overall success of the policy and its assumptions, however defined, cannot be assessed fairly by rising or falling test scores and one-year ratings—misdirected metrics. And that is because these structures, once they've been put in place, adapted to each school's setting, and given sufficient time, are expected to personalize and diversify classroom instruction. Is there any evidence that changes in classroom practices occurred?

2. Have teaching practices changed in the intended direction? Every urban district has an "architecture for learning," where leaders put systems in place to give teachers and principals opportunities to learn. Most districts have professional-development structures that offer individual staff members the opportunity to take courses, attend workshops, and find out about new program-related materials. A few districts have created "communities of practice," academic-speak for sessions in which teachers and principals learn together about a new subject curriculum, cross-disciplinary teaching, and other projects.[6]

Since 2000, AISD district leaders have introduced Disciplinary Literacy, First Things First, and installed new structures for professional learning communities in high schools and for principals. The idea is that these new systems of learning will influence directly and indirectly what teachers do in their classrooms.[7]

In Disciplinary Literacy and First Things First (as well as in high schools blending both approaches), the driving idea has been that teachers should cultivate questions leading to deeper understanding of academic subject matter, conduct engaged discussions, and introduce project-based teaching. As one principal vividly put it: "It is about designing lessons that are rich and kids being engaged in learning and thinking. . . . I joke that we should measure school on the 'drool factor.' How many kids do you see in the classroom sitting there, falling asleep with drool running out of their mouth . . . ? [We need] opportunities like project-based learning, . . . interdisciplinary instruction [with] rich conversation."[8]

A science teacher in one of the Akins High School academies saw connections between his work and that of a core teacher of English. "My students in health/science and the English teacher right across the hall—she was doing *Frankenstein* and we were doing cloning, and we kind of meshed it with, okay, *Frankenstein* in the past—what are you doing *now*, with cloning? The kids really got into that."[9]

Based on the materials that DL and FTF distribute to teachers, there is little question that these programs champion more adventurous teaching that pushes teachers to design activities involving students in active learning and in getting students to think independently, analyze situations, and solve problems. Yet both DL and FTF have implemented new teaching practices unevenly.[10]

For those Austin schools that have implemented FTF and DL in the past few years, created professional learning communities to incorporate such approaches into lessons, and assigned coaches to help teachers expand their repertoire of daily activities, intense pressures to meet state standards on tests and avoid negative school ratings in four of the eleven high schools have dominated the discussions and actions of teachers and administrators. Such pressures, on both secondary and elementary schools, often reinforce traditional teaching practices making it even more difficult (but not impossible) for schools to institute adventurous teaching and progressive classroom activities.[11]

This has been the case across the country since the late 1980s, but especially since NCLB became law in 2002. Many surveys in urban districts and elsewhere have documented the dissatisfaction of teachers who say that, because of these state and national pressures, they have had to narrow the curriculum, increase time during the school year for test preparation, teach remedial classes in math and reading for low-performing students, and focus daily lessons on commonly tested knowledge and skills. To date, however, few observational studies of classrooms have been done in urban districts, including AISD.[12]

Teacher survey responses to accountability pressures only underscore the dilemma-producing tug-of-war teachers face over preparing lessons that focus on raising test scores while also teaching lessons that dig deep into ideas and get students to think beyond textbook assignments. Surveys of Austin teachers do suggest that they feel the tensions arising from conflicting pressures—for example, the tension between teaching rigorous conceptual lessons that embed DL principles and getting students to perform well on tests. But as for actual classroom observations or connecting what occurs in PLCs to teacher lessons, no studies have been done thus far. It is, then, premature to say whether the emphasis placed by DL and FTF on ambitious teaching has altered routine practices in Austin or caused teachers to succumb to the press of test preparation, as it has in most urban districts.[13]

District administrators and principals who engage in frequent and systematic "learning walks," as now occurs in AISD elementary schools, could document the degree to which classroom lessons contain inquiry questions and active learning. Also useful would be shadowing a few teachers from PLCs to see how much of what they learn gets put into classroom lessons. Except for those schools rated Academically Unacceptable, where classroom observations and inspection of lessons do occur, no district-wide documentation exists.[14]

Moreover, surveys of teachers and principals on classroom practices, while useful, cannot capture actual changes in lessons that in-class observers can perceive. Systematic classroom observational studies are essential in determining the impact of DL, FTF, and those small learning communities committed to project-based teaching on lessons. Such studies establish whether implementing an "architecture of learning" (SLCs, advisories, block scheduling) has led to changes in daily teaching routines.[15]

3. Did the changes in classroom practices account for what students learned? Without any systematic and sustained inquiry into the degree to which classroom lessons have changed in desired or undesired directions, it is impossible to determine whether student learning, even that measured only by test scores, is due to a close match between teacher lessons and state curriculum standards, or to specific teaching practices (such as deeper probing into subject-matter content and focusing on test preparation), or to both in combination, or to some other factors.

What do exist are correlational studies where researchers show strong or weak linkages between, say, test scores and a new superintendent, or new curriculum standards, or accountability regulations. While strong correlations between key variables hint at causation, and may even ring with the clarity of "commonsense" observations, such studies fall well short of proving that teacher lessons caused students' scores to rise, decline, or remain stable. And this is especially true of those studies which try to show that new boards and superintendents adopting reform policies yielded test score gains while leapfrogging over what teachers do in their classrooms.[16]

Austin, of course, is not the only urban system lacking much inquiry into the degree to which teaching practices have changed and whether those changes in daily practices are linked to student learning, as measured by test scores or other metrics. The absence of such critical data is common, leaving unanswered the question of whether the assumptions inherent in the logic of reforms such as High School Redesign do, indeed, produce better student outcomes.[17]

4. Did what students learn achieve the outcomes that policy makers desired? Do higher test scores for students translate into a reduced achievement gap between minorities and whites, fewer students dropping out of high schools, and more graduating seniors going on to college? In Austin, the trustees and the superintendent often stated these desired outcomes at meetings; the Strategic Plan and many other public documents stated these outcomes for all students.

Since 1999, district annual reports and news releases have pointed out that the test score gap between minorities and whites has lessened and that more students are receiving their diplomas and attending college. Moreover, magnet schools and the schools appearing in Tables A.I, A.2, and A.5 (in the Appendix) show clearly that there are high-flying schools that are in the top 25 percent of AISD performance on state tests. Yet despite what AISD leaders would like to say publicly, none of these obvious gains can be clearly attributed to the Board of Trustees' policies establishing new reform structures, curricula, and professional learning communities, or to accumulated actions by superintendents. At best, the policies and actions of AISD leaders suggest a strong relationship but not a causal one. How can that be?[18]

Other factors may have caused the improvements. To cite one example: family socioeconomic status, as researchers have shown for decades, exerts a strong impact on academic achievement. Among the eleven cities participating in the National Assessment of Educational Progress Trial Urban Districts, the highest performers in reading and math at two grade levels were Austin and Charlotte. Both districts also had the highest family income among the eleven cities.[19] And here's a second example: many of the elementary schools that perform at the highest levels year after year (see Table A.5) have low percentages of poor and minority students. Furthermore, these schools have many more experienced teachers than do high-minority, high-poverty schools, a factor that is associated with gains in student test scores. These are but a few of the other school characteristics that can cause some schools to do better than others.

Yet a handful of high-poverty, high-minority elementary schools have achieved special recognition for their strong test results. Isn't this evidence that reform policies produce desired student outcomes? It could be, especially if such schools sustain the academic gains over time. But unless we know what happens in those particular schools (were the new program structures and curricula fully implemented?

does the school culture prize academic learning?) and classrooms (have teacher practices of questioning, explaining, and engaging students changed? how much test preparation goes on?), we cannot say with confidence that these schools prove the case for the board's reform-driven policies. Here again are strong correlations that hint at causation but fail to prove it.

Confirming Policy Assumptions

As evaluators have tried to assess AISD reforms by asking the four questions above, many of the new policies have been put into place in district offices and schools. AISD has set up an instructional infrastructure that includes curricular guidelines, coaches, and professional learning communities. High School Redesign structures are present in all eleven high schools, and half of these schools have already established advisories and small learning communities. Beyond this obvious evidence, however, concrete data on whether these new structures have confirmed the assumptions embedded in the policy logic of the reforms remain scattered or unavailable. The situation in AISD is common to other urban districts: no one can say with confidence that the new structures have altered teaching practices, or that improved classroom lessons have led to higher student performance on tests and other intended outcomes of policy initiatives.

To many policy makers, however, such concerns are irrelevant. They're likely to ask: What's all the fuss about? It's the students outcomes that count. If test scores rise, if the achievement test score gap between minorities and whites closes, if more students graduate and go to college, it matters little whether the assumptions driving the reform are accurate or not. What matters is getting the right results.

The rebuttal to this line of argument is that not knowing *why* metrics move in the direction policy makers seek makes it very difficult to recommend what to do when the numbers sour. If we cannot say with reasonable confidence which policies caused which outcomes, then we negate the value of evidence, critical thought, and analysis of assumptions when public policies are formulated, staff hired, and budgets spent. This is why the lack of data on teaching practices and their influence on student learning is significant. The dearth of district data for judging the success of these initiatives, however, may not be the major threat to overall reform in AISD, especially High School Redesign.

Threats to High School Redesign

As described earlier, since the mid-1980s a three-tiered system of schooling has reemerged in Austin, echoing earlier decades of segregated practice. There is a bottom tier of chronically low-performing schools, largely poor and minority, that are rated Unacceptable year after year; there is a middle tier of schools that, more often than not, meet state standards and in some years achieve ratings of Recognized and Exemplary, but that in other years slide into the bottom tier as Unacceptable; and finally, there is a top tier of schools frequently ranked by the state as Recognized and Exemplary. Unaddressed since the mid-1980s except for Blueprint Schools and High School Redesign, this three-tiered school system is in danger of hardening into steel-lined bunkers that are impervious to even the most ambitious reform-minded staff.[20]

This multi-layered system of schooling has emerged amid signal achievements. Beginning in 2000, more schools have received ratings of Acceptable, Recognized, and Exemplary than did schools in the turbulent 1990s. Yet the number of schools rated Unacceptable or Low-Performing has remained steady, with an occasional spike upward (see Table A.2 in the Appendix).

From 2003 to 2006, the percentage of students meeting the state standard increased each year in reading, math, writing, and social studies, but there were only slight reductions in the achievement gap between whites, Hispanics, and African Americans. When AISD students are compared to those of ten urban districts on the National Assessment of Educational Progress at the fourth and eighth grades in 2005 and 2007, Austin scored first or second. The graduation rate increased from 71 percent in 2000 to 81 percent in 2005—though, again, blacks, Hispanics, and poor students lagged behind whites. Graduating seniors who went on to college increased from 55 percent in 2002 to 63 percent in 2006, but with disturbing differences in the rates for whites, Hispanics, and African Americans.[21]

These notable gains have come at a price. Ever-rising state and federal demands for higher test scores have steered courses in bottom-tier schools toward meeting benchmarks on state tests and avoiding TEA's rating of Academically Unacceptable to prevent closures (for example, at Reagan High School and Pearce Middle School). In these low-performing schools, far-reaching educational goals and a broad-based curriculum have been narrowed, so as to focus only on the topics covered by the state exam.[22]

The shrill calls for test-based accountability according to Texas-style ratings or NCLB bookkeeping, and increased enrollments of English-language learners and students from poor families, have squeezed the superintendent and the board into a corner. Caught between a rock and a wall, board members and top AISD staff implicitly accept (though none have said this publicly) that chronically low-performing high schools, unlike top-tier schools, have basically be-come test-taking factories.[23]

At least one fact has become clear: test-driven accountability cloaked in threats and penalties cannot, in and of itself, turn low-performing schools into high-performers. What such accountability can do, however, is fortify a three-tiered system of schooling that was anchored in decades of segregated schools and poverty but that had gone largely unnoticed by the media and by civic and business leaders (see Tables A.3 and A.4).[24]

If bottom-tier schools continue to be test-taking factories—as current signs indicate they will—then the core idea that education is broader than items on a state test, a notion that both Pat Forgione and the Board of Trustees have advocated, will risk being strangled. The Board of Trustees and the superintendent say again and again that they want an Austin education to be equitable and high-quality, one that produced graduates who are engaged citizens ready for college and the job market. They want students to be well-rounded human beings who can think for themselves, solve problems, and are aware of the arts and humanities. They also want to reduce social inequalities by closing the gaps in academic achievement between minority and white students. Many parents, board members, and AISD educators —including Forgione—have sought these goals for years, yet Austin's three-tiered system makes such goals operationally incompatible for the bottom tier.[25]

Not so, however, for the top-tier schools. In many AISD schools, those competing goals are being achieved. Elementary and secondary schools that are unthreatened by state and federal sanctions, and that tend to be largely white and of middle to high socioeconomic status, often receive ratings of Exemplary and Recognized from TEA (see Table A.5). Parents move to particular neighborhoods so they can send their children to these schools, and they become outraged when district officials even whisper about changing the attendance boundaries. These schools offer an education very different from the one provided in Eastside's poor and minority schools. Parents, of course, realize that "academic excellence" and "equity" are grand words, and they want more than words. This is why newspapers annually report that parents pitch tents late at night, so that the next morning they can be first in line to get transfers to particular schools.[26]

The fact that AISD is actually three districts—rich, middle-class, and poor—mirrors the reality that existed in the decades of segregated schools and the subsequent reform efforts during and after desegregation. Then, as now, the goals of achieving academic excellence and achieving equity in low-performing elementary and secondary schools were basically in conflict.

I mention those earlier AISD reforms, when boards and superintendents struggled with chronically low-performing schools, because nowadays there is another threat to the success of High School Redesign. It's the prevailing social belief that expertly managed and efficient schools alone, apart from the effects of poverty, segregation, and other social problems, can reduce the achievement gap and prepare graduates of high-poverty, high-minority schools to enter college and the labor market. Contemporary policy elites in Texas and across the nation, including mayors, governors, and various urban superintendents, champion the idea that schools by themselves can overcome obstacles. And Austin, whose school enrollments are still growing, is no exception.

Earlier descriptions of Austin's decades of segregation, its years of "deliberate slowness" in desegregation, increased poverty in the city, changes in student population, and spurts of newly arrived immigrants point to deeper factors—the metaphor of the peat bog again comes to mind—that make it impossible for schools to overcome these legacies unaided. It is here that the prevailing belief that public schools can ignore the spillover of societal ills on families and children becomes troublesome and even malign.

All of this is to say that such widespread beliefs in the power of efficiently managed schools to attain academic excellence and achieve equity through closing the achievement gap, reducing dropouts, and increasing college-bound graduates—particularly for those schools in the bottom 25 percent that are in danger of being shut down—raise expectations far beyond what these historically low-performing schools have done in the past and can do now. Such inflated beliefs about the power of schools make it almost inevitable that eager parents, policy makers, and students—listening to hype by the champions of High School Redesign—will be disappointed, even angry, over school closings by the state, continued reports of unsatisfactory test scores, high dropout rates among minorities, and low rates of high school graduation. Thus, beliefs among parents, educators, and policy elites about what schools can and cannot do matter a great deal when evaluators are assessing a school district's reform actions and its leaders.

5

The Future of Austin Reform
and Three-Tiered Schooling

> Just as the sun was comin' up, Stuart saw a man seated in
> thought by the side of the road. Stuart steered his car along-
> side, stopped and put his head out.
>
> "You're worried about something, aren't you?" asked Stu-
> art.
>
> "Yes, I am," said the man, who was tall and mild.
>
> "Can I help you in any way?" asked Stuart in a friendly
> voice.
>
> The man shook his head. "It's an impossible situation,
> I guess," he replied. "You see, I'm the superintendent of
> schools in this town."
>
> "That's not an impossible situation," said Stuart. "It's
> bad, but not impossible."
>
> —E. B. White, *Stuart Little*

In February 2008, Pascal (Pat) Forgione announced that he would
retire in 2009 after completing ten years as Austin's school chief—a
"bad but not impossible" situation. He had equaled the benchmark
tenures of two previous district superintendents (Jack Davidson, who
served during the years 1970–1980, and John Ellis, 1980–1990).
His performance in Austin matched that of big-city superintendents
who have received national awards for their district's improvements,

134

such as Carl Cohn in Long Beach, Calif., Beverly Hall in Atlanta, and Tom Payzant in Boston.[1]

Given the chaotic decade of the 1990s, with its cascade of untoward events in 1998–1999, few close observers of AISD could have predicted that Forgione would be any better at coping with the Board of Trustees and Austin politics than his predecessors. Part of the surprise at the length of his tenure comes from the fact that this short, portly, voluble, enthusiastic, East Coast Italian Catholic parachuted (with no entourage) into Austin's politically liberal, largely Protestant, elite-run capital, where a Texas brand of conservative culture prevailed and where local and state politics were considered blood sport on a par with dogfighting.[2]

An ex-seminarian who once taught social studies in a Baltimore public high school, Forgione had never served as a principal or district office administrator. These were credentials that his predecessors had had and whose absence veteran AISD staff quickly noted. After earning a doctorate at Stanford University, he worked for years as a state educational administrator in Connecticut and eventually moved to Delaware to become state superintendent. The Clinton administration tapped him to become head of the National Center for Education Statistics, where, by all reports, he performed well. After being bumped out of that post—he was a political appointee—he applied for urban superintendencies and landed the Austin post on his second try, after the top candidate withdrew from consideration.[3]

As the new guy on the block, Forgione was hungry to learn and eager to act. He was constantly on the phone, talking to state senators, colleagues across the nation, and academics to try out his ideas; he emailed experts to get the latest research and advice on AISD issues. His fervor to help staff members teach better and all students learn better appeared contrived initially, in the eyes of colleagues and sub-ordinates, but his unfailing support for hardworking principals and teachers who improved student performance convinced many that his zeal was not tactical but real.[4]

Forgione had to tiptoe through the maze of conflicting goals the Board of Trustees prizes, just as other superintendents do with their school boards across the nation. They seek to promote *excellence* in aca-demic achievement for each and every student by setting standards that all must reach, regardless of family and neighborhood disadvan-tages; and they want to ensure *equity* for all students in access to knowl-edge and skills, such that the schools will get high-quality results in a residentially segregated district with large numbers of poor and im-migrant families.

The board and the superintendent supported district-wide racial and ethnic diversity, seldom acknowledging publicly that residentially segregated neighborhoods had produced racially and ethnically iso-lated schools, such as Eastside and Westside. They supported equity in allocating the same resources to all schools, yet experienced teachers earning high salaries had clustered in schools where the children came from mostly white middle-income and upper-middle-income homes, a fact that made it very difficult to equalize the distribution of effec-tive teachers—the most important resource available to children. They resolved publicly to close the achievement test score gap by sending more resources to particular schools, knowing full well that most English-language learners enter school unprepared, academically and socially, for routine lessons and face too many teachers who lack the bilingual and bicultural experience to deal with them. Behind the rhet-oric of "closing the gap" is a sobering reality, one that policy makers seldom voice publicly: lower-achieving students have to *exceed* the gains that white students make in order to reduce the discrepancy in test scores—a tough leap for students being taught by less experienced teachers.[5]

Forgione, like his AISD predecessors and like his peers across the nation, wrestled with this conundrum. Austin's unbending residential segregation by race and class, and the lack of any political push from civic and business elites (or, for that matter, from the elected Board of Trustees) for city-wide desegregation or efforts to lift families out of poverty, left Forgione, an appointed official, with little room to maneuver. He did what his peers across the country have done. He reaffirmed his pledge to raise student achievement for all students—the pledge he'd made when he arrived in Austin. "While desegregation has always been important, the more significant challenge for educators now is high achievement. . . . In achievement, there's much to be done. We have to ensure that every classroom has clear, high standards, no matter what your ZIP code is."[6]

A year after Forgione took office, Reverend Sterling Lands and his Eastside Social Action Coalition attacked AISD for its inaction over persistently low-performing Eastside schools, and the controversy was amplified by the media. Forgione and the board, startled by the fracas, resorted to a quick political solution to quell a potentially ugly racial situation. In response to the initial charges, and to Lands's subsequent flirtations with the idea of forming a separate district and hiring Edison Schools Inc., Forgione hastily presented the Board of Trustees with his Blueprint, a latter-day version of the mid-1980s Priority Schools.

Claudia Tousek, a veteran elementary principal who had earned the reputation of a turnaround expert, headed the project. She worked closely with the six principals and coaches for three years, substantially improving elementary test scores, teacher retention, school climate, and parental support. Although improvements occurred as well in the two middle schools, the results were more mixed. By 2005, with the reform of all eleven high schools on the table, Reagan and LBJ in East Austin were added to the Blueprint Schools. Thus far, there is no evidence that the gains made in Blueprint elementary and middle schools have affected these two high schools. The speedily contrived Blueprint carries the taint of being a hasty top-down political response to a crisis, rather than a considered move to unlock the conundrum of how to achieve equity and academic excellence in a segregated school district.[7]

Even as a hasty solution, the Blueprint mirrored the overall strategy that other district leaders across the country had pursued in striving for system-wide reform. Like their peers in big cities elsewhere, Austin leaders began with elementary schools and largely succeeded there. Except in a few schools, elementary school achievement, state ratings, and overall performance have climbed. As in other big cities, Austin leaders then turned to improving achievement in high schools and middle schools.

Just as in Boston and other urban districts, Austin leaders soon ran into trouble because of the size, structure, and staffing of high schools. In the late 1990s, the team of superintendent Alan Bersin and chancellor of instruction Anthony Alvarado had directed an ambitious reform of San Diego's schools. Alvarado had bluntly declared that high schools were "bastions of inaction." One top official estimated that, of the sixteen San Diego high schools, only two had "bought into the reform."[8]

Compared to elementary schools, secondary schools are larger and more rule-driven. They have teachers who are trained in subject-matter specialties and who work within schedules that allow them little time to work with individual students. In secondary schools with large percentages of middle-class white students, the structural and staff differences between lower-grade and upper-grade schools matter less when it comes to academic performance. But in high-poverty, high-minority comprehensive high schools, these structural and staff characteristics matter, as the high dropout rates and low graduation rates attest. Thus, the creation of small urban high schools, which was fueled initially by the Bill and Melinda Gates Foundation and soon became a national movement, has led to the conversion of big traditional high schools into small learning communities or stand-alone small high schools in separate facilities.

In AISD, there has been a similar pattern of success in elementary school performance but stumbling in high-poverty, high-minority middle and high schools. It is too early to say whether High School Redesign and the recent launching of another wholesale reform of middle schools in 2009 might succeed in these low-performing secondary schools. In some instances, sheer persistence in pursuing reforms can turn faltering steps into desired outcomes. At other times, that same perseverance may be criticized as a stubborn clinging to failed policies. Forgione experienced both.[9] His doggedness in reaching district goals through top-down decisions and frequent checking with key stakeholders (but not necessarily affected neighborhood groups) produced small victories alternating with occasional defeats. Forgione's project resembled a major renovation of a rambling old house: he shored up the foundation, fixed the leaky roof, torn down walls, moved stairs, and installed new appliances, creating a smartly outfitted home that still needed more work.

In doing the renovations, Forgione also stepped on some rakes and got smacked in the face. His sudden top-down decisions with little consultation and his flip-flopping on issues led to public scoldings at board meetings, in budget hearings, and in newspaper editorials. Those who watched him at meetings or listened as his critics lambasted him admired his ability to face criticism without losing his temper, at least in front of audiences and cameras.[10]

Part of his public equanimity stemmed from the lesson that all superintendents must learn in order to survive and be effective: do not give your opponents wood that they can use to start a fire and burn you up. Instead, Forgione questioned critics, looked for flaws in their arguments, and used data to bolster his case without probing at opponents' less savory motives. He also learned early that taking critics' words and actions personally or acting defensively, especially in public, would seldom help him achieve his goals. Forgione absorbed the boot-camp lesson of state and district politics: someone who loudly criticizes you today may come to your office next week asking for a favor.

Still, bouts of impulsiveness, in both word and deed, afflicted the superintendent. Time and again, board members, staff, and friendly critics rescued him from foot-in-mouth disease and from hasty, ill-considered decisions. But those lapses and rescues scarcely slowed him down between the time his plane landed in Austin in 1999 and the time he departed a decade later.[11]

Assessing the Forgione Years

Judging the success or failure of superintendents has been a time-honored ritual. A century ago, most superintendents served one-year contracts on a handshake with the school board president—the post was a swinging door. Nowadays superintendents have multi-year, inch-thick contracts negotiated by attorneys acting on behalf of the superintendent and the board.

Whether a superintendent has met the terms of a contract, however, is only one factor in judging his or her success. Another factor is that school boards invest the hopes of a community in a superintendent, who is charged to sustain a successful system, improve a middling one, or resuscitate a collapsed district. As happens in this last case, when a school board expects the chief to turn around a failing district, the new superintendent, after a few years, disappoints patrons mostly because he or she has piled up enemies by implementing tough decisions and making political slips with the school board, the teachers, or the community (or all three). The school chief is fired according to the terms of the contract, or leaves for a better job, or receives a buyout package from the board. Having served in Chicago and Philadelphia before taking the top post in New Orleans, Paul Vallas put the saga of urban superintendents in vivid terms: "What happens with turnaround superintendents is that the first two years you're a demolitions expert. By the third year, if you get improvements, do school construction, and test scores go up, people start to think this isn't so hard. By year four, people start to think you're getting way too much credit. By year five, you're chopped liver."[12] This has occurred so many times in the past four decades that the average tenure of an urban school chief is just over five years.[13]

It is easier to judge superintendents who spend only a year or two in a district and hastily depart, since—aside from the skidmarks they leave when pulling out of the parking lot on their last day—they seldom leave traces that endure. It is much harder to determine the worth of a superintendent who has served nearly a decade. Yes, such long-serving school chiefs were beset with problems that went unsolved, and they were showered with criticism that stung. And, yes, those superintendents could point to achievements for students, teachers, parents, and the larger community. Such superintendents were more like long-distance runners than flashy sprinters who falter just before the finish line. They defied the dominant image of the turnstile superintendency.

How, then, can I explain Forgione, Payzant, and others who are exceptions to the rule of short-tenured urban school chiefs? Three stories offer different explanations for their long service.[14]

The Superintendent as Superman or Wonder Woman

Some long-tenured superintendents are extraordinary individuals. They have revived urban districts that were nearly dead as a result of chronically low student performance, bureaucratic resistance to change, and managerial incompetence. These superintendents convinced their respective mayors or boards to install new structures of parental choice and instructional support for teachers and principals, refocus bureaucracies on improving teaching and learning, and redesign large comprehensive high schools into small learning communities. And test scores have risen.

These urban districts, once graveyards for superintendents, have become magnets attracting the best and the brightest among young professionals who want to be part of the Herculean effort to reclaim children and youth from the despair of stunted lives.

By sheer force of will, political smarts, and enormous expenditures of energy, these stellar superintendents ignored the conventional wisdom and succeeded. They are remarkable individuals.

Success Comes from Aligning the Time, Place, and Person

Being in the right place at the right time is crucial. After New York State gave New York City's mayor Michael Bloomberg the authority to take over the schools, he appointed Joel Klein chancellor in 2002. By 2009, Klein had been in that office longer than any New York City school chief since the post was created in the early 1970s. Yet Bloomberg's predecessor, Rudy Giuliani, who sought to control the schools in the 1990s without state authority, had engineered the appointment of three seasoned big-city superintendents as chancellors:

Joseph Fernandez, Ramon Cortines, and Rudy Crew. And he had engineered the departure of each within eight years. If timing is crucial, so is context. The three chancellors that Giuliani wanted in the top job had all been praised as heroes in their former districts. Yet in the mayor's eyes, they didn't fit him or the city.[15]

Now consider Long Beach superintendent Carl Cohn, who shepherded his district through a decade of changes that yielded gains in student achievement impressive enough to win the Eli Broad award for urban district excellence. In 2002, Cohn retired. In 2005, the San Diego Unified School Board forced the exit of superintendent Alan Bersin after seven years of struggle marked by contentious 3–2 votes and a poisonous relationship with the teachers' union. A year later, the school board appointed Carl Cohn to heal battle wounds with the board and the teachers. In December 2007, Cohn left San Diego. His forty years of urban experience and his awards for improving the Long Beach district could not find traction in San Diego.[16]

Bringing in superstars who made their reputation in other districts may not be an effective way to improve troubled schools. Leadership depends on finding the right person for the right place at the right time. Examples of good pairings between chief and district were Tom Payzant in Boston, Carl Cohn in Long Beach, and Joel Klein in New York City; imperfect matches were Fernandez, Cortines, and Crew in New York City and Cohn in San Diego. When the match is off-kilter by time, place, and person, then individuals labeled heroes in one city fall flat in another.

Coping Smartly with Conflict and Limits of Change

Improving urban students' academic performance is hard work, filled with struggles, defeats, and small victories. Long-serving superintendents, working closely with their school boards, have accomplished a great deal through tough decisions, energetic actions, and political savvy.

Dilemma-filled conflicts inevitably arise whenever superintendents introduce major changes, such as expanding parental choice, firing slackers, pressing principals to be instructional leaders, and redesigning comprehensive high schools. Tensions over the highly prized values embedded in these changes arise because every policy initiative must compete for limited funds, competent people, and scarce time. Here are a couple of classic dilemmas:

- How can districts get better test scores and higher graduation rates quickly, so as to avoid state and federal penalties, while also building teacher and principal capacities that will lead to those better numbers?

- How can district officials ensure that all schools follow policies and meet uniform standards, while also giving principals and teachers sufficient autonomy to make school-based decisions, even if those decisions produce district-wide variations when it comes to meeting uniform standards?

In managing these common dilemmas, veteran superintendents find few clear-cut victories because the tensions require them to make unattractive choices and forge unappealing political compromises that please their bosses and key stakeholders some of the time, and offend them at other times. Superintendents whose tenure lasts five to ten years have learned to sell these compromises to powerful influentials in and out of the district. They push skillfully for what has to be done, given the circumstances, while acknowledging both the strengths and shortcomings of the deal.

The dirty secret that successful, long-tenured urban superintendents know well is that they cannot permanently erase conflicts over desired values or solve all problems with the resources they have, particularly when the goal is to turn around chronically low-performing, high-poverty schools and keeping them turned around. They can certainly do better than their predecessors have done in coping with conflicts while achieving signal triumphs—but they also know that with all of their political moxie, they still bump up against limits as to what they can do.[17]

Sifting the Three Explanations

Of the three stories, the saga in which Superman and Wonder Woman perform monthly miracles is the most popular. That story is embedded in every job description advertising superintendent vacancies and every news article greeting a new school chief. Everyone wants a savior dressed up as a hero.

This belief in Superman motivated the Miami-Dade school board, facing serious problems of academic achievement, to hire former New York City chancellor Rudy Crew on an 8–1 vote in 2004 and pay him a compensation package of almost $500,000. In 2008, the American Association of School Administrators chose Crew as its national superintendent of the year.[18]

Reflecting society's deep desire for a heroic leader to save the city, state, or nation from overwhelming problems, the idea of a superstar superintendent turning around a declining system by virtue of extraordinary personal traits has created far-fetched expectations that few flesh-and-blood humans can meet. In August 2008, six months after Crew was named national Superintendent of the Year, Miami-Dade board members forced a vote on whether to fire him; he barely kept his job, on a 5–4 vote. Weeks later, however, after constant back-

and-forth sniping with the school board, Crew accepted a buyout of his contract.

Even the best-match explanation of superintendent success and longevity in urban districts, one where a person is nicely aligned with the particular time and place, still must come to terms with the inevitable conflicts over competing values and the limits of fundamental changes. Few urban school boards and superintendents can implement deep changes in their districts. Instead, they traffic in incremental changes, hoping they can accumulate a sufficient number that might add up to a worthwhile, profound, and abiding change in district climate and performance. Short of a natural disaster—such as Hurricane Katrina in New Orleans in 2005 and the San Francisco earthquake in 1906—school districts change slowly, in small increments. And that is because social institutions are strongly affected by a city's demography, history, and economy.

Consider Washington, D.C., and San Antonio, Texas—districts that are roughly the same size in enrollments and clearly urban in texture. Yet racially and ethnically, they are far apart; they spend different amounts of money per student; and they face issues in educating their students that look similar on the surface but differ substantially when examined closely, because the arcs of their individual histories as cities diverge considerably.

Moreover, urban public schools each reflect their city's social structures and the deeply embedded social beliefs about what schools can achieve for the community and for individual families. Chicago is a rigidly segregated city where neighborhoods of whites, Hispanics, and African Americans still adhere to street-by-street demarcations of turf. Nonetheless, poor families expect their neighborhood schools, no matter how well or inadequately provisioned with experienced teachers and materials, to take their sons and daughters and get them ready for jobs and college, just like the schools that the children of middle- and upper-class white and minority parents attend. Thus, many deeply embedded factors may constrain the actions of long-tenured superintendents, even when they've been blessed to be in the right place at the right time and are a good match with their board and their mayor.

For a decade, the fit between Pat Forgione and the Austin Board of Trustees was as snug as that between chilled fingers and a fleece-lined glove. The incremental changes Forgione recommended and the board approved, most of which headquarters staff, principals, and teachers implemented, produced many gains for the district over the years but left some unresolved issues, particularly over chronically low-performing schools. Toward the end of the decade, the fit between glove and hand had become uncomfortable.

The nine-person board that hired Forgione in 1999 turned over more than once: he served under twenty-six different members during the decade. None of the board members in 2008 had hired Forgione. Many of them bristled at the notion that they might "rubber stamp" the superintendent's recommendations as earlier trustees had. One trustee said that when he had announced he was running for a vacancy on the board, a representative of the Chamber of Commerce asked him only one question: Could he work with Forgione? The candidate was upset and resented the question. He thought the question should be the other way around: Could Forgione work with *him?* Also, trustees wanted to be more "hands-on" in making local school decisions and wanted more community involvement from minority parents than Forgione had sought in the past. As one board member told me in confidence during the search for the next superintendent, "If Pat was applying now for the Austin superintendency, we wouldn't hire him. We need someone different now."[19]

Given these explanations for the small band of superintendents who serve upwards of a decade, evaluating a district superintendent becomes more complicated when one considers whether the match between a board and superintendent fits the place and times. There is little doubt that the match between Forgione and AISD worked for the decade that he served. But the necessary ability simply to survive as a superintendent—often the default (and only) standard for judging a school chief's record—is hardly a sufficient criterion for determining success.

Other criteria, such as achieving the goals set by the board and the superintendent publicly (and put into negotiated contracts as objectives to meet), matter as well. Yet whereas CEOs can point to profit margins, stock values, and other "bottom-line" measures, big-city superintendents have a mix of concrete and ambiguous metrics: test scores, the size of the achievement gap between minorities and whites, teacher and principal turnover, dropout rates, percentages of graduates attending college, relations with school board, contacts with neighborhood groups and elite business and civic leaders, ability to manage personnel. Intangibles such as a superintendent's political smarts, temperament, social skills, and self-presentation easily get entwined in the assessment of his or her record. Very little agreement exists on how much weight should be given to each of these soft and hard measures, even when they are specified in contracts.

In the absence of such agreement, one option is to use the indicators of success that appear in the research literature and upon which professional administrators rely. The usual markers of a superintendent's success are a tenure of at least five years (a sign of a district's political stability) and the passage of tax levies and bond referenda. These are clear signs of school board and voter support for a leader's actions. Professional administrators also view reducing principal and teacher turnover and increasing staff stability as prerequisites for school improvement. Finally, improved student outcomes over time and across a range of indicators suggest that board and superintendent actions may have borne fruit in classrooms, even though few existing theories or studies can directly link school board and superintendent actions to students' test scores.

On this last point, some skepticism is in order. Taking credit for a rise in test scores that occurs after you've been appointed district chief is, at best, a dubious *post hoc* claim. The correlation is as shaky as the one examined in a recent study which showed that eating pizza reduces the incidence of cancer. Jumping to the conclusion that school officials' actions caused a test score gain is an impulsive leap that too many boards and superintendents make.[20]

What is the evidence for Forgione's success? In a vote of confidence in his leadership in 2007, the Board of Trustees extended his contract until 2011. Voters approved hikes in tax rates—the most recent in 2008, to fund teacher salary increases—and passed major bond referenda in 2004 and 2008. These are clear signs of restored political stability and respect for district leadership, after the turmoil of the 1990s.[21]

The instructional infrastructure established by the central-office staff apparently helped hardworking principals and teachers to erase the rating of Unacceptable that AISD had received in 1999. It also contributed to higher district test scores year after year in elementary schools, marginally higher graduation rates, lower dropout statistics, and increased college attendance for most secondary schools.

Yet there are important caveats to these gains. Even though every year state and federal ratings show that nearly 90 percent of Austin schools meet ever-rising benchmarks in these accountability systems, a half-dozen or more predominantly poor and minority middle and high schools—and an occasional elementary school—show up on these lists of low-performing or Academically Unacceptable schools (see Tables A.1–A.4 in the Appendix). To put this bluntly, nine schools were rated Academically Unacceptable in 2000, Forgione's first year on the job. In 2008, the last full year of his superintendency, eleven schools received that rating.

There are, of course, many possible reasons for the mixed record of achievement. But one in particular needs to be considered, since it lies at the heart of contemporary urban school reform in Austin and big cities across the nation. The AISD board-approved policy logic of the decade-long reforms contains a fundamental assumption that policies creating new structures (such as Blueprint Schools, High School Redesign's small learning communities, and advisories) will reshape teaching practices, and that those different classroom lessons will produce better student outcomes. The assumed links between structures, classroom practices, and student outcomes are crucial. The problem, as described above, is that no one in AISD or other urban districts embracing the same policy logic knows whether routine classroom lessons have indeed changed, and, if they have, in what direction.

Reports by others, and the observations that I made in my brief visit to one high school, suggest strongly that current teaching practices lean heavily on test preparation in chronically low-performing schools. Moreover, in the newly reopened Eastside Memorial High School (formerly the Johnston High School), new programs are being considered that depend upon project-based teaching, a pedagogy quite different from the one teachers routinely use when preparing students for state tests.

Furthermore, in those elementary and secondary schools where Disciplinary Literacy has extended its reach, a consensus over best instructional practices is forming. But variation among these schools (and across classrooms within these schools), plus the reality that not all AISD schools are involved with DL, makes that emerging consensus very shaky. Taken together, these points add up to a basic dilemma of instruction: How can you encourage student inquiry and raise test scores? AISD top staff have failed to reconcile the contradiction between test preparation lessons and ambitious teaching, when guiding professional development and annually inducting 20–25 percent new teachers.[22]

In AISD, except for occasional stories told by administrators and teachers, few top officials know what kinds of teaching occurs in the district's nearly 6,000 classrooms. No systematically collected classroom data exist. Without such evidence, no one can say with confidence that board policies over the past decade, particularly for Blueprint Schools, High School Redesign, and Disciplinary Literacy, have led teachers to depart from their routine practices to embrace adventurous, demanding lessons—as the policy logic of these reforms assumed would happen.

Without classroom data, no AISD official can point to the causes of the district's increasingly positive test results and school ratings during the Forgione decade. Guesswork proliferates. Doubts arise when AISD officials claim that the test score gains and improved ratings resulted from the new reform-driven structures that were put into place. The assumption that there is a tight link between board policies designed to establish new structures that alter teaching practices, and the subsequent gains in student achievement, remains unquestioned.

That guesswork and those doubts about the linkage, I should add, are not restricted to Austin; they infect most big cities engaged in similar reforms. For example, in Prince George's County, Md., an urban district of 130,000 students has done poorly on state achievement measures for years. From 1999 to 2006, three superintendents had moved in and out of the post. In 2006, yet another new hire made swift top-down changes in headquarters staff, expanded the Advanced Placement program, transferred extra staff to low-performing schools, and started a pilot pay-for-performance program for teachers. District results on 2008 state tests of elementary and middle school students' reading and math skills improved at every grade level. The number of poorly performing schools on the state list declined from seventy-six in 2006 to fifty-eight in 2008. Moreover, Prince George's County outpaced the state average in test score gains.

Shortly thereafter, the superintendent announced that he would leave in a few months to take another job with a national foundation. The newspaper report of his departure—here's the punch line— said that "overall, his effort seemed to make a difference." The word "seemed" hints that the departing superintendent *may* have been responsible for the gains, and thereby conveys the uncertainty that accompanies board and superintendent actions when they trickle down into classrooms and the unknown influence those policies have upon daily teaching.[23]

The missing link between superintendent actions, altered teaching practices, and student outcomes, important as that is, should not diminish a signal achievement by Austin's board, superintendent, and staff since 1999. AISD administrators and teachers, in effect, took schools that were below the median in academic achievement (that is, in the bottom 50 percent) and raised them to the top 25 percent, not once but repeatedly, so that they achieved state ratings of Recognized or Academically Acceptable—an uncommon feat for most urban districts (see Tables A.1 and A.5).

Too many urban school critics and policy pundits discount the importance of such victories. I do not. Even without knowing fully which policies and which actions made the difference in these victories, such sustained successes can help to restore confidence in the abilities of urban students, teachers, principals, superintendents, and boards, improving schools academically for many more students than critics of urban schools thought possible.

While Forgione accomplished much in his tenure, there are two abiding issues that neither he nor his predecessors (nor current school chiefs elsewhere in the country) could solve: chronically low-performing secondary schools, and the ill effects of the tight grip that state and federal accountability systems have on districts.

Both are part of the unfolding story of High School Redesign. How the district-wide reinvention of high schools will play out in three to five years, no one can say. Serious questions need to be continually asked, prickly dilemmas need to be carefully managed, and classroom effects have to be documented.

After Forgione's decade as superintendent, local and national observers, using both popular and professional indicators, have already judged his record as successful. Austin's daily newspaper heartily congratulated the retiring superintendent for serving the city well. In 2008, the Council of the Great City Schools (representing sixty-six urban districts) awarded Forgione its highest honor, naming him the nation's Top Urban Educator.[24]

Forgione's record—like the records of his peers in other districts, including those who have received national awards—is weakest in two areas. First, the district still has a bottom tier of schools with high dropout rates, low numbers of seniors graduating, and stark achievement gaps between white and minority students—problems that existed when he arrived in 1999. Second, it is still difficult to use state and federal accountability rules, as punitive and unforgiving as they have turned out to be, in constructive ways. AISD has considered using test scores to target resources (such as building administrator and teacher skills), bolster the community's will to alter the three-tier system (by, for example, urging parents to become more involved in school improvement, especially in low-performing schools), and prod staff to accept more ambitious, even unsettling, changes (such as more school options for parents). The district has even tried these methods in small ventures, but has not fully exploited them.

Nonetheless, Forgione plowed forward, trying hard to put out the inevitable peat bog fires that flared up from deep strata of earlier reforms and the inequalities embedded in Austin's segregated past, ones still unrelentingly present. In some cases he succeeded, in some instances he failed, and in other situations he simply crossed his fingers and hoped that things would improve. The Board of Trustees appointed Meria Carstarphen, the school superintendent of St. Paul, Minn., to succeed Forgione beginning in July 2009. At thirty-nine, Carstarphen is the first woman and the first African American to head the 82,000-student district. Whether she can consolidate the various systems that have been established in AISD, complete the work of High School Redesign, improve AISD middle schools (the next item on Austin's reform agenda), and sustain district gains already made is a question that cannot yet be answered.[25]

6

Urban District Reform Strategies

Common Errors and Assumptions

In 1948, Harvard president James Bryant Conant appointed a new dean of education. He brought the young man, Francis Keppel, to a tea to meet the other academic deans. After everyone was seated, Conant described an experiment that had been conducted at the London Zoo: a researcher had put a lion and a lamb in the same cage. Scientists had come from far and wide to study the experiment, and Conant had asked the investigator whether any problems had arisen. The scientist had replied: "Not really. Of course, from time to time we have to replace the lamb." After telling this story, Conant introduced Keppel to the group.[1]

The tale is every bit as germane to the precarious position of a newly appointed big-city school superintendent. For the past half-century, urban districts striving to "fix the system" have been afflicted with constant policy churn and personnel turnover. Mayors take charge of the schools; boards of education thirst for the right superintendent to turn around failing districts; entrepreneurs dream they can rejuvenate schools with a magic elixir of idealism mixed with business competence; policy elites champion strategies such as Effective Schools and Districts, and Improved Schools and Community.

Three Policy Options

Amid this vigorous churning, three basic options aimed at achieving the competing values of equity and academic excellence have dominated policy makers' agendas.

- Change the racial, ethnic, and socioeconomic mix of students within particular schools.
- Alter the governance of schools, streamline bureaucracies, install reform models in schools, improve principal and teacher performance, and hold staff and students accountable for achievement.
- Disrupt the system through market-driven competition from without and within, by means of vouchers, charter schools, and similar ventures.

Austin, like most other big cities, has largely concentrated on the second strategy, with a sprinkling of initiatives from the other two approaches and, of course, from time to time replacing the "lamb."[2]

Change the Mix of Students

After the U.S. Supreme Court's *Brown v. Board of Education* decision in 1954, desegregating schools became a policy pursued by the federal government to equalize educational chances for people who were historically banned from full participation. For a few decades, desegregation expanded and black students across the nation experienced better staff and facilities for the first time. By the mid-1980s, however, the federally driven equity surge had sputtered; by the end of the century, it was gasping for breath. Yet a distinct residue of those desegregation-driven reform policies that were in force from the 1960s to the 1980s can still be seen in big-city magnet schools and specialty alternative programs, including many offered in AISD.

Much evidence has accumulated showing that there are strong links between racial and socioeconomic integration of students and improved academic and nonacademic gains. The policy argument that neither academic excellence nor equity suffers when schools are desegregated is based on many research studies. And there have been many recent efforts to bring together students from different socioeconomic backgrounds. In places such as Montclair, N.J., where magnet schools arose during desegregation, every school in the district has been turned into a magnet school. In other districts, such as Raleigh, N.C., Cambridge, Mass., and San Francisco, planned variations of racial and ethnic desegregation have been put into practice. All of this is further confirmation that who goes to school with whom matters and that equity and academic excellence are not competing values.

Yet Supreme Court decisions since the 1980s and popular discontent with initiatives that took students from their neighborhood schools have stalled racial desegregation and slowed the socioeconomic mixing of students, while accelerating the resegregation of urban schools by race, ethnicity, and class. Very few elected officials have been eager to promote racial or socioeconomic integration when the current political support for neighborhood schools remains staunch.[3]

Except for a few smaller urban and suburban districts, this equity-driven policy of mixing children in schools is seldom pursued now by either outside entrepreneurs or hardy urban reformers. In Austin, a handful of magnets from the desegregation years and a few new schools aimed at drawing students from across the district (such as the Ann Richards School for Young Women Leaders) do have a mix of white and minority students from different social classes. But in the two years I spent examining Austin press clippings, interviewing community and school leaders, and analyzing public records, I found no public officials, business leaders, or community groups who publicly called for either socioeconomic or racial integration in AISD schools.

Improve Governance, Bureaucracies, Reform Models, Teaching, and Accountability Structures

Some big cities have adopted mayoral control, while others have left school board governance untouched. Most urban boards of education have opted for picking the best superintendent they could find to chart a course for school improvement and, in many cases, inviting educational entrepreneurs to join them.

With or without governance changes, urban superintendents across the United States have reorganized bureaucracies, borrowed and created reform models to change schools one at a time, and accepted state and federal accountability regulations that both prod and punish schools. Some districts have collaborated with Teach for America, New Leaders for New Schools, and other entrepreneurial organizations to supply teachers, principals, and other staff. A few districts (such as Washington, D.C.) have moved further and challenged union contracts on tenure. Others, such as Denver, have adopted pay-for-performance plans in order to motivate teachers and principals to increase their students' test performance. In short, most urban districts tilt toward the Effective Schools and Districts end of the reform strategy continuum.[4]

Austin mirrors these districts in many ways. No major governance changes have occurred—though there has been a minor shift, in that the Board of Trustees now elects its own president (formerly elected by the voters). Under the board leadership of Doyle Valdez, who was president from 2002 to 2006, Pascal (Pat) Forgione had the backing of a strong trustee majority in making decisions, even unilateral ones, although after Valdez left the board in 2006, some of those decisions (such as the proposed closing of Becker and Oak Spring elementary schools and Webb Middle School) ricocheted hard enough to dent Forgione's credibility with new members.

Forgione reorganized the central office, abolishing five area super-intendents and concentrating authority for instruction under a deputy for instruction. He thus achieved a measure of control over what happened instructionally in schools. High School Redesign brought further reorganization of central-office tasks. It ensured that the right hand knew what the left hand was doing when the district converted eleven comprehensive high schools into smaller units with advisories and professional communities.[5]

The superintendent and staff spent a great deal of time inventing, finding, and establishing models of reform for individual schools. The process of changing one school at a time, called "whole-school re-form," dates back to superintendent Jack Davidson's Design for Excellence program for low-performing schools during desegregation, the establishment of Priority Schools in the mid-1980s, and John Ellis' endorsement of Effective Schools. In the past decade, AISD has plowed funds into Blueprint Schools, which were homegrown versions of borrowed models. Also, federal funds came to Johnston, LBJ, and Travis high schools through the Texas High School Initiative. First Things First, implemented in three AISD high schools, was a whole-school reform model that all high schools in Kansas City, Kans., had adopted.[6]

In building an infrastructure to help principals and teachers work effectively within these whole-school reform models, AISD staff created teacher collaboratives across the district through Disciplinary Literacy workshops and within individual high schools undergoing conversion into small communities. Similarly, new district-wide communities were formed for principals and assistant principals, so they could discuss details of daily work and share ideas.

Forgione, however, had little choice when it came to federal and state accountability regulations and, like his peers, did his best to massage the rules. Clearly, fear of earning a state rating of Unacceptable and a federal sticker of Needs Improvement does get school officials and staffs to work harder in figuring out ways of improving students test scores. The coercive and punitive measures built into state and federal bureaucratic rules that fix blame do seem to prod many AISD schools. Yet fear and shame were never enough to yank chronically low-performing schools out of the bottom tier. The board and the superintendent pursued other inside-the-system approaches to improve teacher and student performance in those schools.[7]

Forgione directed staff to come up with a pay-for-performance plan. In 2007–2008, a pilot program was instituted in nine schools and was anticipated to extend to more than forty schools by 2011. Called REACH, the plan seeks to improve the quality of new teachers, retain experienced ones especially in high-poverty, high-minority schools, and spur professional growth. For example, with regard to student achievement, teachers and principals jointly set goals and objectives focused on student performance. At the end of the pilot year, AISD paid out roughly $1 million in bonuses (ranging from $1,000 to $3,000) to nearly 500 teachers; nine principals received $3,500 to $4,500 each.[8]

Another strategy that Forgione used sparingly, and probably too late, was encouraging community involvement in turning around persistently low-performing schools. Where such neighborhood participation worked, it was by pure chance. The superintendent, for example, threatened Webb Middle School with closure in 2007 because of chronic low performance. After the community reacted strongly, parents and the St. Johns Neighborhood Association became involved in preventing closure, and then in collaborating with Webb staff to gain a TEA rating of Academically Acceptable. The community also became involved with Johnston High School, but this occurred much too late in the process. The same was true for Pearce Middle School and Reagan High School as they approached the deadline for improvement: AISD officials invited the St. Johns Neighborhood Association to work with the school, but there was not enough time for the efforts to take hold.[9]

For urban districts, such strategies—changing governance, rearranging bureaucracies, changing one school at a time, building infrastructures for helping teachers and principals while dealing with the pluses and minuses of union contracts and accountability structures—are painstakingly slow, better measured in spans of five years to a decade, rather than a year or two. Impatient with the slowness of improvement, some urban leaders have turned to a third option in their effort to transform schools.

Disrupt the System

Irritated with one-school-at-a-time methods and annoyed at officials' slow pace in getting changes into gear, eager reformers and outside entrepreneurs over the past few decades have tried outflanking cumbersome, often inefficient, urban district bureaucracies by betting on fast-moving superintendents who believed in allowing parents and teachers to run schools (as with community control and "free schools" in the 1960s and 1970s, and in charter schools since the 1990s), or who let principals and teachers operate schools (as with site-based management in the 1970s and 1980s), or who implemented combinations of these approaches. Devising structures to give parents more choices beyond their neighborhood school, reform-driven school boards and superintendents established alternatives to neighborhood schools and gave individual schools enough breathing room and flexibility to establish innovative programs aimed at improving academic performance.[10]

With the collapse of the Soviet Union in the early 1990s and the defeat of a thoroughly regulated command economy, U.S. policy makers who favored deregulated markets took a page from the corporate catechism on market economies and pressed school leaders to expand parental choice, so as to increase competition for students among public schools. Such competitiveness, choice-driven leaders believed, would lead to innovation, greater organizational efficiency, and higher academic performance.

Many big-city districts adopted this strategy beginning in the mid-1990s and bet on the right superintendent to follow through. Paul Vallas, for example, became Chicago superintendent when Mayor Richard Daley moved him from the city's budget office to head the schools. Chicago saw a proliferation of school choices for parents. After Vallas left Chicago, a Pennsylvania state commission appointed him superintendent in Philadelphia, where he again contracted with for-profit and nonprofit companies to operate schools and give parents a diverse menu of choices. After a few years, he left Philadelphia to rescue the post-Katrina New Orleans schools; again, he created charters, contracted with companies to run schools, and pursued similar ventures. In each case, Vallas worked closely with entrepreneurs and external organizations to build new structures that would jolt the traditional system. Joel Klein in New York City, Michelle Rhee in Washington, and Arne Duncan in Chicago have followed a similar strategy.[11]

In Austin, Forgione pursued neither a strategy of disruption nor alliances with entrepreneurs in his first five years. He was far more interested in bringing coherence and efficiency to a district addicted to chasing various reforms. Meeting state standards, building an instructional infrastructure, expanding professional development, and establishing accurate data systems were at the top of his reform agenda. After 2005, under High School Redesign, a growing portfolio of parent choices of schools became apparent but was never intended to be disruptive.

Transforming the eleven comprehensive high schools into small learning communities meant establishing schools-within-a-school. Most students living in the attendance zone continued at their current high school, exercising choice among the options within the school. Alumni and booster clubs at mostly white, higher-socioeconomic-status schools such as Bowie, Anderson, and Austin high schools continued to see the same buildings, sports teams, and school colors. Surely, the slow emergence of schools-within-a-school alleviated the fears of white middle-class parents that there would be major changes at already high-flying schools. A new school here and there (such as the Ann Richards School for Young Women Leaders) and the continuance of a few magnets from the desegregation years were the extent of the board's and superintendent's effort to inject more competition into AISD.

AISD's Strategies

Of these three policy options, AISD leaders, like most other urban district school boards and their superintendents across the nation, have largely forsaken the first policy: changing the mix of students. Except for existing magnets, the creation of a few new schools open to all students, and a policy of allowing parents to transfer their children, I have seen no political will—in the AISD Board of Trustees, organized parent groups, business and civic leaders, or the larger community—to challenge the primacy of the neighborhood school and the existing high level of residential segregation in Austin. Including more choices of schools and providing transportation for those parents willing to send their sons and daughters outside their neighborhoods will slowly, but only slightly, alter AISD's three-tiered segregated schools for a small percentage of involved middle-class white and minority parents.

Thus, the strategies of renovating district structures, whole-school reform, teacher and principal improvement, and adhering to state and federal accountability rules dominated Forgione's decade of service to AISD. With High School Redesign, First Things First, and homegrown creations, the Board of Trustees and the superintendent gingerly and slowly fashioned a slightly larger menu of choices for parents.

After 1999, the AISD Board of Trustees bet on choosing the right superintendent to fix the system and convert the tired rhetoric of achieving equity and academic excellence into reality. But like a dead body in a peat bog, the three-tiered system of schooling has resurfaced in a residentially segregated Austin, and this means that persistently low-performing, high-poverty secondary schools still need fixing. The renovation of AISD that began in the 1990s remains unfinished.

Before concluding this discussion of the policy options facing big-city school districts such as AISD, I need to point out a surprising finding. Except for the large body of positive evidence on student outcomes from racial and socioeconomic desegregation, there is very little research or experience that clearly marks one strategy as superior to another in achieving the desired student outcomes cherished by reformers. Why is that?

First, few decision makers can say with assurance whether new structures (small learning communities, district infrastructure of professional development), new curricula, and new models (Disciplinary Literacy in Austin, Balanced Literacy in New York City, New Tech High reform models in Sacramento, Portland, and Indianapolis) altered classroom lessons.[12]

Second, unless we know for sure what teachers did differently as a consequence of reform-driven policies, determining whether new forms of teaching and materials led to student learning becomes nearly impossible. And if classroom-driven reforms cannot be shown to have produced intended gains, imagine how much harder it is to demonstrate whether changes in city government, expanded parental choice, bureaucratic streamlining, merit-pay plans, and similar big-ticket policy items paid off down the line, in the form of better classroom lessons and student test scores. The policy chain comprising a mayor, a school board, a superintendent, district administrators, principals, and teachers is hardly like a whip that can be snapped. It is more like a wet string of spaghetti that cannot be pulled or pushed easily. It stretches a long distance, winds around corners, gets stuck in cul-de-sacs, and occasionally breaks.

Few school boards and superintendents, if any, can point with confidence at that policy pasta and say, yes, the reforms are working and we have the evidence to show for it. In 2008, after six years as New York City chancellor, Joel Klein pointed out that "despite our progress, we haven't achieved yet in New York . . . a school district that people from other cities can come to and say: 'This works.'"[13]

Unsurprisingly, then, no large district has yet achieved a decade-long success for other cities to copy. Districts that were seen as models to copy—such as Seattle, San Diego, or Philadelphia in the late 1990s and early 2000s—lost their luster when new superintendents took the helm. The sticky issue of how to consolidate the remarkable gains achieved under one board of education and superintendent, as leaders exit and enter, has baffled policy elites for decades.[14]

Yet choice-driven reformers and their business allies who often favor a "disrupt the system" strategy seldom have doubts about what to champion. To fix the broken system, entrepreneurial leaders say, districts should expand parental choice through charter schools and other options to create market competition and edgy innovations. Within a competitive market, district leaders will quickly see which are the best schools and replicate them, while closing failing ones. Frederick Hess points out the shortcomings of the arguments proposed by the more-choice-the-better crowd.

> [They say,] "Look, let's just create options, and more good alternatives will emerge." It's a little bit like the mistake we made in planning for the Iraq War in 2002 and 2003: if we create a vacuum, good stuff will happen. Well, you know, effective markets aren't created by vacuums. Markets are ways to channel human energy and ingenuity, but only when they're transparent, when they're structured, when you're building on human social capital, when you've got talent and investment capital. If we really want to think about new solutions, it's not just identifying the right people and the right programs; we need to create an environment where these people and solutions are able to thrive. . . . The most important strategy is not . . . funding the five best charter operators. It's attracting aggressive human-resource operations like New Leaders for New Schools or the New Teacher Project. It's providing the kind of legal and business support that those programs need in order to expand and grow. These are things that philanthropists tend not to invest in because they're not sexy but that are actually going to determine whether we're able to make reforms work or not.[15]

Hess and other business-driven educational entrepreneurs assume that even if "human-resource operations" and other structures were put into place, then classroom practices would improve and student learning would flourish. But the long spaghetti strand called policy-to-practice, which stretches from policy makers to classroom lessons, bends, weaves, and often breaks. The assumption has little evidence to support it.

Listening carefully to these confident entrepreneurs, I can only conclude that their convictions about success come from their own experiences in the corporate world, from stories they have heard from other risk takers about turning around urban districts, and from shrewd guesses based on impressions. For the fact remains that most school board members, superintendents, entrepreneurs, researchers, and donors have little direct classroom experience and very little reliable research to justify such robust certainties that mayoral control, managing bureaucracies, and more charter schools will make classroom lessons lively. What does unite the current crop of urban district reformers is their confidence that values and skills drawn from successful well-run businesses and taken-for-granted beliefs in the power of a deregulated market can solve not only economic but also educational problems.

Also taken for granted is the assumption that the primary goal of public schools is to prepare all students for college and for the workplace because the economy needs graduates who have "soft" and "hard" skills and who can find their niche in an ever-changing labor market. That other goals such as civic engagement, community service, and strong moral values might be on the menu is often dismissed as unquantifiable, of lesser importance, or unrealistic in a market-driven society.[16]

These words and views about how to fix urban schools are worlds away from what principals and classroom teachers experience and consider important in their daily work. Missing in these policy exchanges over strategies to improve schools are parents' views about schools, as well as the experiences of teachers and students—their familiarity with the gritty school processes that create classroom relationships and shape the quality and results of learning. Missing, too, is an awareness of how the goals and structures of schooling have changed over time, and the ways in which schooling as an institution has remained constant. Instead, what are often served up in these debates over fixing the broken system are policies that resemble business plans, with projections for different rates of return for each strategy.[17]

Any suggestions for improved urban districts in student outcomes, then, should take into consideration not only past reforms but also the unquestioned assumptions that urban school reformers held and the mistakes that flowed from those unexamined beliefs.

Knowing the Past

Most policy entrepreneurs and elite leaders are ahistorical in their thinking about school reform.[18] They are seldom familiar with previous urban reforms, or with the way urban districts evolved (absorbing waves of earlier immigrants), or with the long history of efforts to improve schooling for the poor. Instead, these policy brokers draw from first-hand or second-hand experiences in schools and the corporate world, while soaking up stories others tell. They assume that nothing can be learned from the past because conditions today are so different from conditions long ago. They err in their assumption.

There are of course no exact lessons to be drawn from particular reform episodes, because while events may appear similar across two points in time (such as the failures of banks in the early 1930s and the federal takeover of commercial and investment banks in 2008), the contexts and consequences differ. But historical trends and patterns of behavior in schools and district organizations do exist, and a knowledge of how those patterns emerged can be instructive. Why, for example, have all public and private schools been age-graded for 150 years? Why have most teachers used textbooks as their primary instructional aid, decade after decade? Why are there thirteen years of schooling (K–12) and not ten? Why is it so hard to deal with race and poverty in classroom teaching? Answers to these questions reveal the stability of the school system.

The constancy of institutional structures, teaching methods, administrative roles, and patterns of behavior is closely linked to the fact that tax-supported schools are financially dependent on their communities, and to the powerful social beliefs and expectations that parents, taxpayers, and voters have about what public schools ought to be doing for students. Few urban school reformers acknowledge that Americans want public schools to achieve multiple, often conflicting, goals (such as teach students to conform to prevailing community values and also teach them to be critical thinkers) that spring from deeply rooted social beliefs about what schools should do to and for children.[19]

When urban school reformers, however, fumble decade after decade in grappling with largely poor and minority low-performing schools, then expectations, beliefs, and institutional structures are no longer trivial nuisances to be dismissed but central to analyzing why urban school reform goes awry. We need fewer superintendents and boards frantically patching urban districts and more historically informed plans that have room for necessary adaptations and that contain careful analysis of which incremental changes make the most sense to those who do the daily work—namely, teachers and students. In short, we need to go from "spinning wheels" to "tinkering toward utopia."[20] To do that, the frequent errors committed in the name of reform need to be made plain.

Common Errors

Nonstop reform results in incoherent direction. Books such as Frederick Hess's *Spinning Wheels* have documented in wrenching detail the helter-skelter way in which districts embraced reforms in the 1990s. Since then, turnover in big-city superintendents and federal and state accountability pressures have caused districts to lurch in different directions seeking those innovations that promised equity and academic excellence. Over time, a consensus has emerged among urban school leaders that standards-based curricula, testing, and accountability constitute a formula for success, yet they don't know for sure whether the formula actually reshapes teaching practices and student learning.

Even within this consensus, urban district leaders pounce on reforms that promise increased equity and academic progress, attaching soaring rhetoric to initiatives such as ensuring every student a laptop, requiring all students to take algebra, thinking of principals as CEOs, and instituting small high schools. Because money often follows these promising reforms, getting started is hardly a problem. It is much harder to sustain the reform and ensure that the changes mesh with standards-based curricula and state tests. Staff members pay a high price for incessant reform. Burnout and loss of commitment often translate into high turnover of teachers, principals, and, of course, superintendents.[21]

In AISD, the constant disorganized and frenetic reforms of the 1990s were propelled by a micro-managing Board of Trustees and accompanied by frequent superintendent turnover. Frenzied grasping of one reform after another left the district wobbly. By mid-decade, with the introduction of High School Redesign and district office reorganization, Superintendent Forgione and his staff directly confronted the disadvantages of flying off in different directions. Teachers surveys continued to note the overload from different district initiatives. But since the late 1990s, the incoherence-threat level has dropped from high-alert red to yellow.[22]

Half-done implementation. When significant policies aimed at both equity and academic excellence are put into practice partially, or so slowly as to make little difference in the daily work of principals, teachers, and students, then this becomes a major failing. In some cases, districts have created small learning communities without changing schedules to provide time for teachers to work together; in others, they have mandated new math curricula without providing many of the textbooks students need and without setting aside sufficient time and money for teachers to learn how to use the various new curricula.

When only policy fragments have been put into place, it is nearly impossible to determine whether the policy influences practice. So when test scores rise, remain flat, or fall over time in an urban district, it is impossible to judge whether those scores resulted from half-done policy implementation in a particular city with particular actors.[23]

After 2000, AISD leaders helped elementary schools by providing them with Instructional Planning Guides, coaches, and professional-development sessions. After 2005, High School Redesign structures were swiftly implemented in high-poverty, high-minority schools ("urgent" and "high priority" categories) and more slowly in low-poverty, low-minority schools ("deliberate priority"). In many ways, Austin officials have thought through and established, after occasional missteps, guidelines about building teachers' and principals' knowledge and skills, gathering data, and monitoring new programs. Whether these guidelines and structures have achieved intended changes in school and classroom practices is, of course, an entirely different issue.[24]

The unknown impact of reform policies on teaching and student learning. Few districts, if any, have undertaken systematic analysis of what happens in classrooms after policies intended to lift student achievement are put into practice. For example, in those districts that have seized upon professional learning communities as a solution to move teaching away from traditional routines, it is rare for evaluators to have studied the connection between these PLCs and classroom practice.[25]

Yet district, state, and federal policy makers can consult the familiar correlational studies that link variations in a school's student test scores to, for example, the dates that accountability structures were put into place. Also, occasional researcher studies and evaluations of scattered districts and classroom clusters provide much data but, again, can only suggest associations—they cannot show that gains, losses, or stability in test scores are attributable to particular teaching practices. These studies reveal much uncertainty over whether new accountability rules, changes in elementary school structures and small high schools with their various communities, and concerted efforts to build communities of professional learning have led to gains in student achievement.[26]

In 2007, AISD staff began providing the Board of Trustees with exhaustive summary reports for elementary and secondary schools—reports that detail changes in these schools arrayed against a full tableau of test scores. They are full of statistics on teacher and principal retention, professional-development activities, and special efforts underway in schools that received a rating of Academically Unacceptable. District staff members make it clear that the relationships between TAKS scores and the changes that have occurred are correlations only. Whether test score gains are due to AISD efforts and resources is an open question.[27]

Of course, hazy correlations have not deterred any urban district policy makers from assuming that their actions have accounted for gains in TAKS scores, reductions in the achievement test score gap, and increased graduation rates.

Leadership succession. Frequent turnover in leaders dooms reform. The literature on urban schools is filled with accounts of new superintendents who leave their thumbprints on a district, only to have them erased by a successor.

Occasionally, there are transitions where incoming superintendents consolidate, adapt, and improve reforms that they inherited from a predecessor. For example, Frank Jackson, the mayor of Cleveland, approved his school board's appointment of Eugene Sanders as CEO in 2006, following Barbara Byrd-Bennett's resignation after eight years. Since then, Byrd-Bennett's reforms (such as K–8 school organization) were continued and adapted, while new ones (such as single-gender academies) were created. Students' academic achievement, the closing of many schools, and other issues continue to be contested, but the leadership succession was not disruptive.[28]

Cleveland, however, remains an exception. More common is what occurred after reform-driven Alan Bersin left the San Diego district: within three years, the school board appointed two superintendents with different reform agendas. And in Philadelphia, after David Hornbeck had served six years heading the schools and implementing his ten-point plan (called Children Achieving), a state commission took

173

over the schools and appointed Paul Vallas, who swiftly dismantled his predecessor's reforms and hired entrepreneurs to run a number of the schools.[29]

Even when a superintendent gives a school board or mayor plenty of notice before departing, this hardly guarantees an easy transition or sustainability of reforms. In Boston, for example, Tom Payzant notified the School Committee and the mayor in 2004 that he would retire two years later. But after the School Committee named the next superintendent in 2006, the candidate withdrew. Not until 2007 did Boston finally install Carol Johnson, from the Memphis system, as its school chief.[30]

While there is much talk among mayors and school boards about the importance of continuity and of sustaining gains made by an outgoing superintendent, words seldom translate into a smooth handing of the baton to the entering executive. AISD's experience after John Ellis' decade-long tenure in the 1980s illustrates the turbulence that occurred repeatedly as superintendents came and went. Pascal (Pat) Forgione, during his decade of service, brought political and institutional stability to Austin's schools. He announced his retirement in 2008, eighteen months before his actual departure, to give the Board of Trustees time to find a successor who would build on the gains of the previous decade while adapting structures to the inevitable changes that occur in districts. A few months before Forgione left office, the Board of Trustees appointed Meria Carstarphen to succeed him. Whether frequent leadership succession and the dismantling of reforms will haunt Austin is for another historian to record.

These common mishaps, which afflict urban districts grappling with largely minority and poor schools stuck in the bottom 25 percent of achievement, did not arise randomly. Urban school reformers, in formulating their policy agendas and pursuing their favorite strate-

gies, have taken little notice of school-reform history, multiple institutional goals, and district officials' political and economic depen-
dence on voters and their social beliefs about schools. While this
myopia matters in how policy elites, including entrepreneurs and
foundation officials, conceptualize and analyze problems in schools,
a much larger mistake is their failure to probe the connections they
assume exist between the macro-policies they push and the micro-
practices teachers use in classrooms.

Common Assumptions

Urban school leaders seldom question the dominant assumptions and
taken-for-granted "common sense" that drive reform policies and
budgeted programs. Few district officials, for example, ever lay out
publicly their reform-driven logic tying policy assumptions to goals,
strategies, and outcomes. The hidden assumptions buried in the policy, of course, form the framework for identifying the problems to be
solved and the solutions—the reforms—to be put into practice.

Inspecting such a framework (if it were made public) could reveal
the flaws in thinking that too often go unexamined. For example, most
urban districts openly support raising all students' achievement and
simultaneously closing the test score gap between whites and minorities. Yet these goals are in conflict. When you raise everyone's achievement to the same degree, the test score gap remains the same. What
district officials and reformers probably mean is that they seek to raise
the achievement of the lowest achievers by larger increments than the
increase in scores of the highest-achieving students. Or they want to
lift students stuck in the bottom 25 percent to the next-higher tier.
The rhetoric of "closing the test score gap" and "raising all students'

achievement" is rich in the language of equity, but it is seriously flawed in logic.

Such faulty assumptions are not the sole province of urban school districts. During the recent meltdown of the world's financial markets, for example, assumptions that drove the housing bubble of the past decade—such as the expectation that prices would continue to rise—were reinforced by the belief that markets are self-correcting and that major companies can manage themselves without a nudge from federal regulators. In 2008, after the U.S. government instituted the largest-ever federal rescue of financial institutions, these assumptions finally came in for sharp inspection. Probing such taken-for-granted beliefs can shed light on different ways to frame urban school problems and different solutions for Austin and other big-city districts.[31]

Following are the most common assumptions.

All urban schools are broken. This is not true. Every big city boasts some elementary and secondary schools that parents are eager to have their children attend.

It is accurate to say that some urban systems have higher proportions of low-performing schools, fewer graduates, and much higher dropout rates than others—Detroit, Washington, and New Orleans, for example. It is also accurate to say, as do champions of better management and equity, that many districts are geared to adult needs and to maintaining the status quo, not to children's learning. Nonetheless, schools that parents and school officials would call good are present in every single district, beyond those public schools that select their students based on examinations, as in New York, Boston, and San Francisco.

This is certainly the case in Austin, where a substantial portion of elementary and secondary schools are considered good, according to parents, AISD officials, and state ratings. One-half of the schools received the highest TEA ratings in 2009 (see Tables A.2 and A.5 in the Appendix).

If the belief that all urban schools are broken is flat-out wrong, then anyone interested in district improvement would design varied strategies to prod high-performing schools to do more, stir mediocre ones to higher performance, and lift up those languishing in the bottom tier of achievement. Districts need more arrows in their improvement quiver, not just one aimed at "broken" schools.

All comprehensive high schools need small learning communities, advisories, and professional community structures. Beginning in the mid-1980s, Theodore Sizer's Coalition of Essential Schools grew into a movement to convert big high schools (those with more than 1,500 students and departmentally organized, with teachers seeing 150 or more students a day) into small high schools where teachers worked with eighty to a hundred students, met with fifteen or so students in advisories, taught interdisciplinary lessons, and assessed students' achievement through portfolios and exhibitions of their work to those inside and outside the school community. Schools-within-schools and separate small high schools spread rapidly in big cities and occasionally in suburbs.

Yet as standards-based testing and accountability spread in the 1990s across big-city districts, the progressive-minded small high schools where staffs taught across disciplines, used project-based teaching, and assessed portfolios mutated into schools where students took traditional college preparatory subjects and sat for state tests. Since 2000, with buckets of money and aggressive marketing, the Bill and Melinda Gates Foundation has invested well over $1 billion supporting more than 1,500 small high schools in nearly 300 districts. State and federal officials have also joined the movement, calling for small urban high schools to become college preparatory academies. Choruses of administrators chanted the magic words "rigor, relevance, and relationships" to get Gates dollars. Austin received a Gates grant in 2006 to convert all eleven of its comprehensive high schools into small learning communities.[32]

With so much money being invested in small high schools, one would think that research studies would provide evidence for such a direction. No such luck. As in so many other instances of reform, the presence or absence of research studies is seldom the determining factor in adopting policies. Too often, the "common sense" and unexamined assumptions of policy elites, plus available monies, steer policy direction. Small high schools may be better places for the well-being of students than large comprehensive high schools—and a strong argument supported by evidence can be made on psychological and social grounds for just that point. But creating small high schools pell-mell in the hope that such inventions will turn around chronically low-performing high schools is a hypothesis, not a fact.[33]

In the case of those AISD high schools that closed or were in danger of closing (such as Johnston and Reagan), the evidence is humbling. Neither First Things First nor academies saved Johnston. For 2008–2009, although Reagan High School student scores improved in many areas, TEA again rated the school Academically Unacceptable for students' low performance in certain academic subjects. TEA commissioner Robert Scott ordered AISD to contract with private companies and take other actions to improve student achievement in 2009–2010. District officials would have one more year to avert the closing of Reagan. As one local pundit phrased it, "First Things First was really Too Little, Too Late."[34]

Questioning the prevailing assumptions that drive contemporary high school reform is vital to any serious effort to improve the academic achievement of high school students. Enlightened district leaders who find the dominant assumptions weak and worthy of rethinking should consider mixes of small and large high schools to match their communities, and other ways of organizing upper-grade schools, rather than an unthinking allegiance to small college prep learning communities with weekly advisories.

Once accountability, choice, and high school structures are in place, teaching practices will shift and students will improve their academic performance. As I've pointed out repeatedly, this assumption simply lacks much evidence beyond occasional surveys, yet remains a cardinal belief of policy mavens and entrepreneurs. Policy elites believe that this link in the policy chain will lead to improved student outcomes as inevitably as the sun rises in the east. But it may well be the weakest link or, to shift metaphors, the strand of spaghetti that is hard to push. Teachers—who are street-level bureaucrats serving the public, just like lawyers, doctors, police officers, and firefighters—cannot do automatically what they are unprepared to do: change daily lessons and practices to fit new policy requirements. But most teachers will try their best, if assisted by people they trust.

Austin and other districts have instituted programs that help teachers in secondary schools gain more knowledge and skills for teaching academic subjects and those in elementary schools acquire skills for teaching math, reading, writing, and science. But probing whether such professional development alters teaching practices remains a rare event. Moreover, surveys and occasional studies show that changes in teaching practices do not always go in the directions policy makers want (say, more test preparation, more direct instruction). In short, policy makers rely too much on new structures for producing the necessary expertise and skills, and too little on directly helping teachers make desired changes in their daily routines. As Geoffrey Canada, head of Harlem Children's Zone Project, says about educating minority and poor children, teachers, and parents, "It's not rocket science we're doing here; it's harder than rocket science."[35]

Standards-based testing, accountability, managerial leadership, and expanded parental choice of schools will achieve equity and academic excellence. At one end of the continuum of urban school reform strategies, Effective Schools and Districts reformers—political liberals as well as conservatives—believe that highly motivated and hardworking entrepreneurial staff who put the interests of children before those of adults can get all students to graduate high school, enter college, and get good jobs. The problem rests not in poverty, culture, or family background; the problem is that urban school systems are adult-controlled, poorly managed reservations where the organizational status quo is maintained.[36]

Efficiency-driven reformers believe that reorganizing district offices, creating new schools and thus more choices for parents, challenging seniority and tenure in union contracts, holding teachers and principals responsible for student performance, and transferring low-performing staff will produce desired results. To such reformers, then, certain solutions will lead to both strong academic achievement and equal opportunity for persistently low-performing schools. The goals are not in conflict. Both can be achieved.

Reformers lodged at the other end of the continuum, however, question this assumption. Improved Schools and Community reformers—conservatives and liberals—believe that highly motivated, entrepreneurial, and managerially smart staff who put the interests of children before those of adults can help students a great deal and are central to reducing the achievement gap. As essential as school improvement is, however, such work remains insufficient. Assigning accountability ratings or giving grades to schools for their performance, for example, can prod some staffs to improve test scores; but fear, blame, and shame have failed to lift poor, minority, and chronically low-performing schools out of the bottom tier of achievers.

Pursuing only school improvement, then, is inadequate. The invidious effects of poverty and racial isolation require additional community-based social and medical services, preschool opportunities, and other resources if children are to do well in school, graduate, and lead full lives. Those who challenge the managerial approach argue that parental involvement and community services have to be included in any strategy seeking to achieve both equity and academic excellence. Families need to be helped, and families need to help their children at home. Parent education, early-childhood programs, medical treatment, and social services become vital links in helping parents support their children. Communities need to provide services to students that schools either cannot afford or choose not to offer.

Urban district leaders are familiar with the views from both ends of the reform continuum. Most say publicly that their schools will raise students' academic achievement, close the test score gap, and create equal access for all students. Quietly and behind the scenes, however, these leaders try to achieve all of these inherently conflicting goals, and with limited resources. They extend schooling for three- and four-year-olds, fund after-school programs, provide nurses and social workers for pregnant teenagers, and offer emergency aid to distressed families.

In Austin, for example, the board and the superintendent know that AISD lacks the resources to solve the serious problems children bring with them to the schoolhouse door. But they also know that if students are to learn, schools must lessen the negative impact of dysfunctional families, poor health, violent neighborhoods, and poverty—problems that students carry in their backpacks along with paper, pens, and books.

Since 1995, for example, AISD has offered prekindergarten classes (with transportation and no waiting list) for students from low-income families and students with limited English proficiency. These programs prepare students for acquiring reading, language, and math skills. In 2006, more than 5,000 four-year olds (75 percent Hispanic, 15 percent African American, 6 percent white, and the rest Asian) attended full-day prekindergarten classes in sixty-six schools. Evaluators followed the four-year-olds who were in pre-K in 2002 through the third grade, and measured how they did on the TAKS reading test. On the English TAKS in reading, 93 percent passed; on the Spanish TAKS in reading, 90 percent passed. Prekindergarten experiences can help level the playing field for many students.[37]

Moreover, AISD employs many support staff linked to neighborhood and city agencies. They intervene in difficult situations, offer tutoring through public libraries and business partnerships, and staff after-school programs. AISD also provides breakfast, lunch, and even a third meal before low-income children go home—meals provided through the Austin Food Bank and the Kid's Café. School nurse and dental programs offered through the Seton and St. David's medical centers help students, as do campus recreation and social services coordinated by the city and AISD.[38]

Thus, like most district managers in the nation, AISD officials are caught in the conundrum of seeking both excellence and equity with limited resources, and with the knowledge that families shape students' attitudes toward learning and inculcate the skills necessary for school success. Officials try to strike a balance—on the one hand, mitigating the harsh effects of poverty and racism upon students, and, on the other, working hard to improve the schools that children attend. The problem of how to reconcile these competing values is hardly new. Previous AISD boards and superintendents faced the same dilemma and compromised by focusing upon school improvement while providing minimal support services to students. They are, in effect, closet members of the Improved Schools and Community crowd, offering a minimum array of services; but they talk publicly about what schools are doing to improve achievement, like the supporters of Effective Schools and Districts.

Of course, in the broad range of the reform spectrum, there are other school board members, superintendents, politicians, parents, teachers, principals, and streetwise activists who hug the middle of the continuum. They draw extensively from the reform agendas of the groups at the two poles, creating mixes of policies that they champion.

Although probing these pervasive assumptions buried in the policy logic of reforms is an important first step in reframing problems and solutions, school districts need actions, not more words. In light of the common errors made in urban districts seeking reform, and the reluctance to question the basic assumptions that drive current leaders, what else can AISD and other urban districts do?

7

What Can Be Done?

"We cannot escape history."

—Abraham Lincoln, annual message to Congress, 1862

"I don't live in the past. I don't think it's a good idea. My motto is: Yesterday's history, tomorrow's a mystery. What are you doing today?"

—Don Nelson, quoted in *San Jose Mercury News*, May 12, 2003

Unlike professional basketball coach Don Nelson, I accept Lincoln's view of the past. I know full well how effectively William Faulkner's famous dictum applies to big-city school systems: "The past is never dead. It's not even past." Yet as a policy historian studying urban districts, I am caught in a dilemma. By this point, many readers may expect me to extract clear lessons from the past and apply those lessons to Austin and other big cities. And I have a strong impulse to do exactly that, since I have spent more than a quarter-century in public schools as a teacher and administrator. I would very much like to offer suggestions that could help reformers—for example, a list of good-conduct vows that they should pledge to follow whenever they begin work in a district. Yet as a scholar who has spent another two decades researching past school reforms and the history of efforts to improve schooling and classroom teaching, I know, as other historians who have wrestled with a final chapter know, that conclusions and recommendations "more often than not . . . appear utopian, banal, not very different from [what] others have suggested"—in short, a waste of time for me and the reader. I am caught between competing values as a practitioner and a scholar.[1]

The risk of making policy suggestions that are banal, simplistic, or unconnected to the preceding analysis runs high, but I have decided that is a risk worth taking, if for no other reason than to illustrate once again that reform-driven policy makers' confidence in focusing on economic purposes for schooling and on spanking new structures is revealed as misplaced when those purposes and structures fail to have the desired effect in classrooms. The compromise I have fashioned is to build on my historical, political, and organizational analysis of urban districts in general, and Austin in particular, and extract a few lessons.

Let me summarize what I have argued in the case of Austin and other big-city school systems. History leaves distinct footprints that can be observed in the present. The consequences of Jim Crow practices for blacks and Hispanic immigrants since the early twentieth century remain noticeable in Austin's schools a half-century after the *Brown* decision. In the early twenty-first century, Austin schools are filled with large populations of poor, minority, and immigrant students, many of whom are learning English as a second language. Most white and minority Austin students still come from segregated neighborhoods—segregated, these days, not by law but by income. Such neighborhoods tend to have chronically low-performing schools that year after year are rated Academically Unacceptable.

Also part of the historical and demographic context is the shift in the state's role in funding and managing its schools. Since the 1980s, Texas governors and legislatures have aggressively expanded state power over schools by increasing funding, setting curriculum standards, mandating testing, and holding districts accountable for students' academic performance. The increase in policy intervention was largely driven by state business and civic leaders who believed that better schools would lead to economic growth, even as the economy shifted from farming, ranching, and mining to knowledge-based industries. Expanded state power over schools has had an undeniable impact on Austin. Historical events in Texas and Austin played a crucial role in the shaping of AISD.

Yet contexts, influential though they are, do not alone determine what happens in district schools and classrooms. If history and demography were deterministic, all Texas big-city systems would be alike. Austin, Dallas, Houston, and Brownsville would operate in the same manner. They do not. And the reason is that district organizational structures, value-driven policies, and persistent patterns of behavior also influence what happens in schools and classrooms.

In some districts, once reformers adopt a policy (say, that teachers should use phonics materials in kindergarten and first grade to teach reading), they initiate sporadic follow-up to determine whether the required materials are in teachers' hands, whether teachers use the books, worksheets, and activities as expected, and whether students are learning. In other districts, principals and officials closely monitor new policy through monthly classroom visits. Districts differ not only because of their histories, demographic profiles, and locations, but also because of particular policies and how organizations put those policies into practice.

Finally, individuals likewise influence the direction and quality of schooling. Inside and outside school systems, individuals (school board members, business leaders, civic elites, superintendents, principals, teachers, parents, community activists) bring different ideas about the goals schools ought to pursue, the definition of "good" schooling, the strategies district and schools should use in making changes, and the most desirable classroom practices.

At certain times, when conditions are ripe for change, particular individuals holding important posts—presidents, governors, superintendents—can lead others to adopt reforms and pursue particular strategies. Politically, people come together to form coalitions around ideas and values as displayed within particular individuals, and to lobby decision makers on behalf of specific changes. If sufficient power is exercised in the political arena, these ideas get converted into reform strategies targeted to alter routine practices in schools and classrooms. Political will exerted upon educators and decision makers, then, melds with organizational strategies to make desired changes in contexts where the conditions are favorable.

No surprise, then, that historical and demographic contexts, organizational structures, patterns of behavior, and individual leadership interact constantly within urban districts. The chemistry of these interactions makes it difficult to isolate exactly how and why a particular reform flies or flops. Is the organizational strategy of top-down direction from a school board and superintendent the best way to turn around a failing district or school? Does granting principals the authority to hire teachers, design curricula, reorganize schools, and spend their budgets turn schools around? Will building political and organizational structures that increase parents' school choices produce higher-achieving students? Researchers cannot yet answer these questions.

Researchers design studies that focus on one or two of these factors, but they can seldom show, with a high degree of confidence, causal connections. They can demonstrate which key factors are related, but not which ones produced specific outcomes. The lack of precise research findings is just another reason that reformers engage in so much guesswork.

A Few Recommendations

This summary of my analysis of Austin and other large districts brings me back to my risky decision to offer specific lessons for urban district policy makers, practitioners, and reform-minded observers. Surely, individual districts are the product of their unique political and socioeconomic histories. The lessons I draw from Austin and other urban districts would need to be tailored to varied circumstances. That is part of the risk in making recommendations. But the educational and political advice I offer does draw from decades of direct experience and applied research in urban districts. Reform-minded readers would need not only to judge whether these lessons are useful for districts they know, but also to consider, in the light of Austin's experience, whether such advice can spur improved teaching and learning in chronically low-performing schools.

1. Systematically monitor whether new structures, programs, and materials aimed at improving academic achievement alter or perpetuate traditional classroom practices. As we have seen, Austin's school reformers assumed that new structures and programs aimed at improving students' academic performance would encourage more ambitious teaching practices and thereby affect student learning. AISD's decisions to align district curriculum standards with those of the state, design Blueprint Schools, and launch High School Redesign are initiatives that expect teachers to change what they routinely do in classrooms in order to engage students in learning more and better than they had previously. That is a critical assumption governing these reform-driven policies.

As in many other urban districts where this assumption prevails, AISD leaders advanced policies that took desired changes in teaching practices for granted. Systematic inquiry by district staff to determine whether the policy assumptions were accurate has not occurred in AISD or in most other urban districts. It should.

2. Raise the ceiling for schools in the uppermost tier of achievement. Too often, high-performing schools in urban systems are left alone because they already meet district and state performance standards. Since resources are limited, district staffs pay far more attention to those schools stuck in the lower tiers. This is understandable but nonetheless may be a political and educational mistake. These high-flying schools provide political muscle for tax levy and bond referenda, while offering incentives for lower-tier schools to do better.

In Austin, at least a dozen schools have repeatedly earned state ratings of Exemplary and Recognized. These top-tier schools, many of which are located in middle- and upper-middle-class neighborhoods, enjoy frequent accolades. Such schools could be designated as special AISD schools. They could be given more autonomy in budgeting and hiring, and granted waivers from certain district constraints. In exchange for such autonomy, they would be expected to reach beyond AISD's Five-Year Strategic Plan and aim toward broader school goals (say, deeper exploration of the humanities) or increase their focus on particular goals (such as critical thinking about media, including video games). Top-tier high schools could be allowed to add electives, while high-performing elementary schools could offer new activities that staff had always wanted to pursue but that were precluded by district rules and the imperatives of test-based accountability. Or as one student in another district put it, "It's letting people learn about what they love, rather than dictating what they should be learning." Of course, these special schools would have to maintain the level of performance that made them eligible for such increased freedom in the first place.[2]

If such top-tier schools were given expanded discretion, their autonomy could become an incentive for principals and faculties in the lower-tier schools to strive for higher state ratings, so that they, too, could enjoy the benefits of greater freedom. While raising the ceiling for high-performers may widen the gap between them and the lower tiers (more about this point below), it is a risk worth taking because middle-class parents supply critical political support for financing district bond campaigns and tax levies. Also, these schools have few ways of unleashing their creative and academic potential when they have to march to the beat of minimum state standards and play it safe academically.

Other cities have used various tactics to achieve such school independence while sustaining the loyalty of politically active middle-class parents. In 2004, New York created an "autonomy zone" comprising nearly fifty schools (principals and staff members volunteered to be part of the zone) with significant discretion to choose their curriculum, manage their budget, and use additional monies to purchase what the school needed. In 2006, the number that volunteered rose to more than 330. Boston's seventeen Pilot Schools, which served about 10 percent of the district's students, have autonomy from district rules and manage their own budget, while being held to both local and state standards. In Milwaukee, superintendent William Andrekopoulos proposed that high-performing high schools be granted budgetary, staffing, and instructional autonomy equal to the freedom that charter schools already have in the district. These examples show that not all urban schools are broken and that high-performing schools could easily be given more autonomy to retain the support of public schools by politically active middle-class parents, while moving beyond the boundaries that have kept particular schools from attaining academic excellence.[3]

3. Lift the floor for the lowest-performing schools. No formula yet exists for turning around big-city schools that have been mired for years in the bottom tier. In fact, just like the few low-performing hospitals, businesses, and government agencies that have been turned around, such resuscitated schools are rare. What is clear, however, is that while state and federal strategies of test-based accountability seem to prod schools in the middle tiers to avoid the stigma of failure, fear and shame have had less success in extricating persistently low-performing schools.[4]

In Austin, for example, the bottom tier contains two kinds of schools: those that have been labeled Academically Unacceptable in consecutive years, that are in various stages of remediation, or that are close to being shut down; and those that risk being repeatedly labeled Unacceptable and that slip in and out of that category. At least three to four high schools, two to four middle schools, and four to six elementary schools are in those categories—in other words, 8–12 percent of AISD schools.

Those schools that slip in and out of the bottom tier because handfuls of students in certain subgroups trip the wire on the annual test need undramatic responses. Ensuring that stable principal and teacher leadership continues at these schools (increased turnover in principals and staff for more than two years is the clearest indicator of impending academic trouble), plus wise application of financial incentives for staff and additional support for students who need extra help, should keep this small number of schools in the Academically Acceptable category and even bump a few up to a rating of Recognized. Along that line, the AISD Board of Trustees has already recognized a form of merit pay (under what's called the Strategic Compensation Initiative) in twelve pilot schools and recently approved bonuses, known as "retention incentives," for thirty-two middle and high school principals and teachers to keep them from leaving their schools.[5]

But for those AISD schools in danger of being shut down in a year or two if students' scores do not meet state standards, turnarounds seldom occur. Yes, shame and fear can prod staffs to work harder and draw in neighborhood activists and parents to help. Recall Webb Middle School and the superintendent's threat to close it in 2007. In the following year, Webb teachers, administrators, and parents turned disgrace into anger and began concrete actions to improve academic achievement. Whether the improvement stemmed from community activists joining with Webb staff to monitor low-performing students or from any number of other actions, no one in AISD or Webb can say for sure. What did happen, however, is that afterward the middle school was rated Academically Acceptable two years in a row. Nonetheless, there is also much evidence showing that state and federal threats about taking over schools, reconstituting schools, or contracting out to companies have failed to resurrect schools into high fliers.[6]

When turnarounds do occur, more often than not a principal and staff figure out, with district office support, what model, what program, what people best fit a school's history and neighborhood. Then they work with parents, day in and day out, to tailor the different components to fit the school, adapting their approach every time a pothole in the road appears. This happens one school at a time. Success spreads when district officials make it possible for turnaround teachers and administrators to share their wisdom with those staff members who are ready and willing to improve.

Such a slow, labor-intensive process runs counter to what many state officials, federal policy makers, and foundation officers champion. They scorn the few individual schools that have been turned around here and there; they want a dozen or a score of schools "going to scale" with a sure-fire model in place as soon as possible—not in five years, not in a decade, but in the next couple of years. Yet as Charles Payne observed, expanding one or two apparently successful schools across a district is like saying, "Let's pretend to do on a grand scale what we have no idea how to do on a small scale."[7]

Some districts, for example, have established "turnaround zones" where clusters of low-performing schools are placed and where prescribed strategies that change traditional operating conditions are required. In such zones, school leaders have more authority over their budgets and the hiring of personnel. They can change the daily schedule, extend the school day, use their resources to hire additional staff members, and place them in nontraditional posts. Chicago, Miami-Dade, New York, and Philadelphia have created such semi-autonomous subsystems within their districts.[8]

Such turnaround zones might well work in particular districts, even though the initiatives in these cities remain experimental. Reforming one school at a time by ensuring that seasoned principals, teachers, and parents help one another is, to the policy makers and donors who tout turnaround zones, like reviving mom-and-pop grocery stores in an age of supermarkets.[9]

4. Expand school choice for middle and high school students. Since the 1970s, AISD has slowly built an informal structure of parental choice, including magnet schools, International Baccalaureate programs, career academies, and other special programs. The Ann Richards School for Young Women Leaders is a recent initiative that appeals to a striking cross-section of Austin students. Both middle- and working-class parents line up early to get transfers to these schools. Still, the district has yet to authorize charter schools, although the state has chartered over a dozen schools in the city of Austin—schools such as KIPP, and the University Charter School started by the University of Texas. The board and the superintendent have been reluctant to allow groups of teachers, parents, and charter management organizations to enter into a contract with the district and take over persistently low-performing elementary or secondary schools stagnating in the lowest tier of the system. Why should they allow this?[10]

First, expanded choice can deepen the political and financial support of parents for public schools. Second, when policy makers are uncertain about what works best to lift the floor of achievement, starting many different new schools under close monitoring is sensible. The schools that succeed in attracting parental support and that achieve their goals will thrive; less successful ones will fade away. Moreover, schools alone cannot remedy the ill effects of poverty or erase the legacies of ethnic and racial segregation; but a broader palette of choices can offer more chances for individual students and schools to succeed than the dismal history of state and federal threats has provided.[11]

If the board and the superintendent shed their reluctance, they might copy experiments from other districts that have gone beyond the conventional college prep model currently in vogue in AISD. Other districts, for example, have made use of the Career Academy, a school-within-a-school that targets students at risk of dropping out. Organized by business leaders and educators, Career Academies stress academics as well as technical preparation for entry-level jobs in high-tech, medical, and other industries. Long-term evaluations of Career Academies have shown that these employer-and-school partnerships promote student persistence toward graduation, engagement in both academic subjects and work, and, after graduation, higher income than is the case among graduates who did not attend such academies.[12]

There are other possibilities. Districts could institute a school-within-a-school or a separate school organized by civic leaders that coordinates academics and social services, to make it a one-stop social-service community-based learning center for both adults and children. Or a district could establish a small, progressive high school that pursues intellectually stimulating ideas and practices, offers cross-disciplinary curricula, and promotes personal well-being in a context where teachers and students work together to improve both the school community and the larger society. Currently there are a number of community-based, democratically governed, and social-action-oriented high schools, such as the Robert F. Kennedy Community High School in Queens, N.Y.; Hanover High School in Hanover, N.H.; and Metropolitan Regional, Technical, and Academic High School in Providence, R.I.[13]

Such openness to different kinds of schools would not preclude considering public boarding schools such as SEED, developed in Washington, D.C., and Maryland. Foundations and private donors in those districts have raised money to provide public residential settings for minority poor students. The obvious attraction is that a total institution—which provides twenty-four-hour supervision of students—increases the impact of caring adults, as private boarding schools do.[14]

All of these suggestions for chronic low-performers in both categories suggest that districts should cultivate different kinds of schools for low-performing students, rather than relying on state and NCLB threats. New school options for Austin students can come from groups of teachers (including Education Austin), parents, and community activists who organize their own small schools; or they can come from charter school organizations or AISD and city officials who venture into entrepreneurial territory and develop alternatives for students in these schools. Akins High School staff, for example, created a New Tech High Academy in 2006, and the AISD Board of Trustees has approved New Tech High models for Eastside Memorial High School (formerly Johnston High School) to be implemented in 2009–2010.

In short, formalizing and monitoring a structured array of school choices—some experimental, some tried elsewhere—that go beyond the existing unplanned growth of informal options for all AISD students would bring political attention and systematic innovation to the urgent process of lifting the floor for low-performing schools.

5. Publicly join reformers who champion both school improvement and the use of community resources to alleviate the effects of poverty and racial segregation. For those reformers who tilt toward the Improved Schools and Community end of the continuum, endorsing those policies publicly, securing funds for their implementation, and adapting programs to fit the local context become the next steps. Most districts, including Austin, recognize that children bring societal inequalities to school. They offer prekindergarten, after-school programs, and support services for parents, pregnant teenagers, and others in need. These services, however, are seldom widely advertised and often operate on shoestring budgets.

In Chicago, Boston, and Long Beach, where mayors are heavily involved in the public schools, closer coordination of a wide array of city and school services has provided help to families. In cities where school boards and superintendents operate independently from mayors and city councils, as in Austin, tighter coupling between school and city services can occur. Private donors can help considerably in bringing together community and civic organizations, both public and private, to sharpen the focus on helping families gain far more from school than they do now, while doing more for themselves and their children. The Harlem Children's Zone remains a sterling example of what can be done, yet also shows how hard it is to gather together the right mix of people and resources to help children and families.[15]

No such massive integration of services as occurs in Harlem Children's Zone exists in Austin or in most big cities. In sorting through data on Austin's high-poverty, high-minority schools involved in repeated reforms over a thirty-year period, I found three elementary schools (but no high schools) that had done reasonably well in state ratings. These three elementary schools rose from Unacceptable to Acceptable, and even earned ratings of Recognized and Exemplary in certain years. These schools focused tirelessly on early literacy and math, from kindergarten to the third grade. For such against-the-odds exceptions, the Effective Schools champions of reform would assert: demography is *not* destiny. And they would be correct, so long as they pointed out that these elementary school staffs received extra people, funds, and training over the years, but saw much less coordination of community-based medical, social, and family services (see Tables A.1, A.3, and A.4). Had Priority Schools in the late-1980s or Blueprint Schools after 2002 received integrated city and district medical, social, family, and other services, perhaps—and this is only speculation—there might have been many more elementary and secondary schools receiving higher academic ratings.

The accumulated research on the long- and short-term effects of poverty on families and the evidence drawn from the experiences of those who see such effects every day have convinced me that urban leaders adopting reforms that harness comprehensive school improvement efforts to existing city services and community institutions, designed to help families at home and in school, can achieve both academic excellence and equity.

Inevitable Dilemmas

Since I know that the foregoing suggestions will create tough political and educational quandaries for reform-driven district policy makers and practitioners, I will end this book by exploring the conflicts that are bound to arise. As with every reform proposal, decision makers can anticipate some outcomes while others are hidden around the corner. Organizational proposals to raise the ceiling for high-performers, lift the floor for the lowest-performing schools, expand the range of school choices, and bring about other improvements will create predictable (and prickly) political dilemmas for leaders seeking to achieve equity in urban districts.

By "dilemmas" I mean situations in which highly prized values are in conflict with one another. For instance, most urban educators want students to score well on state tests and want schools to receive favorable ratings from state and federal officials. Yet educators also want teachers to go beyond covering content and skills on tests—to teach in ambitious ways that get students to ask questions, inquire into topics, and enjoy learning.

Such conflicting yet prized values require administrators and teachers to make choices about how much time, energy, and funds can be spent on trying to fulfill desired but competing values. Because organizational resources are limited, administrators craft compromises that permit tradeoffs between rival values. In the tradeoff between doing well on state tests and teaching students to think and ask questions, some school staffs, for example, decide to work only on getting their students to score higher on state tests and give extra credit to those students who want to investigate questions and projects they design. Other staffs incorporate project-based teaching activities into their daily repertoire, while squeezing in test preparation once a week. And in other schools, staff members identify those students who are on the cusp of doing well on tests and tutor those students, leaving teachers more time to engage the majority of students in adventurous learning tasks. These compromises involve tradeoffs between prized values. They work for a while and then have to be renegotiated as conditions, resources, and people change.

Both organizational and political dilemmas and their compromises are a steady presence in every district, school, and classroom across the nation; they take no holidays. Dilemmas arising from reform initiatives are as natural as day following night. So is conflict.

District leaders, always aware of their local setting, have to figure out politically palatable and creative tradeoffs between conflicting values as they move from crisis to crisis. Unlike problems that can be solved, dilemmas can only be identified and then managed through astute negotiations and crafted compromises. Leaders have to work through these organizational and political dilemmas.[16]

Enlarging the autonomy of high-performing schools and expanding school choice increase variation among schools in resources, curricula, and outcomes but undercut equity, whereas adherence to uniform district standards decreases variation among schools but promotes equity. If districts allow high-achieving schools (mostly located in middle- and upper-middle-class neighborhoods) to pursue additional goals and if they expand the range of choices open to parents, more schools will diverge from district standards.

High-performers that choose to use their newly granted autonomy often hire staff to explore different content, invest in new programs, and prod their students to develop skills not currently in AISD Instructional Planning Guides. In doing so, they vary even more from other schools in the district. Such exercise of autonomy can easily lead to wider test score gaps between white and minority students. District leaders seeking both equity and academic excellence will then have to face tough decisions: How much variation in school operations and outcomes is acceptable to district leaders—who want system policies to be followed, yet also want innovative and experimental academic and nonacademic programs that perpetuate strong test performance? If more low-performing schools rise to higher tiers yet the median achievement score gap between whites and minorities widens, is this an acceptable tradeoff? If upwardly mobile and politically forceful parents across the district are pleased that some schools have more autonomy and want even more schools to have such freedom (so long as they meet state performance requirements), while other schools slip and receive ratings of Unacceptable, is this a manageable compromise? No easy answers appear, since this dilemma is packed with political dynamite and managing its explosive potential requires exquisite political tap-dancing. The following dilemma poses a similar risk.

Satisfying the public's demand for test score gains that meet state and federal accountability standards, versus building the capacity of school staffs to implement reforms that will produce those gains. This tension exists in every urban district. Unrelenting pressure from state and federal accountability rules presses district staff and school practitioners to produce swift results, yet teachers, principals, district office staff, and superintendents need to have the skills and the knowledge base that will engage students sufficiently to score higher on the annual tests.

In Austin, as in all Texas districts, test scores and state ratings released by TEA are published in local newspapers. Pressures on school boards and administrators intensify when a rating of Academically Unacceptable pops up, or when a school is listed as Needs Improvement according to NCLB criteria. Educating school board members and the media about the byzantine system of state and federal rules governing school-by-school ratings becomes a superintendent's major task.

For example, TEA will rescind a rating of Unacceptable if a school makes substantial gains in test scores the next year. Recall that Webb Middle School students' scores improved in 2007, leading to a rating of Academically Acceptable. After putting Webb on notice for one year, TEA restarted the clock. Not so for NCLB regulations, which specify that a school has to meet an absolute percentage—say, 70 percent of the students must pass fifth-grade math. Even if the school has gone from 45 to 69 percent passing, that school still gets labeled as a failure in math and moves to the next step of sanctions. Not understanding this NCLB rule, school board members, editorial writers, TV producers, bloggers, teachers, and parents end up blaming the school for failing, when students have actually made progress.

This double-bookkeeping system of accountability—district administrators keep one set of books for the state and another set for federal regulators—causes concern for AISD educators and their peers in big cities across the nation. The AISD Board of Trustees, like boards in many other urban districts, hates to see any school labeled Academically Unacceptable or wind up on the NCLB list. District leaders, like school staffs, feel the shame and blame from such labels. When the ratings of Unacceptable are released, the board presses its superintendent to turn the school around quickly. It is no easy task.

No school can turn around on a dime; teaching, homework, and scheduling practices cannot be altered in a brief period. An AISD official pointed out to me that one high school, at the start of a particular school year, had received a hundred transfer students, many of whom had academic difficulties. Those students did not do well on the state test a few months later. Raising test scores for low-performing groups of students prior to the next round of tests is nearly impossible. A crash intervention of tutors for one-on-one work and double-period test preparation will help in some cases, but not for most of these students.[17]

Some Texas districts other than Austin get state waivers to hold back ninth-graders who failed one or more of their core subjects. These students reduce the cohort taking the tenth-grade test; scores tend to be higher for the shrunken cohort than they would have been had those absent ninth-graders been included. Worse yet is that ninth-graders retained in grade tend to drop out, a situation documented fully in Houston.[18]

Beyond trying to game the state system's accountability rules for schools in danger of closing, most urban districts turn to systematic professional development. This highly valued strategy builds the knowledge and skills of teachers and administrators, and promises payoffs in the form of demanding classroom lessons aligned with state standards. Such efforts, implemented through PLCs, coaches, and SWAT-like teams sent to schools to work with teachers, require patience. It takes time for what is learned in these sessions to percolate into schools and end up changing practices in classrooms. Time has become the enemy of ambitious teaching and improved student achievement. Thus, the tension between securing swift test score improvement and fostering sustained staff development persists.

Like many urban superintendents, Pascal (Pat) Forgione recognized this dilemma and did his best to manage the ever-shifting state and federal accountability rules. He plowed grants and AISD funds into

professional learning communities and other forms of staff development, confident that the compromises he fashioned would help in the
long run. In the short run, however, central-office help was useless to
Johnston High School. Such quick-fix help failed to stop the closure
of Pearce Middle School, with Reagan High School in the final stages
of state and federal sanctions.[19]

Forgione clearly made progress in figuring out compromises for
this and other dilemmas, but the stubbornness of chronic poor academic performance will require many years of service from the next
superintendent. As Forgione said, "I can't be here long enough to do
everything we must do, so we must find another good leader who can
stay another ten years." It remains to be seen whether his successor
will build on Forgione's decade of gains by adapting existing structures to changing conditions, so as to both raise the ceiling and lift
the floor—a feat that few, if any, big-city districts have ever accomplished.[20]

*Publicly endorsing the task of making chronically low-performing schools effective
while also addressing poverty in minority communities through school and city programs, versus continuing the low profile of school-based programs addressing poor and
minority students' needs.* The conflict here is over public endorsement of
a broader community-based approach for persistently failing schools
with mostly poor and minority students. Like most districts, AISD
already has an array of small, quietly run programs addressing students' health, family problems, and the like. These efforts are largely
peripheral to schools' instructional programs. A larger presence and
integration of city and AISD social, medical, and psychological services within particular low-performing schools offers a one-stop center for improved instruction as well as help to families. Yet raising the
profile of these services within particular schools runs the risk of

creating sharp political conflict over scarce AISD dollars, when these are used to supply services that other institutions are better equipped to provide.

Other than under-the-radar agreements made between AISD, city agencies, and private groups, district leaders have kept these social services peripheral to the main instructional program. A bolder, broader approach to raising academic achievement in low-performing schools could easily spark political conflict over the best way to spend educational dollars. It is a gamble, but may be worth the effort for persistently failing schools.

None of these complicated and tension-filled dilemmas will disappear. They are constantly beneath the surface, creating political and educational conflicts because each of the values at issue is prized within the district and the community. Effective leadership identifies and manages these inevitable tensions, and finds ways to support constructive compromises that benefit students. These dilemmas are not hidden around the corner; they are predictable. Leaders who ignore these organizational and political dilemmas pay a price in the end.

Yet the issues of persistently low-performing schools and threatened closures will endure because Austin and other urban districts are deeply entangled in histories of segregation, poverty, and continuing immigration. Well-intentioned reforms aimed at freeing students from the effects of poverty exacerbated by segregation, desegregation, and resegregation have fallen flat in Austin and across the nation.

Although public schools have contributed much to the nation's civic, economic, social, and political life by reducing inequalities among low-income minorities and whites in the rates at which they graduate from college, enjoy full employment, own property, and raise children, much remains to be done for those without the political muscle or voice to get a better schooling.

Nor is it clear that further reductions in the test score gap between minorities and whites will occur, even when schools are charged by policy elites to reduce those societal inequities. From time to time, crises erupt—sudden peat bog fires such as a natural disaster or a huge spike in unemployment. The fires reveal deep and broad socioeconomic inequalities. Reform policies are swiftly adopted to remedy the dismal records of bottom-tier schools. Firefighters douse the blaze, yet the embers will continue to smolder underground until the next flare-up.

Austin "is not a success story," Superintendent Forgione concluded when leaving his post. It "is a progress story." Yes, it is a progress story—but one that offers a mixed picture of significant victories amid stubborn losses, muscular optimism along with bouts of enervating pessimism, astute district leaders unaware of historical patterns, and school board members determined to reduce inequalities while micro-managing staff. This is why Austin is as good as it gets in urban districts.[21]

Appendix

Table A.I. Historically low-performing high-poverty, high-minority elementary schools involved in previous AISD improvement efforts (1978, 1987, 2002).

School	Year	Ratings[a]	Minority (in percent)	Poverty (in percent)
Blackshear	1999	U	98	94
	2000	A	97	80
	2001	U	99	91
	2002	R	98	94
	2004	A	98	96
	2005	A	98	96
	2006	A	100	97
	2007	A	99	98
	2008	R	100	95
	2009	A		
Metz	1999	A	97	90
	2000	A	95	83
	2001	A	96	81
	2002	R	96	85
	2004	A	98	91
	2005	A	99	90
	2006	A	98	91
	2007	R	98	93
	2008	R	98	95
	2009	R		

Table A.I.   (continued)

School	Year	Ratings[a]	Minority (in percent)	Poverty (in percent)
Sims	1999	A	95	96
	2000	A	97	95
	2001	A	96	92
	2002	U	97	93
	2004	A	99	94
	2005	A	99	96
	2006	R	99	96
	2007	A	99	97
	2008	A	99	97
	2009	A		

a. E = Exemplary; R = Recognized; A = Academically Acceptable; U = Academically Unacceptable.

Table A.2. Big picture of AISD ratings, 1994–2009.

Year	AISD schools	Exemplary	Recognized	Acceptable	Low-Performing
1994	91	0 (0%)	1 (1%)	88 (97%)	2 (2%)
1995	96	4 (4%)	8 (8%)	65 (68%)	15 (17%)
1996	93	5 (5%)	8 (9%)	67 (72%)	11 (12%)
1997	91	7 (8%)	10 (11%)	73 (80%)	1 (1%)
1998	94	8 (8%)	8 (8%)	72 (77%)	4 (4%)
1999	94	9 (10%)	7 (7%)	64 (68%)	14 (15%)
2000[a]	97	10 (10%)	9 (9%)	69 (71%)	9 (9%)
2001	101	14 (14%)	24 (24%)	58 (58%)	5 (5%)
2002	102	17 (17%)	31 (30%)	51 (50%)	3 (3%)
2003[b]					
2004	103	7 (7%)	16 (15%)	75 (73%)	5 (5%)
2005	103	4 (4%)	17 (16%)	77 (75%)	5 (5%)
2006	102	6 (6%)	21 (20%)	68 (67%)	7 (7%)
2007	104	7 (7%)	18 (17%)	70 (67%)	9 (9%)
2008	108	15 (14%)	19 (18%)	63 (58%)	11 (10%)
2009	108	24 (22%)	30 (28%)	45 (42%)	9 (8%)

a. Ratings are known by June, the end of the school year. The Board of Trustees appointed superintendent Pascal (Pat) Forgione in August 1999. His first full year in office was 1999–2000.

b. The Texas Education Agency gave no ratings in 2003 because the state was moving from one test (Texas Assessment of Academic Skills) to another (Texas Assessment of Knowledge and Skills). A common pattern emerges here, as elsewhere: schools and districts "learn" to do better on tests, and ratings of Exemplary and Recognized become more frequent the longer a test is used. Note the numbers for the years prior to 2003, and the differences in these ratings for the years 2004–2008.

Table A.3.   Historically low-performing, high-poverty, high-minority middle schools in AISD.

School	Year	Rating[a]	Minority (in percent)	Poverty (in percent)
Dobie	1999	U	83	77
	2000	U	86	68
	2001	U	89	70
	2002	A	91	77
	2004	A	95	88
	2005	A	95	90
	2006	U	96	89
	2007	A	95	92
	2008	A	96	95
	2009	A	96	95
Pearce	1999	U	95	75
	2000	U	95	69
	2001	A	96	76
	2002	U	97	78
	2004	A	97	86
	2005	U	97	89
	2006	U	98	90
	2007	U	98	92
	2008	U	98	95
	2009	U		
Webb	1999	A	89	84
	2000	A	89	82
	2001	A	93	79
	2002	A	94	85
	2004	U	94	92
	2005	U	95	92
	2006	U	95	92
	2007	A	95	94
	2008	A	98	96
	2009	A		

a. E = Exemplary; R = Recognized; A = Academically Acceptable; U = Academically Unacceptable.

Table A.4.   High-poverty, high-minority high schools in AISD.[a]

School	Year	Ratings[b]	Minority (in percent)	Poverty (in percent)
Akins	2001	A	70	33
	2002	A	71	36
	2004	A	77	48
	2005	A	77	51
	2006	A	80	54
	2007	A	81	56
	2008	A	83	62
	2009	A		
Crockett	1999	U	59	26
	2000	A	60	22
	2001	A	62	25
	2002	A	63	26
	2004	A	64	41
	2005	A	66	48
	2006	U	68	50
	2007	A	71	51
	2008	U	76	58
	2009	A		
Lanier	1999	U	76	52
	2000	U	78	46
	2001	A	80	48
	2002	A	85	56
	2004	A	89	70
	2005	A	91	74
	2006	A	91	78
	2007	A	93	79
	2008	A	93	77
	2009	A		
Reagan	1999	U	93	60
	2000	U	93	58
	2001	U	95	61
	2002	A	97	60
	2004	A	97	71
	2005	A	97	77
	2006	U	98	80

Table A.4.   (continued)

School	Year	Ratings[b]	Minority (in percent)	Poverty (in percent)
	2007	U	98	83
	2008	U	98	80
	2009	U		
Travis	1999	U	84	53
	2000	U	85	47
	2001	A	88	55
	2002	A	90	63
	2004	A	92	75
	2005	A	93	79
	2006	A	93	79
	2007	U	94	80
	2008	A	95	78
	2009	U		

a. Johnston High School is excluded. It was rated Unacceptable for eight of the nine years. Formally closed in spring 2008, it reopened as Eastside Memorial High School in September 2008. LBJ High School was also excluded because the TAAS and TAKS scores of the middle-class magnet school Liberal Arts and Science Academy (LASA), located in LBJ since 2002, bumped up the annual rating to Acceptable in subsequent years. In 2006–2007, LBJ became a First Things First school, and LASA, still housed on the campus, was thereafter rated separately from LBJ.

b. E = Exemplary; R = Recognized; A = Academically Acceptable; U = Academically Unacceptable.

Table A.5. AISD schools rated Exemplary and Recognized, 1999–2009.

School	Number of times	Minority[a] (in percent)	Poverty[a] (in percent)
Sampling of elementary schools rated Exemplary			
Baranoff	8 of 10 years	31	5
Casis	10 of 10 years	17	3
Doss	8 of 10 years	33	12
Highland Park	10 of 10 years	18	5
Sanchez	1 of 10 years	93 (2002)	91
Campbell	1 of 10 years	99 (2008)	92
The only secondary schools rated Exemplary			
Anderson H.S.	1 of 10 years	29 (2002)	10
Bowie H.S.	1 of 10 years	28 (2002)	4
(No middle schools)			
Sampling of schools rated Recognized			
Anderson H.S.	1 of 10 years	24 (2001)	9 (2001)
Bowie H.S.	2 of 10 years	30	8
Small M.S.	3 of 10 years	30	16
Murchison M.S.	1 of 10 years	29	19
Bryker Woods E.S.	6 of 10 years	24	12
Cowan E.S.	6 of 10 years	39	15
Summitt E.S.	6 of 10 years	37	34
Ortega E.S.	5 of 10 years	99	98
Pease E.S.	5 of 10 years	75	30
Kocurek E.S.	6 of 10 years	64	55

a. Except where noted, minority and poverty percentages are for 2007.

Notes

Introduction

1. "Burns Bog Fire Likely to Burn for Another Day," Canada.com, May 30, 2007, www.canada.com/theprovince/news/story.html?id=83de97cc-2f93-4b17-a11d-67ac8d3b77aa&k=68247 (accessed June 24, 2009).

2. Jennifer Viegas, "Ancient Scots Mummified Their Dead," *ABC News*, September 17, 2007, www.abc.net.au/science/articles/2007/09/17/2035481.htm?site=science&topic=ancient (accessed June 24, 2009).

3. For histories of progressive education prior to World War II, see Lawrence Cremin, *Transformation of the School* (New York: Vintage, 1961); David Tyack, *The One Best System* (Cambridge, Mass.: Harvard University Press, 1974); Sol Cohen, *Progressives and Urban School Reform* (New York: Teachers College Press, 1964); William Reese, *Power and Promise of School Reform: Grassroots Movements during the Progressive Era* (New York: Routledge and Kegan Paul, 1986).

4. Diane Ravitch, *The Troubled Crusade* (New York: Basic Books, 1983), ch. 2. Also see David A. Gamson, "Rethinking Progressivism: The District Perspective," *Paedagogica Historica*, 39 (2003): 417–434; The degree to which these progressive school practices penetrated the classroom is less apparent. See Larry Cuban, *How Teachers Taught*, 2nd ed. (New York: Teachers College Press, 1993).

5. The film *Blackboard Jungle*, based on the book by Evan Hunter, appeared in 1955; *West Side Story* appeared in 1961. Diane Ravitch, *The Great School Wars* (New

York: Basic Books, 1974), p. 261; Kenneth Jackson, *The Crabgrass Frontier: The Suburbanization of the United States* (New York: Oxford University Press, 1987).

6. Peter Daniels, *Lost Revolutions: The South in the 1950s* (Chapel Hill: University of North Carolina Press, 2000); James Patterson, *Brown v. Board of Education: A Civil Rights Milestone and Its Troubled Legacy* (New York: Oxford University Press, 2001), ch. 1.

7. David Labaree, "Public Goods, Private Goods: The American Struggle over Educational Goals," *American Educational Research Journal*, 34, no. 1 (1997): 39–81. For the phrase "educationalizing social problems," see idem, "The Winning Ways of a Losing Strategy: Educationalizing Social Problems in the U.S.," unpublished paper. David Tyack, Diane Ravitch, Carl Kaestle, Marvin Lazerson, and other historians of education have likewise commented on this phenomenon.

8. Diane Ravitch, *The Troubled Crusade* (New York: Basic Books, 1983), pp. 228–230; Eileen White, "Sputnik at 25," *Education Week*, October 13, 1982, at www.edweek.org/ew/articles/1982/10/13/02090031.h02.html (accessed June 24, 2009).

9. Patterson, *Brown v. Board of Education;* Hugh Davis Graham, *The Uncertain Triumph: Federal Education Policy in the Kennedy and Johnson Years* (Chapel Hill: University of North Carolina Press, 1984).

10. Frank Reissman, *The Culturally Deprived Child and His Education* (New York: Harper and Row, 1962); Larry Cuban, *To Make a Difference: Teaching in the Inner City School* (New York: Free Press, 1970); Mario Fantini and Gerald Weinstein, *The Disadvantaged* (New York: Harper and Row, 1968).

11. Business Roundtable, *K–12 Education Reform* (Washington, D.C.: Business Roundtable, 2001); Thomas Friedman, *The World Is Flat* (New York: Farrar, Straus and Giroux, 2005); Norton Grubb and Marvin Lazerson, *The Education Gospel* (Cambridge, Mass.: Harvard University Press, 2004); Larry Cuban, *The Blackboard and the Bottom Line: Why Schools Can't Be Businesses* (Cambridge, Mass.: Harvard University Press, 2005).

12. By "policy elites" I mean loose networks of corporate leaders, public officials (including top educational policy makers), foundation officers, and academics who circulate ideas consistent with their views of problems and solutions, champion particular reforms, use both public and private funds to run projects, and strongly

influence decision making. Not unlike policy elites in business and civic affairs who are involved in growing a stronger economy, improving health care, protecting national security, strengthening foreign policy, and safeguarding the environment, policy entrepreneurs and reformers have ready access to media, are capable of framing problems, and set a public agenda for discussion. Or as one member in good standing wrote: "In public policy, it matters less who has the best arguments and more who gets heard—and by whom" (Ralph Reed, cited in Dana Milbank, *Homo Politicus: The Strange and Barbaric Tribes of the Beltway* [New York: Doubleday, 2008], p. 68).

Political party labels do not define these elites, although there are clearly Republican and Democratic members who wear their affiliation on their sleeve and, when administrations change, move in and out of office. I do not use the phrase "policy elites" to suggest conspiratorial groups secretly meeting and designing action plans. Nor do I bash elites. I suggest only that these overlapping networks of like-minded individuals share values and tastes and seek school improvements aligned with those values and tastes. As "influentials," they convene frequently in different forums, speak the same policy talk, and are connected closely to sources of public and private influence in governments, media, businesses, academia, and foundations. They help to create a climate of opinion that hovers over no more than a few hundred national policy leaders and smaller numbers at state and local levels. Familiar with the ways of the media, these policy elites extend and shape that climate of opinion by closely working with journalists who report what they say, write, think, and do. Few members of these loosely connected policy elites, however, have had direct or sustained experience with school principals or teachers, much less engaged in the teaching of children. Yet their recommended policies, their "common sense" about what the nation, state, district, and teachers should do, touch the daily lives of both educators and children. See John Kingdon, *Agendas, Alternatives, and Public Policies* (Boston: Little, Brown, 1984); James Fallows, *Breaking the News* (New York: Random House, 1996); William Safire, "Elite Establishment Egghead Eupatrids," *New York Times Magazine*, May 18, 1997, p. 16. For a more recent survey of experts as to who are the "influentials" currently shaping reform policy, see Christopher Swanson and Janelle Barlage, "Influence: A Study of the Factors Shaping Educational Policy," (Washington, D.C.: Editorial Projects in Education Research Center, December 2006).

13. Policy elite and educator rhetoric about the need to raise every student's aca-

demic achievement while "closing" or "ending" the test score discrepancy between minority and white students has a conceptual problem that is only occasionally aired in public. That these two goals are in conflict—when you raise everyone's achievement to the same degree, the achievement test score gap remains the same—too often goes unnoticed, as school board members, superintendents, teachers, parents, and other reform-minded fellow travelers advocate both without missing a beat. What most of these well-meaning reformers probably seek is to raise the achievement of the lowest achievers by larger increments than the increases in the scores of the higher-achieving students. Or they want to take those district students lodged in the bottom quartile of achievement and raise their scores to the next-higher one. For a recent news article on this conflict over closing the racial gap in achievement test scores, see Sam Dillon, "'No Child' Law Is Not Closing a Racial Gap," *New York Times*, April 29, 2009, pp. A1, A16.

14. Policy elites view equity and academic excellence, so often fused together to look like a bumper-sticker slogan, as harmonious values. They are not. Just as the prized values of liberty and equality are often thought by Americans to be in sync with each other, yet are likewise in conflict. Consider an example. Democrats often want to raise personal income taxes; they do not see this as a restriction on individual liberty. Republicans want to cut those same taxes, yet do not see this as increasing inequality. See Dick Meyer, "Myths about Good Old American Values," *Washington Post*, November 2, 2008, p. B3.

"Academic excellence" generally means all students are exposed to rigorous content and skills in schools—that is, they have equal access to knowledge and skills (e.g., every student who wants to take Advancement Placement courses can do so) and then perform equally well regardless of race, ethnicity, social class, gender, or religion (e.g., if each student works hard, he or she can get A's in school and score high on the Scholastic Assessment Test).

Because the word "equity" has many meanings among school reformers and is used differently by them in different contexts and at different times, friction between "academic excellence" and "equity" arises.

The most common view of "equity" is that everyone gets the same chance to go to school. This is equal access to schooling. Over a century ago, every child was expected to have a chance to attend elementary school; after World War II, every young person was expected to complete high school; since the 1990s, every student has been expected to earn a diploma, enter college, and get a Bachelor's degree. Rising expectations for attaining school credentials that made a difference in the workplace meant that over the past century no distinctions based on color, ethnicity, religion, gender, or social class were to mar young people's access to schooling. The prevailing metaphor was the race in which everyone has the same chance to win a gold medal. Yet decades of residential segregation and unequal allocation of funds and teachers to schools based on social class, ethnicity, and race, as high school dropout rates rose and graduation rates declined, undercut equal access time and again.

A competing definition of "equity" is the condition in which there is a level playing field where students compete for school credentials. In this version of equity, schools acknowledge that race, class, ethnicity, and gender are embedded in adult attitudes, social practices, and socioeconomic structures to such an extent that they shape what children bring to school. It is, then, the school's job to provide unequal amounts of help to students who—through no fault of their own—need assistance in schools. Here is the basis for the post-1965 compensatory school programs (e.g., Head Start, Upward Bound, Job Corps) which offered programs strong enough to crack the strong link between poverty and underachievement. While such compensatory programs have helped many students, insufficient funds and staff have for decades prevented many eligible students from participating in these programs.

Since the 1970s, there have been determined efforts to provide additional resources to largely low-income minority schools to close the test score achievement gap between minority and white children. It is this task of helping such low-performing minority students to raise their scores to those of higher-performing white students that frames another perspective on equity: equal results. That is, each racial and ethnic group in society is represented equally in the distribution among the four quartiles of academic achievement. Thus "with group proportional equality, race and ethnicity tell you nothing about . . . past, present, or future achievements." The history of the national test score gap reveals that differences in achievement have narrowed in certain decades and then widened again, leaving a substantial distance between white and minority group test scores. See Ronald Ferguson, *Toward Excellence with Equity: An Emerging Vision for Closing the Achievement Gap* (Cambridge, Mass.: Harvard Education Press, 2007), pp. 284–285.

Thus, at least three versions of "equity" get entwined in the language of school reformers, policy elites, and media analysts. Obviously, these three different meanings have different consequences for both district and school policy and practice. When policy makers and district leaders use the word "equity," they seldom parse which meaning of the concept they intend for the public to know. Nor do these opinion leaders see how these various definitions of equity conflict again and again with the prized value of academic excellence.

I found the following sources helpful in thinking through these different meanings of equity: James Coleman, "The Concept of Equality of Educational Opportunity," *Harvard Educational Review*, 38(1), 1968, pp. 7–36; Christopher Jencks, "Whom Must We Treat Equally for Educational Equality to Be Equal?" *Ethics*, 98, no. 2 (1988): 518–533; David Kirp, "Changing Conceptions of Educational Equity," in Diane Ravitch and Maris Vinovskis, eds., *Learning from the Past* (Baltimore, Md.: Johns Hopkins University Press, 1995), pp. 97–112; Christopher Jencks and Meredith Phillips, eds., *The Black-White Test Score Gap* (Washington, D.C.: Brookings Institution Press, 1998).

15. The quote ("The sad reality . . .") comes from the fourth of ten principles stated in a manifesto from the Education Equality Project, an organization of "non-partisan . . . elected officials, civil rights leaders, and education reformers that has been formed to help insure that America finally brings equity to an educational system that, fifty-four years since *Brown v. Board of Education*, continues to fail its highest-need students." Superintendents, mayors, governors, and former federal officials signed the Ten Principles and Mission Statement. See the organization's website at /www.educationequalityproject.org (accessed June 24, 2009). These managerially driven reformers who tilted toward business-oriented solutions to school problems are first cousins to the efficiency-minded reformers a century earlier who focused on school improvement through creating numerical measures of success and touting those numbers as evidence of success or failure in school reform. See description of "Administrative Progressives" in David Tyack, *The One Best System* (Cambridge, Mass.: Harvard University Press, 1974), pp. 126–129.

16. Clay Risen, "The Lightning Rod," *The Atlantic*, November 2008, p. 85.

17. On effective schools, see Barbara Taylor and Pamela Bullard, *The Revolution Revisited: Effective Schools and Systemic Reform* (Bloomington, Ind.: Phi Delta Kappa Books, 1995); David Whitman, "An Appeal to Authority: The New Paternalism in

Urban Schools," *Education Next*, 8, no. 4 (2008), at www.hoover.org/publications/ednext/26967964.html (accessed June 24, 2009). I have visited East Side Prep in East Palo Alto, Calif., numerous times.

18. Note that the "Effective Schools and Districts" reformers generally use "equity" to mean equal access to high-quality programs and equal results, while "Improved Schools and Community" reformers generally lean on unequal help inside and outside schools to achieve equal results.

The quote ("There is no evidence . . .") comes from a published statement and newspaper advertisement touting a "Broader, Bolder Approach to Education." The signers of this statement are academics, former and sitting superintendents, state and federal officials, and civil rights leaders. See www.boldapproach.org (accessed June 24, 2009). These "whole child" reformers are akin to those educational progressives a century earlier who saw the school as an agency providing not only intellectual development for every child but also children's physical, psychological, emotional, and civic development.

19. See Lawrence Cremin, *The Transformation of the School* (New York: Vintage, 1961). For the Mott Foundation's support of community schools, see www.mott.org/Home/about/programs/pathwaysoutofpoverty/improvingcommunityeducation.aspx (accessed June 24, 2009). Descriptions of School Development program schools can be found at www.med.yale.edu/comer (accessed June 24, 2009). On the Coalition of Community Schools, see www.communityschools.org (accessed June 24, 2009). Geoffrey Canada's Harlem Children's Zone Project, covering nearly 100 city blocks and including more than 8,500 children, has classes for low-income expectant parents, preschools, charter schools, and dozens of other programs that reach out into the community to give children and youth the middle-class skills to succeed. Canada, however, did not sign the call for a "Broader, Bolder Approach to Education," though his efforts are clearly consistent with that call. Instead, he signed the "Education and Equality" manifesto. On Canada's work, see Deborah Pines, "Thriving in the Zone," *U.S. News and World Report*, October 31, 2005, at www.usnews.com/usnews/news/articles/051031/31canada.htm (accessed June 24, 2009). Also see Paul Tough, *Whatever It Takes: Geoffrey Canada's Quest to Change Harlem and America* (Boston: Houghton Mifflin, 2008).

20. Frederick Hess, *Spinning Wheels: The Politics of Urban School Reform* (Washington, D.C.: Brookings Institution Press, 1999); Paul Tough, How Many Billionaires Does

It Take To Fix a School System?" *New York Times Magazine,* March 9, 2008, pp. 50–54, 70, at www.nytimes.com/2008/03/09/magazine/09roundtable-t.html?sq =philanthropists%20education%20March%202008&st=cse&scp =1&pagewanted=all (accessed June 24, 2009). Consider one obvious inequality, the lopsided distribution of income in the United States during the past century. In 1910, the top 1 percent of the population in the United States received one-third of all personal income, while the bottom 20 percent earned 8.3 percent. The high-water mark of disparities in income in the twentieth century was in 1929, when the top 1 percent held 44 percent of all personal income. The gap decreased during the Great Depression and World War II to its lowest level in the mid-1970s, when that same 1 percent possessed nearly 20 percent of all personal income. In the 1990s, the high-income 1 percent steadily increased its share to reach 40 percent, even higher than 1910 and almost reaching the level of 1929. The 1910 figures come from David Tyack and Elisabeth Hansot, *Managers of Virtue* (New York: Basic Books, 1982), p. 109; later figures come from Kevin Phillips, *Wealth and Democracy* (New York: Broadway Books, 2002), pp. 122–123.

21. Patterson, *Brown v. Board of Education;* Daniels, *Lost Revolutions.*

22. Gary Orfield and John Yun, *Resegregation in America* (Cambridge, Mass.: Harvard University Civil Rights Project, 1999); Robert Linn and Kelvin Welner, eds., *Race-Conscious Policies for Assigning Students to Schools: Social Science Research and the Supreme Court Cases* (Washington, D.C.: National Academy of Education, 2007); Russell Rumberger and Gregory Palardy, "Does Segregation Still Matter? The Impact of Student Composition on Academic Achievement in High School," *Teachers College Record,* 107, no. 9 (2005): 1999–2045; Richard Kahlenberg, *Using Socioeconomic Diversity to Improve School Outcomes* (New York: Century Foundation, 2007).

23. Hess, *Spinning Wheels;* Jonathan Supovitz, *The Case for District-Based Reform: Leading, Building, and Sustaining School Improvement* (Cambridge, Mass.: Harvard Education Press, 2006); New Schools Venture Fund, "2007 Summit: Envisioning New Public Education Systems for the 21st Century," May 8, 2007; Larry Cuban and Michael Usdan, eds., *Powerful Reforms with Shallow Roots* (New York: Teachers College Press, 2003); Frederick Hess, ed., *Urban School Reform: Lessons from San Diego* (Cambridge, Mass.: Harvard Education Press, 2005).

24. New Schools Venture Fund, "2008 Summit: From Innovation to Transformation—Connecting Entrepreneurs to Systems Change," May 20, 2008.

25. Ross Perot quoted in McNeil, *Contradictions of School Reform*, p. 186; Alan Bersin quoted in Amy Hightower, "San Diego's Big Boom" (Seattle, Wash.: University of Washington, Center for Study of Teaching and Policy, 2002), p. 10.

26. Anthony Russo, "The Bostonian," *Education Next*, 6, no. 3 (2006), at www.hoover.org/publications/ednext/3211646.html (accessed June 24, 2009); Martha Bryant, "Michelle Rhee: Unconventional, Bee-Swallowing Reformer," *Newsweek*, December 31, 2007, at www.newsweek.com/id/81617 (accessed June 24, 2009). On Paul Vallas, who served six years as superintendent in Chicago and five in Philadelphia, and who is now in New Orleans, see Dale Mezzacappa, "The Vallas Effect," *Education Next*, 8, no. 2 (2008), at www.hoover.org/publications/ednext/16109997.html (accessed June 24, 2009).

Adam Nossiter, "A Tamer of Schools Has Plan in New Orleans," *New York Times*, September 24, 2007, at www.nytimes.com/2007/09/24/education/24orleans.html?_r=1&oref=slogin (accessed June 24, 2009).

27. Frederick Hess, "Reforming Reform," *HGSE News*, August 1, 2004, at www.gse.harvard.edu/news/features/hess08012004.html (accessed June 24, 2009).

28. Quoted in Tough, "How Many Billionaires Does It Take To Fix a School System?"

29. See, for example, ibid.; Charles Lindblom and David Cohen, *Usable Knowledge: Social Science and Social Problem Solving* (New Haven, Conn.: Yale University Press, 1979); David Cohen and Michael Garet, "Reforming Educational Policy with Applied Social Research," *Harvard Educational Review*, 45, no. 1 (1975): 17–43; Frederick Hess, ed., *When Research Matters* (Cambridge, Mass.: Harvard Education Press, 2008). For a different view of the relationship between policy and evidence, see Denis Phillips, "Adding Complexity: Philosophical Perspectives on the Relationship between Evidence and Policy," in Pamela Moss, ed., *Evidence and Decision Making* (Chicago: National Society for the Study of Education, 2007), pp. 376–402.

30. Helen Ladd, "Rethinking the Way We Hold Schools Accountable," *Education Week*, January 23, 2008, pp. 26–27; New Schools Venture Fund, "2007 Summit." See www.educationequalityproject.org (accessed June 24, 2009). In 2009, President Barack Obama appointed Arne Duncan, former Chicago school chief, as U.S. secretary of education. Duncan had signed appeals from both the "Effective Schools and Districts" and "Improved Schools and Community" groups. See list of signatories for Education Equality Project and "Broader, Bolder Approach to Education."

31. To say that researchers are split over what strategies work in urban district improvement of academic achievement is to restate a cliché. Advocates of one policy or another can pick from various research studies to support their positions. For a sampling of the disagreement among researchers and policy analysts, see Kenneth Wong, "District-Wide Framework for Improvement," in Herbert Walberg, ed., *Handbook on Restructuring and Substantial School Improvement* (Lincoln, Ill.: Center on Innovation and Improvement, 2007), pp. 23–36; Cross City Campaign for Urban School Education, "A Delicate Balance: District Policies and Classroom Practice" (Chicago, 2005); "High-Performing School Districts," Bill and Melinda Gates Foundation, June 2005; Stephen Smith and Roslyn Mickelson, "All That Glitters Is Not Gold: School Reform in Charlotte-Mecklenburg," *Educational Evaluation and Policy Analysis*, 22, no. 2 (2000): 101–127; Jeff Lowenstein, "School Districts Often Use Top-down Approach to Improve Instruction," *Catalyst Cleveland*, June–July 2005; Chrysan Gallucci, et al., "Converging Reform 'Theories' in Urban Middle Schools: District-Guided Instructional Improvement in Small Schools of Choice," *Teachers College Record*, 109, no. 12 (2007): 2601–2641; Kenneth Wong and Francis Shen, "City and State Takeover as a School Reform Strategy, *ERIC Digest*, at www.ericdigests.org/2003-2/city.html (accessed June 24, 2009); Cuban and Usdan, *Powerful Reforms with Shallow Roots.* Yet there is general agreement that local context is a critical variable that must be taken into consideration. This, in effect, means that models for school improvement are adapted frequently to fit local differences.

32. John Goodlad, *A Place Called School* (New York: McGraw-Hill, 1984); David Labaree, *How To Succeed in School without Really Learning: The Credentials Race in American Education* (New Haven, Conn.: Yale University Press, 1997), ch. 1. Labaree nicely distinguishes between three competing private and public goals: Democratic Equality, Social Efficiency, and Social Mobility. Those often-conflicting goals are in this paragraph, though I do not use Labaree's labels.

33. Grubb and Lazerson, *The Education Gospel;* Labaree, *How To Succeed in School without Really Learning*, ch. 1. President Obama's quote comes from "Remarks by the President to the Hispanic Chamber of Commerce on a Complete and Competitive American Education," March 10, 2009, in Washington D.C. at www.nytimes.com/2009/03/10/us/politics/10text-obama.html (accessed June 24, 2009).

School board members, the general public, and superintendents have views of purposes that differ from those of policy elites. See a recent survey done by the

American Association of School Administrators in Richard Rothstein and Rebecca Jacobsen, "A Test of Time: Unchanged Priorities for Student Outcomes," *School Administrator*, 64 (March 2007): 36–40. All three groups ranked "basic academic skills," "critical thinking," and "social skills and work ethic" first, second, and third, respectively. School board members ranked "preparation for skilled employment" fourth in a tie with "citizenship," while the general public ranked it in a tie for fifth with "emotional health." Superintendents ranked it fifth in a tie with "physical health" and "the arts and literature."

34. In the interests of full disclosure, I have known Pat Forgione since 1974, when I was at Stanford University completing my doctorate; Forgione was an entering graduate student. As students, we overlapped in a few courses. Since 1974, I have seen Forgione several times at national conferences as our careers diverged considerably. I served as a school superintendent and, later, a professor at Stanford. Forgione worked in state departments of education in Connecticut and Delaware before moving to a federally appointed post as Commissioner of Education Statistics. He became Austin's superintendent in 1999. Our relationship was, at best, distant but cordial the few times we met.

In 2006, Professor Linda Darling-Hammond and Director Raymond Pecheone headed Stanford's School Redesign Network initiative, which included Austin and a half-dozen other big cities. Forgione asked Darling-Hammond and Pecheone about the possibility that someone could write a case study of Austin's reform involving all eleven high schools. They approached me—a professor emeritus since 2001—and after conversations with them, a telephone call with Forgione, and negotiations over the scope and time span the case study would cover, I signed a Memorandum of Understanding (MOU) with Stanford University to research and write the case study for the School Redesign Network. The MOU made clear that I would take a longer view of AISD's reforms than only the years that Forgione had served the district, the superintendent's initial idea for the case study. The MOU provided that Forgione and his staff would help me arrange interviews with AISD staff and community leaders, collect documents, and provide resources to help me complete the study. It further made clear that while I would show drafts of the case to the superintendent and other top administrators in AISD, as well as Darling-Hammond and Pecheone, I retained control over the final content of the case study.

In addition, during the three summers of 2006–2008 I was hired to speak at School Redesign Network conferences held at Stanford that brought together Austin and a half-dozen other urban district officials to discuss high school redesign. In June 2008, I presented to the assembled administrators a comparison of high school redesign in Austin and one other district. I offered my interpretations of the two districts' experiences with high school reform. Forgione and the director of Austin's high school redesign were given time to respond to my talk. They did so vigorously. Finally, in September 2008, Forgione arranged for the University of Texas at Austin to hold a seminar on the initial report I wrote about Austin's experience with reform. Professor Angela Valenzuela (University of Texas-Austin) and Professor Lauren Resnick (University of Pittsburgh) critiqued the report. After the seminar, I met with AISD principals and central-office administrators to discuss the report, ending the day at an informal, private meeting with five members of the Board of Trustees, again, on the report and my views of reform in the district. From all of these encounters, AISD personnel, officials, and researchers have had opportunities to critique the views contained within the original report.

Basically, the methodology I used to complete this case study was to visit Austin three times, for a week on each occasion between April and December 2007. In Austin, I collected AISD official documents, went through newspaper clipping files at the district office for the years 1999–2007, used the Texas History Center for additional clippings and documents extending back to the 1950s, and read masters theses, histories of Austin, and official documents at the University of Texas libraries at Austin. I interviewed fifteen community leaders, a former board member, and AISD administrators. Interviews were recorded and transcribed. In addition, I conducted telephone interviews with AISD administrators and took notes during those conversations; I exchanged emails, which I kept in my records. I observed two board meetings and spent two mornings at Reagan High School. Peter Ross, a Stanford University doctoral student, was completing his dissertation on the impact of High School Redesign upon the district office. He interviewed many teachers and administrators in three high schools and the district office. Following Stanford's rules for using a fellow researcher's data and protecting the confidentiality of his informants, Ross stripped away information that might identify a teacher or administrator in any of the schools or district office. When quoting, I used his identifying numbers and occupations of interviewees, so confidentiality was not breached. I am most grateful to Ross for having access to his data.

35. Austin statistics come from Austin Independent School District, "Close-Up on Austin Schools, 2008–2009," at www.austinisd.org/inside/factsfigures (accessed June 24, 2009).

36. William Faulkner, *Requiem for a Nun* (New York: Random House, 1951), p. 92.

I. The Past Is Never Dead

1. Anthony Orum, *Power, Money, and the People* (Austin: Texas Monthly Press, 1987), pp. 174–176; quotations from J. J. McDonald, "Race Relations in Austin, Texas, c. 1917–1929" (diss., University of Southampton, U.K., 1993), vol. 1, pp. 218–219.

2. McDonald, "Race Relations," vol. 1, pp. 204–209; David Humphrey, *Austin: A History of the Capital City* (Austin: Texas State Historical Association, 1997), p. 42.

3. Humphrey, *Austin*, p. 40; McDonald, "Race Relations," vol. 1, p. 219.

4. City of Austin, "Austin's Total Population, 1850–2000," www.ci.austin.tx.us/library/ahc/population.htm (accessed July 5, 2009); David Humphrey, *The Handbook of Texas Online*, www.tsha.utexas.edu/handbook/online/articles/AA/hda3.html (accessed July 5, 2009).

5. Anna Wilson and William Segall, *Oh, Do I Remember: Experiences of Teachers during the Desegregation of Austin's Schools, 1964–1971* (Albany: State University of New York Press, 2001), p. 39.

6. Humphrey, *Austin*, p. 42; Orum, *Power*, p. 135.

7. Humphrey, *Austin*, p. 37.

8. Humphrey, *Handbook*; McDonald, "Race Relations," vol. 2, pp. 261–262.

9. Humphrey, *Austin*, p. 42.

10. McDonald, "Race Relations," vol. 1, p. 270.

11. Humphrey, *Austin*, p. 37.

12. Orum, *Power*, pp. 255–256; Humphrey, *Austin*, p. 42.

13. McDonald, "Race Relations," vol. 2, pp. 413–430; Wilson and Segall, *Oh, Do I Remember*, p. 40; Heman Sweatt, an African American letter carrier in Austin, wanted to attend law school at the University of Texas at Austin in 1946. Knowing that *Plessy v. Ferguson* (1896) required the state to provide equal facilities, University of Texas administrators set up a room with a few law texts on the campus of a

nearby all-black college, arguing that this makeshift "university law school" was equal to the facilities and traditions of its Austin campus. The university rejected his application again and again as the case worked its way through the local and state courts. Sweatt's lawyers, including Thurgood Marshall, who at that time was working for the NAACP, argued that the university had not satisfied the *Plessy v. Ferguson* standard of separate-but-equal facilities for Sweatt. Finally, in *Sweatt v. Painter* (1950), the U.S. Supreme Court agreed with Marshall's reasoning and ordered the university to admit Sweatt to its law school. The rest of the university remained closed to black undergraduates until 1956. See Orum, *Power*, pp. 195–198.

14. McDonald, "Race Relations," vol. 2, pp. 393–396.

15. Ibid., vol. 2, p. 399.

16. Ibid., vol. 1, p. 224; Humphrey, *Austin*, p. 36.

17. McDonald, "Race Relations," vol. 2, pp. 301–302, 344.

18. Ibid., vol. 2, pp. 306–309.

19. Ibid., vol. 2, p. 301 for quote.

20. City of Austin, "Austin's Total Population, 1850–2000"; AISD, *The Messenger*, 14 (March 1965): 4; Andy Alford, "A Dream Deferred," *Austin American-Statesman*, May 16, 2004, pp. A1, A7; Debra Irwin, "Resegregation of Austin Public Schools (thesis, University of Texas, 1994), p. 48. Figure for Mexican American students is for 1955.

21. Ada Anderson, interview with Larry Cuban, August 29, 2007; Wilson and Segall, *Oh, Do I Remember*, pp. 40–42; Vanessa Walker, *Their Highest Potential: An African American School Community in the Segregated South* (Chapel Hill: University of North Carolina Press, 1996).

22. McDonald, "Race Relations," vol. 1, p. 224.

23. Ibid., vol. 2, pp. 280–299; Orum, *Power*, p. 254.

24. Ada Anderson, interview with Larry Cuban, August 29, 2007; Walker, *Their Highest Potential*; Adam Fairclough, *Teaching Equality: Black Schools in the Age of Jim Crow* (Athens,: University of Georgia Press, 2001); Barbara Shircliffe, "'We Got the Best of That World': A Case for the Study of Nostalgia in the Oral History of School Segregation," *Oral History Review*, 28, no. 2 (Summer–Fall 2001): 59–84.

25. McDonald, "Race Relations," vol. 1, p. 186; Louis Harlan, *Booker T. Washington: The Making of a Black Leader, 1856–1901* (New York: Oxford University Press, 1972); Booker T. Washington, *Up from Slavery* (New York: Doubleday, 1901). The phrase "racial capitalism" refers to a white agricultural elite (and, in cities, industrial

leaders) committed to low taxes, little government intervention, workplaces free of unions, and—for laborers—few political rights and little formal schooling. They created a socioeconomic system where segregation was just another tool to keep blacks and Mexican Americans confined to domestic service, menial labor, low-skilled factory jobs and other work viewed as fit for minorities but not for white people. Some historians and social scientists use the phrase. See Jacquelyn Dowd Hall, "The Long Civil Rights Movement and the Political Uses of the Past," *Journal of American History*, 91, no. 4 (March 2005): 1233–1263.

26. McDonald, "Race Relations," vol. 2, pp. 404–409.

27. Ibid., vol. 2, pp. 405–406.

28. David Tyack, *The One Best System* (Cambridge, Mass.: Harvard University Press, 1974); Charles Johnson, *Patterns of Negro Segregation* (New York: Harper Brothers, 1943).

29. On distinguishing between the rare fundamental changes that occur in educational institutions and the more common incremental changes, see Larry Cuban, "Reforming Again, Again, and Again," *Educational Researcher*, 19, no. 1 (1990): 3–13; idem, *How Teachers Taught*, 2nd ed. (New York: Teachers College Press, 1993); and idem, *How Scholars Trumped Teachers* (New York: Teachers College Press, 1999), pp. 62–74.

30. For analyses of national patterns of desegregation, I have used the following sources: James Patterson, *Brown v. Board of Education* (New York: Oxford University Press, 2001); Matthew Lassiter, *The Silent Majority: Suburban Politics in the Sunbelt South* (Princeton, N.J.: Princeton University Press, 2006); Gary Orfield, *Must We Bus? Segregated Schools and National Policy* (Washington, D.C.: Brookings Institution, 1978); Reynolds Farley, Toni Richards, and Clarence Wurdock, "School Desegregation and White Flight," *Sociology of Education*, 53 (July 1980): 123–139; Guadalupe San Miguel Jr., "The Struggle against Separate and Unequal Schools: Middle-Class Mexican Americans and the Desegregation Campaign in Texas, 1929–1957," *History of Education Quarterly*, 23, no. 3 (1983): 343–359; Gary Orfield and Susan Eaton, *Dismantling Desegregation: The Quiet Reversal of Brown v. Board of Education* (New York: New Press, 1996).

31. Cass Sunstein, "Did *Brown* Matter?" *New Yorker*, May 3, 2004, www .newyorker.com/archive/2004/05/03/040503crbo_books (accessed July 5, 2009).

32. San Miguel Jr. "The Struggle against Separate and Unequal Schools," p. 355.

33. Orfield, *Must We Bus?* pp. 11–39.

34. Patterson, *Brown*, pp. 175–182; Farley, Richards, and Wurdock, "School Desegregation"; Lassiter, *The Silent Majority*, pp. 121–147 (chapter on Charlotte).

35. Orfield and Eaton, *Dismantling Desegregation*, pp. 9–16; Patterson, *Brown*, pp. 146–158; Lassiter, *The Silent Majority*, pp. 276–279.

36. Patterson, *Brown*, pp. 180–181.

37. The phrase "color-blind conservatism" comes from Hall, "The Long Civil Rights Movement," pp. 1234–1235. Orfield and Eaton, *Dismantling Desegregation*, pp. 9–16.

38. Robert Barnes, "Divided Court Limits Use of Race by School Districts," *Washington Post*, June 29, 2007, www.washingtonpost.com/wp-dyn/content/article /2007/06/28/AR2007062800896_3.html (accessed July 5, 2009).

39. "All deliberate slowness" is a play on the phrase "all deliberate speed," words used in the U.S. Supreme Court's 1955 *Brown II* pronouncement following the previous year's landmark decision. In this book, "all deliberate slowness" characterizes the pace at which the AISD Board of Trustees desegregated its schools grade by grade and transferred teachers to serve in previously segregated high schools. In *Oh, Do I Remember*, Anna Victoria Wilson and William Segall describe the "cross-over teaching" of eighty-five black and white teachers who were assigned to desegregate Austin's all-white and all-black schools in the years 1964–1971.

40. Wilson and Segall, *Oh, Do I Remember*, pp. 5–7; Alford, "A Dream Deferred," p. 1.

41. Quote is in Orum, *Power*, p. 262.

42. Alford, "A Dream Deferred," p. 1

43. National Education Association, *Three Cities That Are Making Desegregation Work* (Washington, D.C.: National Education Association, 1984), p. 41.

44. Kent Ewing, interview with Larry Cuban, December 4, 2007.

45. Darlene Westbrook, interview with Larry Cuban, August 30, 2007; Kent Ewing, interview with Larry Cuban, December 4, 2007.

46. *Austin Citizen*, May 30, 1978, p. 3; *Austin American-Statesman*, May 30, 1978, p. B1.

47. John Egerton, "Profiles in Change," *Southern Changes*, 1, no. 8 (1979): 10–12;

National Education Association, *Three Cities,* pp. 38–52; Joseph Feldman et al., *Still Separate, Still Unequal: The Limits of Milliken II's Educational Compensation Remedies* (Cambridge, Mass.: Harvard Project on School Desegregation, 1994), pp. 46–50.

48. Egerton, "Profiles in Change," pp. 10–12.

49. National Education Association, *Three Cities,* pp. 45–46.

50. Differences of opinion among blacks and whites were stark when a jury found black sports star O. J. Simpson innocent of killing his wife and a friend in 1994. In a 1995 Gallup opinion poll, five of ten whites thought the Simpson verdict was wrong, while eight of ten blacks felt the jury's verdict was right. See www. law.umkc.edu/faculty/projects/ftrials/Simpson/polls.html (accessed July 5, 2009).

More recently, white and black perspectives differed in the 2008 Democratic primary, when Barack Obama was attacked for being a congregant in a Chicago church whose pastor was quoted often as saying that the United States was a racist nation. Obama's response was a national speech pointing out that both whites and blacks drew heavily from the U.S. history of race when they formed their perspectives on their experiences in America. See Janny Scott, "Obama Chooses Reconciliation over Rancor," *New York Times,* March 19, 2008,, www.nytimes.com/2008 /03/19/us/politics/19assess.html (accessed July 5, 2009).

W. E. B. Du Bois wrote about the "veil" and the "double consciousness" that give blacks a distinct perspective on race in America. See Du Bois, *The Souls of Black Folk* (New York: Norton, 1999; orig. pub. 1903).

51. National Education Association, *Three Cities,* pp. 46–52, quote on p. 46.

52. Perry Sailor, "Looking at Magnet Programs in AISD, 1987–1988," AISD, Department of Management Information, Office of Research and Evaluation, July 1988; Laura Heinauer, "Separation Anxiety at LBJ and Magnet Program?" *Austin American-Statesman,* October 25, 2007.

53. Some black parents, concerned about the under-resourced neighborhood black schools, drove their children to schools on the other side of Interstate 35. One parent wrote an op-ed piece telling readers of her children's better academic experiences in mostly white schools. See Alberta Phillips, "Why *Brown* Mattered to My Family and Others," *Austin American Statesman,* May 25, 2004, p. A7.

54. Orfield and Eaton, *Dismantling Desegregation,* pp. 166–168; Geoff Rips, interview with Larry Cuban, August 27, 2007.

55. Catherine Christner et al., "Priority Schools: The Fifth Year," Executive Summary, Austin Independent School District, Office of Research and Evaluation, 1992.

56. Sarah Reber, "Court-Ordered Desegregation Successes and Failures Integrating American Schools since *Brown v. Board of Education*," *Journal of Human Resources*, 40, no. 3 (2005): 559–590.

57. Alford, "A Dream Deferred," p. A7. For an opposing point of view, see Phillips, "Why *Brown* Mattered" (on the same page with Alford's piece).

58. Debra Irwin, "Resegregation of Austin Public Schools" (thesis, University of Texas at Austin, 1994), p. 48; Alford, "A Dream Deferred," p. A7. For a different take on the degree of resegregation that occurred in AISD—and a more generous definition of schools that were considered racially and ethnically balanced and schools that were segregated—see Richard Valencia, "Inequalities and the Schooling of Minority Students in Texas: Historical and Contemporary Conditions," *Hispanic Journal of Behavioral Sciences*, 22, no. 4 (2000): 445–459. Valencia found AISD schools in 1999–2000 "highly segregated." Seventy-eight percent of elementary schools, for example, were unbalanced toward either the white or the minority end of the spectrum. Valencia computed similar percentages for secondary schools (p. 448).

59. Ron Edmonds, "Effective Schools for the Urban Poor." *Educational Leadership*, 37 (October 1979): 15–24; Donald Thomas, former superintendent of the Salt Lake City schools, contracted with AISD to train principals and teachers in Priority Schools. In 1989, Larry Lezotte, a national leader of the Effective Schools movement, came to Austin to speak to all administrators. See AISD, "Effective Schools Research Impacts Education," *The Messenger*, 36 (January–February 1988): 1; and AISD, "Superintendent's Perspective," *The Messenger*, 37 (March–April 1989): 2.

60. Thomas Timar and David Kirp, "State Efforts to Reform Schools: Treading between a Regulatory Swamp and an English Garden," *Educational Evaluation and Policy Analysis*, 10, no. 2 (1988): 75–88; Frank Lutz, "Education Politics in Texas," *Peabody Journal of Education*, 63, no. 4 (1986): 70–89; Angela Valenzuela, *Subtractive Schooling: U.S.-Mexican Youth and the Politics of Caring* (Albany: State University of New York Press, 1999); Walter Haney, "The Myth of the Texas Miracle in Education," *Education Policy Analysis Archives*, 8, no. 41 (2000), epaa.asu.edu/epaa/v8n41 (accessed July 5, 2009); Linda McNeil, *Contradictions of School Reform: Educational Costs of Standardized Testing* (New York: Routledge, 2000); Jennifer Booher-Jennings, "Below the Bubble:

'Educational Triage' and the Texas Accountability System," *American Educational Research Journal*, 42, no. 2 (2005): 231–268.

61. Bryce Bayles, Robert Crawley, and David Mass, "The Texas Landscape: A Snapshot from the 2000 Census," *Texas Labor Market Newsletter*, October 2002, pp. 3–4, 11.

62. McNeil, *Contradictions of School Reform*, p. 186; Emily Pyle, "Te$t Market," *Texas Observer*, May 13, 2005, www.texasobserver.org/article.php?aid=1947.

63. A history of Texas finance reform can be found in Andrew Reschovsky and Jennifer Imazaki, "School Finance Reform in Texas: A Never-Ending Story?" in John Yinger, ed., *Helping Children Left Behind: State Aid and the Pursuit of Educational Equity* (Cambridge, Mass.: MIT Press, 2004), pp. 251–281. For more than 1,000 Texas school districts, local property taxes are the main source of funds. But property wealth in these districts varies from $142,700 to $4.6 million per student (2001). To equalize this variation among districts in funding schools, the legislature and the Texas Supreme Court limited each district's tax rate to $1.50 per $100 of property wealth. Districts that exceeded $295,000 per student were considered "high-wealth" districts and had to share that wealth with districts below $295,000 per student ("low-wealth"). Thus, the label "Robin Hood" became attached to the legislation that created these distinctions. See Hakimeh Saghaye-Biria, "Robin Hood Is Working," World Internet News, University of Houston, Housing and Education, April 22, 2001, soc.hfac.uh.edu/artman/publish/article_137.shtml.

64. Geoff Rips, memo to Larry Cuban, February 15, 2008.

65. The initial Texas system of accountability ratings began in 1993 and lasted until 2002; subsequent revision began in 2003. See www.tea.state.tx.us/perfreport/account/2005/manual (accessed July 5, 2009). On escalating state sanctions administered by the commissioner, see AISD, "Overview of the State and Federal Accountability Systems," www.austin.isd.tenet.edu/inside/docs/upclose/20071004/accountability.pdf, pp. 16–20 (accessed July 5, 2009).

66. On pledge policy, see R. G. Ratcliffe, "Why Do Public School Students Say the Texas Pledge?" *Houston Chronicle*, September 23, 2007, www.danbranch.com/media/HoustonChronicle/hc_20070923.htm (accessed July 5, 2009). On obesity policy, see Coordinated Approach to Child Health, "School Health Legislation," www.sph.uth.tmc.edu/catch/Legislation.htm#SB19 (accessed July 5, 2009). On discipline, see Larry Abramson, "Disciplinary Policy in Texas Schools Raises Con-

cerns," *NPR*, June 25, 2007, www.npr.org/templates/story/story. php?storyId=11363621 (accessed July 5, 2009). On instruction, see Michael May, "Naked City," *Austin Chronicle*, September 14, 2007.

67. AISD, "From the Superintendent," *The Messenger*, 38 (March–April 1990): 2.

68. For typical policy advice about business and schools in Texas, see the website for the Texas Business and Education Coalition, tbec.org, especially "History" and "Mission and Strategic Plan" (accessed July 5, 2009). Also Sandy Dolchen (IBM executive and member of Texas Business and Education Coalition's executive committee), interview with Larry Cuban, August 24, 2007.

69. On the experiences of Houston, another Texas district, see McNeil, *Contradictions of Reform*; and Valenzuela, *Subtractive Schooling*. Enacted in 1965 as part of the Elementary and Secondary Education Act, Title I is aimed at districts with high percentages of students from low-income families. Such districts usually have at least 40 percent of their students qualified to receive free and reduced lunch. Funds can be used for preschool through high school students, but nearly three-fourths of the funds go to low-income children in preschool through grade six. In 2007, more than $12 billion was allocated to the nation's schools. See U.S. Department of Education, "Fiscal Year 2008 Budget Summary," February 5, 2007, www.ed.gov/about /overview/budget/budget08/summary/edlite-section2a.html#title I Iea.

70. What may have jolted the Board of Trustees into some bad choices of superintendents during this decade was the abrupt way that John Ellis left the district (according to Cheryl Orth, who had just begun working in the superintendent's office). Ellis had quietly applied for the post of New Jersey Commissioner in early 1990 and had not told any of the trustees that he was seeking employment elsewhere. After interviews in New Jersey, he was offered the job. Over a June weekend, Orth and Ellis' chief of staff typed up dozens of letters that would inform AISD trustees, key administrators, and community members that Ellis would be leaving. But the *Austin American-Statesman* received a tip and did a front-page story on Ellis' departure before the letters could go out. Board members, subordinates, and the community read about Ellis' sudden exit in the newspaper and were upset. Although there was a hastily arranged retirement party for Ellis, AISD and the superintendent parted company without any preparation for sustaining the reforms that he had initiated during a decade of service to the district. Did Ellis' abrupt departure trigger a subsequent decade of bad choices of leaders by the Board of Trustees and erratic

adoption of reform after reform? That the board subsequently engaged in micro-managing its school chiefs during these years may or may not have been a coincidence. The fact that an unsettled, upset board appointed a short-term interim school chief and subsequently hired Jim Hensley (who lasted a mere two years) and then Jim Fox (who served three years) provides only limited support for the speculation. Pat Forgione, phone interview with Larry Cuban, March 6, 2008; Cheryl Orth, phone interview with Larry Cuban, March 7, 2008. For Board of Trustees oversight of superintendents in the 1990s, see Jason Spencer, "School Board Chief Leaving after Ten Years," *Austin American-Statesman*, February 13, 2002, p. AI, AI2.

2. Turning Chaos into Stability, 1990–2009

1. I interviewed fifteen individuals who had each spent nearly twenty years working inside and outside the district. Only one business leader remembered Hensley. One administrator recalled Hensley as "Jim Bob" after I mentioned his last name.

2. Geoff Rips, interview with Larry Cuban, August 27, 2007.

3. Roseana Auten, "School of Hard Fox," *Austin Chronicle*, December 13, 1996, www.austinchronicle.com/gyrobase/Issue/story?oid=oid%3A525786 (accessed July 8, 2009).

4. Fox quotes come from AISD, "Superintendent James H. Fox Will Lead AISD," *The Messenger*, 43 (Winter 1994): 2–3; Auten, "School of Hard Fox."

5. Kent Ewing, interview with Larry Cuban, December 4, 2007; Ariel Cloud, interview with Larry Cuban, December 5, 2007. Statistics for principal turnover come from "Naked City," *Austin Chronicle*, August 2, 1996.

6. Darlene Westbrook, interview with Larry Cuban, August 29, 2007; AISD, *The Messenger*, various issues, 1990–1994.

7. Jason Spencer, "School Board Chief Leaving after Ten Years," *Austin American-Statesman*, February 13, 2002, pp. AI, AI2.

8. Steven Stark, "A Detour on the Way to Being a Priest," *Oak Hill Gazette*, February 14, 2003, pp. I, 10; *Austin Chronicle*, April 9, 1998. Geoff Rips, memo to Larry Cuban, February 15, 2008.

9. *Austin Chronicle*, September 17, 1998.

10. Ibid., January 22, 1999.

11. Barbara Whitaker, "Prosecutor Says Indictment of Austin Schools Will Help Deter Test Tampering," *New York Times*, April 8, 1999, query.nytimes.com/gst /fullpage.html?res=9403E7DD1438F93BA35757C0A96F958260 (accessed July 8, 2009).

12. *Austin Chronicle*, June 18, 1999.

13. Ibid., June 24, 1999

14. AISD Press Release, "Statement by Austin School Board President Kathy Rider," July 7, 1999.

15. *Austin Chronicle*, August 5, 1999.

16. Pascal Forgione Jr., "A District-Wide Approach to High School Conversion: An Urban Superintendent's Perspective," Paper presented at AERA conference, San Francisco, April 8, 2006.

17. Jason Spencer, "Rider Led School Board in Turbulent Times," *Austin American-Statesman*, February 17, 2002, pp. B1, B3; Sandy Dolchen, interview with Larry Cuban, August 28, 2007; Pascal Forgione Jr., phone interview with Larry Cuban, March 6, 2008.

18. Texas House Research Organization, "The Dropout Data Debate," November 2, 1999, p. 4. Pascal Forgione Jr., memo to Larry Cuban, February 13, 2008.

19. Raven Hill, "School Chief Gets 'A' for Longevity," *Austin American-Statesman*, August 23, 2004, p. B1, B3.

20. Kevin Fullerton, "Man of the Hour," *Austin Chronicle*, October 29, 1999.

21. Pascal Forgione Jr., "Open Letter to the AISD Community," January 7, 2000; AISD Press Release, "Community Forum with Dr. Pat Forgione," May 16, 2000; AISD Press Release, "Superintendent Forgione to Propose $1.5486 Tax Rate," September 3, 1999. For editorial support and occasional criticism, see, for example, *Austin American-Statesman*, editorials dated February 5, 2002, March 24, 2002, and January 15, 2003.

22. Michelle Martinez, "New School Board Leader Brings Quieter Approach," *Austin American-Statesman*, May 14, 2002; Del Stover, "A Remarkable Turnaround for Austin School Board," National School Boards Association, *School Board News*, October 12, 2004, www.nsba.org/HPC/Features/AboutSBN/SbnArchive/2004 /October2004/AremarkableturnaroundforAustinschoolboard.aspx (accessed July 8, 2009). Pascal Forgione Jr., interviews with Larry Cuban, April 24, 2007, and August 27, 2007. Ed Sharpe, interview with Larry Cuban, August 27, 2007; private

meeting with five members of the Board of Trustees to discuss my report on Austin reform, September 10, 2008.

23. Kevin Fullerton, "A Little Off Schedule," *Austin Chronicle*, April 14, 2000; "Statement by Dr. Pat Forgione, Jr. on Accountability Ratings for AISD," August 17, 2000.

24. Jim Haviland, "Trustees Show Support for Forgione," *Oak Hill Gazette*, January 17, 2003, p. 3.

25. Geoff Rips, memo to Larry Cuban, February 15, 2008.

26. The sentence "Austin is a liberal city in a conservative state" was repeated often to me in interviews and informal conversations. Both "liberal" and "conservative," of course, are relative terms and vary from one region of the country to another. The phrase "heat shield" comes from Pascal Forgione Jr., interview with Larry Cuban, April 24, 2007. Data on Democrats and Republicans in Texas come from Andrew Ferguson, "The Birthplace of Bush Paranoia," *Weekly Standard*, October 25, 2004, www.weeklystandard.com/Content/Public/ Articles/000/000/004/788nkdai.asp (accessed July 8, 2009).

27. On the program in "character education," see Matthew Obernauer, "Austin Kids Set to Learn Reading, Writing, and Respect," *Austin American-Statesman*, August 16, 2005, pp. A1, A7; Forgione quote on MTV is from "Fighting the War against Pop Culture" (editorial), *Austin American-Statesman*, April 2, 2005, p. A16; Forgione quote on teachers is from "Austin Teachers Should Dress Like the Professionals They Are" (editorial), *Austin American-Statesman*, July 8, 2004; Janet Wilson, "230 Girls Get Ann Richards' Wish Come True," *Austin American-Statesman*, August 19, 2007. On removing Cokes from vending machines: Geoff Rips, memo to Larry Cuban, February 15, 2008.

28. Pascal Forgione Jr., interview with Larry Cuban, April 24, 2007.

29. Ibid., December 3, 2007.

30. Ibid., April 24, 2007, and August 29, 2007.

31. "Forgione's Lesson: Speeding in School Zone Isn't All Right," *Austin American-Statesman*, October 25, 2002, p. B1.

32. This description of the three stages is drawn from Pascal Forgione Jr., "A District-Wide Approach to High School Conversion: An Urban Superintendent's Perspective," Paper presented at the American Educational Research Association Annual Conference, San Francisco, April 8, 2006. I added titles for each phase of the reforms. No such titles were in the speech.

33. Ibid.

34. Ibid.

35. Ibid.

36. Ibid. Ariel Cloud, interview with Larry Cuban, December 5, 2007.

37. Forgione, "A District-Wide Approach." Darlene Westbrook, interview with Larry Cuban, August 28, 2007; Ariel Cloud, interview with Larry Cuban, December 5, 2007.

38. Forgione, "A District-Wide Approach."

39. AISD, "Priority Schools: The Fifth Year," Office of Research and Evaluation, 1992; Jennifer Jordan, "Looking beyond Priority Schools: Accountability and Funding in Austin Independent School District," (thesis, University of Texas, 1994); Michael Shear, "Money Was No Cure-All, Officials in Austin Found," *Washington Post*, October 26, 1997, p. A17; Darlene Westbrook, interview with Larry Cuban, August 29, 2007.

40. Pascal Forgione Jr., "Austin's Trajectory of Progress and a Unique Opportunity for Investing in Our Community's Future: Its Children," Report to AISD Board of Trustees, April 23, 2007.

41. In San Diego during the years 1998–2005, for example, superintendent Alan Bersin and chancellor Anthony Alvarado spent their initial years working to raise scores in elementary schools, before turning to high schools. That pattern was evident in many other cities as well. See Larry Cuban and Michael Usdan, *Powerful Reforms with Shallow Roots* (New York: Teachers College Press, 2003).

42. On Texas Education Agency ratings of AISD schools, see "Austin Insider" annual reports for the years 2000–2005 and "TAKS Results" for ratings since 2003, at www.austinisd.org/inside/accountability/taks (accessed July 8, 2009). Forgione quote from AERA presentation, April 8, 2006, p. 6.

43. Pascal Forgione Jr., AERA presentation, April 8, 2006; Southern Regional Education Board, "Audit Review and Benchmarking Study," September 2004; Juanita Garcia and Robert Donmoyer, "The Future of Austin's High Schools," University of Texas at Austin, Cooperative Superintendency Program, 2004.

44. Private meeting with five members of the Board of Trustees to discuss report on Austin reform by Larry Cuban, September 10, 2008.

45. Pascal Forgione Jr., AERA presentation, April 8, 2006, pp. 7–9.

46. AISD, "High School Redesign Initiative Evaluation, 2007–2008," Office of Research and Evaluation, 2007.

47. Forgione acknowledged these unexpected crises in his AERA presentation. And in subsequent interviews with me, he made it clear that unexpected events continually put a crimp in his plans.

48. Sterling Lands to Kathy Rider, October 30, 2000, reprinted in *Austin Chronicle*, January 12, 2001, p. 26.

49. Ibid.

50. Jordan Smith, "Can Edison Pass the AISD Test?" *Austin Chronicle*, January 23, 2002, www.austinchronicle.com/gyrobase/Issue/story?oid=84462 (accessed July 8, 2009).

51. Maeve Reston, "District Proposals Flunk Eastside Test," *Austin American-Statesman*, March 14, 2001, pp. B1, B3. Roxanne Evans, "ESAC Sets New Deadline for AISD," *African American News and Issues*, April 4, 2001, pp. 1, 3.

52. Maeve Reston, "East Austin Group Wants School Split," *Austin American-Statesman*, June 20, 2001, pp. B1, B5; "Breaking Up AISD Won't Fix School Problems" (editorial), *Austin American-Statesman*, June 23, 2001, p. A10; Smith, "Can Edison Pass the AISD Test?"; Janet Jacobs, "Forgione Moving Forward with Plan," *Austin American-Statesman*, April 24, 2002, pp. B1, B6.

53. Michelle Martinez, "Trustees Say No to For-Profit Schools," *Austin American-Statesman*, February 26, 2002, pp. B1, B3; Michael King, "A New AISD Blueprint," *Austin Chronicle*, April 5, 2002, www.austinchronicle.com/gyrobase /Issue/story?oid=85491 (accessed July 8, 2009).

Michelle Martinez, "Forgione Finalizes School Reform," *Austin American-Statesman*, April 23, 2002, pp. A1, A5.

54. Ron Edmonds, "Effective Schools for the Urban Poor," *Educational Leadership*, 37, no. 1 (1979): 15–27; Barbara Taylor and Pamela Bullard, *The Revolution Revisited: Effective Schools and Systemic Reform* (Bloomington, Ind.: Phi Delta Kappa Educational Foundation, 1995). Recall that John Ellis had likewise anchored much of the Priority Schools plan in Effective Schools research.

55. Jacobs, "Forgione Moving Forward with Plan."

56. Michael May, "No Bilingual Blueprint?" *Austin Chronicle*, May 3, 2002.

57. Emily Pyle, "Fund and Games: Will the Lege Cheat on School Finance?" *Texas Observer*, December 19, 2003, www.texasobserver.org/article.php?aid=1524 (accessed July 8, 2009).

58. Terrence Stutz, "Fed Up with School Funding, Austin Joins Suit," *Dallas News*, October 25, 2003.

David Hoff, Texas Judge Rules Funds Not Enough," *Education Week*, September 22, 2004, pp. 1, 30.

59. Stutz, "Fed Up with School Funding."

60. Terrence Stutz, "School Financing Fought on Two Fronts," *Dallas Morning News*, July 5, 2005, pp. 1, 2; "A Compromise on School Finance Texas Can Live By" (editorial), *Austin American-Statesman*, May 14, 2006, p. G2.

61. Rachel May, "Forgione Now Suggests Closing Becker and Oak Spring Outright," *Austin Chronicle*, March 24, 2006, www.austinchronicle.com/gyrobase/Issue/story?oid=oid:349750 (accessed July 8, 2009); AISD News Release, "Superintendent Withdraws Recommendation to Close Becker and Oak Springs," March 31, 2006.

62. What I call "errors in judgment" others could easily interpret as cases where the superintendent was "getting too far out front of his board." Darlene Westbrook, interview with Larry Cuban, August 29, 2007.

63. Laura Heinauer, "Plan to Close Webb Draws Public Scorn," *Austin America-Statesman*, January 26, 2007, pp. 1, 2; AISD calendar of testing, www.austinisd.org/academics/testing (accessed July 8, 2009).

64. Ibid. Also see Michael May, "Left Behind," *Austin Chronicle*, February 16, 2007, www.austinchronicle.com/gyrobase/Issue/story?oid=446970 (accessed July 8, 2009); Board of Trustees decision in Laura Heinauer, "Trustees Vote to Keep Webb Open," *Austin American-Statesman*, February 27, 2007. In May 2007, TEA informed AISD that Webb Middle School was designated Academically Acceptable, after three years in which it was labeled Academically Unacceptable. Webb was not closed in 2007–2008.

65. Peter Ross, "Summary Notes of Observations of High School Redesign Steering Committee and Districtwide High Schools Principals Meeting on Professional Learning Communities," unpublished paper, School of Education, Stanford University, May 2007. Peter Ross is a Ph.D. candidate studying the relationship between High School Redesign and the District Office.

66. High school teacher, interview with Peter Ross, March 2007.

67. Principal, interview with Peter Ross, March 2007.

68. Joan Talbert and Jane David, "Evaluation of the Disciplinary Literacy–Professional Learning Community Initiative in Austin Independent School District," Final Report, August 2008, p. 37.

69. Parthenon Group, "Executive Steering Committee Interim Update," Decem-

ber 19, 2006. Pascal Forgione Jr., interview with Larry Cuban, August 29, 2007; Kent Ewing, interview with Larry Cuban, December 3, 2007; Kent Ewing, letter to Larry Cuban, December 11, 2007.

70. Talbert and David, "Evaluation"; Pascal Forgione Jr., interview with Larry Cuban, August 29, 2007.

71. Pascal Forgione Jr., interview with Larry Cuban, August 29, 2007; NAEP urban district scores can be found in Raven Hill, "Austin Students Near Top Again on National Test," *Austin-American Statesman*, November 15, 2007.

72. AISD, "TEA Announces 2007 Accountability Ratings: Austin ISD Continues To Be Rated 'Academically Acceptable,'" press release, August 1, 2007, www .austinisd.org/newsmedia/releases/index.phtml?more=1353.

3. Reinventing the High School, 2005–2008

1. AISD, "Strategic Plan for 2005–2010," Executive Summary, August 2005, pp. 1–2.

2. When I met with five board members on September 10, 2008, to discuss my report on Austin reform, one member pointed out that I had made an error in the March 15, 2008 report. I had stated that the Board of Trustees had approved the five-year Strategic Plan in 2005; board members told me they had not. I met with Forgione on September 10 and he confirmed that it was his Strategic Plan for AISD that had been on the table. While he had consulted with the board many times for their suggestions, he had submitted it to the board for their information, not their approval. In short, the Strategic Plan was the superintendent's initiative, not the board's.

3. Pascal Forgione Jr., interviews with Larry Cuban, April 24, 2007, and August 27, 2007; idem, "School Redesign Network Presentation," April 29, 2005, p. 2.

4. Pascal Forgione Jr., interviews with Larry Cuban, April 24, 2007, and August 27, 2007. Also see Southern Regional Education Board, audit of AISD high schools, September 2004.

5. On San Diego, see Amy Hightower, "San Diego's Big Boom: Systemic Instructional Change in the Central Office and Schools," in Amy Hightower et al., eds., *School Districts and Instructional Renewal* (New York: Teachers College Press, 2002),

pp. 76–93. On New York City Chancellor Rudy Crew, see *New York Times* editorials, September 1, 1997, query.nytimes.com/gst/fullpage.html?res=9D00E4DD1F31F 932A3575AC0A961958260, and June 24, 1999, query.nytimes.com/gst/fullpage. html?res=9E07E6DC173AF937A15755C0A96F958260 (both accessed July 10, 2009).

6. Chrysan Gallucci et al., "Converging Reform Theories in Urban Middle Schools: District-Guided Instructional Improvement in Small Schools of Choice," *Teachers College Record*, 109, no. 12 (2007): 2601–2641. New York City no longer has thirty-plus community districts.

7. Seymour Fliegel, *Miracle in East Harlem: The Fight for Choice in American Education* (New York: Random House, 1993); Deborah Meier, *The Power of Their Ideas: Lessons from a Small School in Harlem* (Boston: Beacon, 1995); Richard Elmore and Deanna Burney, "Investing in Teacher Learning: Staff Development and Instructional Improvement in Community District 2, New York City," Report prepared for the National Commission on Teaching and America's Future, 1997.

8. Alexander Russo, "The Bostonian," *Education Next*, 6 (2006), www.hoover .org/publications/ednext/3211646.html (accessed July 10, 2009).

9. While LBJ High School was placed in the "urgent priority" category, it was not rated Academically Unacceptable, because its magnet school population scored well on state tests, masking the low scores from the rest of the school. In 2008, the magnet was rated separately from the school. Geoff Rips, memo to Larry Cuban, February 15, 2008.

10. Raven Hill, "Schools Given $1.5 Million for Redesign," *Austin American-Statesman*, November 28, 2005, pp. B1, B7; Raymond Pecheone, Paul Tytler, and Peter Ross, "Austin Independent School District and the School Redesign Network at Stanford University: A Partnership for Successful School Redesign," School Redesign Network, Stanford University, 2006, Appendix 5, pp. 50–56.

11. On components of High School Redesign in various high schools, see Pecheone, Tytler, and Ross, "Austin Independent School District."

12. This paragraph comes from my analysis of the assumptions embedded in the goals and strategies of High School Redesign. Other large urban districts using donor dollars and other sources of funding for small high schools containing this policy logic include Philadelphia (www.thenotebook.org/editions/2007/spring/ small.htm), New York City (www.carnegie.org/reporter/15/reform/index.html),

Chicago (www.edweek.org/ew/articles/2006/06/07/39size.h25.html), Boston (www.bostonpublicschools.org/node/911), and Albuquerque (newmexicoindependent.com/701/albuquerque-high-schools-go-from-big-to-small-reflecting-a-trend) (all accessed July 10, 2009).

13. Recall that in 2000, in a budget cut, Forgione had had principals drop block scheduling. But after academies and schools-within-a-school were mandated, fifty-minute classes in a seven- or eight-period day proved insufficient to accommodate advisories and small learning communities. Block scheduling returned.

14. Pascal Forgione Jr., interview with Larry Cuban, April 24, 2007; Kent Ewing, interview with Larry Cuban, December 5, 2007; Glen Nolly, interview with Larry Cuban, December 5, 2007.

15. See Institute for Research and Reform, www.irre.org/ftf (accessed July 10, 2009); Michelle Gambone et al., *Turning the Tide: The Achievements of the First Things First Education Reform in the Kansas City, Kansas, School District* (Philadelphia: Youth Development Strategies, 2004); James Connell and Julie Broom, *The Toughest Nut to Crack: First Things First's (FTF) Approach to Improving Teaching and Learning,* Report prepared for the U.S. Department of Education (Philadelphia: Institute for Research and Reform in Education, 2004).

16. Janet Quint et al., "The Challenge of Scaling Up Educational Reform: Findings and Lessons from First Things First," MDRC (Manpower Demonstration Research Corp.), New York, N.Y., and Oakland, Calif., July 2005, www.mdrc.org/publications/412/full.pdf (accessed July 10, 2009). AISD Office of High School Redesign, "Four AISD High Schools to Work with First Things First," www.austinisd.org/inside/initiatives/redesign/ftf.phtml (accessed July 10, 2009); Pascal Forgione Jr., interview with Larry Cuban, August 27, 2007. A recent evaluation of FTF's effectiveness cast doubt on claims that the program reduces dropout rates. See Debra Viadero, "U.S. Review Finds No Proof That Reform Model Works," *Education Week,* February 6, 2008, p. 6.

17. Ismael Villafane, "Focused Plan to Improve Student Learning at John H. Reagan H.S.," report submitted to Dr. Glenn Nolly, Associate Superintendent, September 2007, Attachment 3b. All figures cited are for 2007. On transfers, see Raven Hill, "Parents Plan Overnight Vigil To Seek School Transfers," *Austin American-Statesman,* February 2, 2008.

18. Villafane, "Focused Plan to Improve Student Learning."

19. Jordan Smith, "Is Reagan High Really Safer?" *Austin Chronicle*, October 3, 2003, www.austinchronicle.com/gyrobase/Issue/story?oid=oid:180125 (accessed July 10, 2009).

20. Ibid. I compiled a chart of turnover among high school principals for the years 1990–2008; this and subsequent statements about changes among high school principals are drawn from that data. In 2008, TAKS scores for Reagan improved in some areas but still fell short of the threshold for "Academically Acceptable" in reading, math, and science. In April 2008, Villafane resigned and an interim principal was appointed. Reagan moved into its second year of "Unacceptable" status, triggering a Reconstitution Plan (including the removal of the principal) that was approved by the Board of Trustees. See Board of Trustees, "Proposed TEA-Required Reconstitution Plan for Reagan High School," Agenda packet, item 6B, June 16, 2008.

21. I spent the mornings of December 3–4, 2007, at the school interviewing the principal, visiting fourteen classes in four major subjects, had brief exchanges with teachers when they were available, and asked students to explain to me what they were doing in their lessons before and after class. The teachers of those classes I visited agreed to having an observer come in for 15–20 minutes. Other than the principal, I do not identify any teachers or students in my notes or in this text.

22. I base this statement on my direct observation in 2004–2005 of high school conversion projects in Mapleton (Colo.) and Oakland (Calif.), where I spent time in high schools in the early stages of putting SLCs, advisories, and block scheduling into practice. In addition, I have read extensively the descriptive and analytic literature on high school conversions. Finally, I have taught in urban high schools in Washington, D.C., Cleveland, and other districts.

23. Dr. Glen Nolly, "School Improvement Restructuring Plans for Reagan High School and Travis High School," Presentation to Board of Trustees Meeting, Austin, February 25, 2008. For Year 2 "Reconstitution" of Reagan, see Board of Trustees, "Proposed TEA-Required Reconstitution Plan for Reagan High School." AISD's Department of Program Evaluation also completed a study of the three high schools, adopting First Things First after the initial year of implementation (2007–2008). While the percentages of students who met the state standard in passing math increased significantly from the previous year, these improvements did not appear evenly across all ethnic groups or remain when comparisons were made

to non-FTF campuses. Similarly, the percentage of students with disciplinary referrals dropped substantially at FTF campuses, but so did the referrals at non-FTF campuses. For other aspects of the FTF program, more than half of the students at LBJ and Travis reported that they had not participated in a conference with their parents/guardians and family advocate. About one-quarter of Reagan students reported no conferences had occurred. One out of three students at FTF campuses reported meeting with the family advocate at least once a week apart from regularly scheduled classes. When observers visited classrooms to determine if lessons were "rigorous," fewer than 30 percent met that requirement. AISD, Department of Program Evaluation, "2007–2008 First Things First Evaluation: Year One Implementation," no. 07.79, November 2008.

24. Johnson High School statistics taken from "School Report Card" for 2006–2007 on the school's website, www.austinisd.org/schools/details. phtml?id=018&opt=ratings (accessed July 14, 2009). Also see Eric Dexheimer, "Pass or Perish," *Austin American-Statesman,* December 3, 2006, pp. A1, A5.

25. Pascal Forgione Jr. to Commissioner Shirley Neeley, Texas Education Agency, June 7, 2007. Superintendent Forgione, in his comments on my draft in a memo to me on February 13, 2008, informed me that Johnston had withdrawn from FTF. I found the distinctions Patti Everitt and Kent Ewing made about Johnston and Reagan helpful: Everitt and Ewing, personal communication, February 19, 2008.

26. AISD, "Trustees Vote To Repurpose Johnston Campus," news release, June 16, 2008; idem, "Trustees Select Eastside Memorial High School at the Johnston Campus," news release, August 11, 2008; Board of Trustees, "Discussion of New Instructional Models for Eastside Memorial High School," agenda item, September 22, 2008. Eastside Memorial website, www.austinisd.org/schools/website. phtml?id=018 (accessed July 14, 2009).

27. In this section describing Lanier, I rely upon Peter Ross, "Moving from 'One Best System' to a Portfolio: A Study of the District-Wide High School Redesign Initiative in Austin Independent School District" (diss., Stanford University, 2008). Ross's study explores the linkage between the AISD district office and the implementation of High School Redesign in Austin, Akins, and Lanier high schools. Page numbers refer to the March 20, 2008, draft of the study. See ch. 5: "High School Case Studies," pp. 331–334.

28. Ibid., pp. 382–384.

29. Ibid., pp. 374–376.

30. Ibid., pp. 377–378.

31. Ibid., pp. 342–343.

32. Ibid., p. 373. Patti Everett and Kent Ewing, "Comments," February 19, 2008. In 2008, the superintendent appointed Oropez to the district office to serve as Executive Principal for High Schools. See "AISD Board Briefs," May 27, 2008.

33. On March 2, 2009, the Board of Trustees discussed the restructuring of Lanier into small learning communities for 2009–2010. A plan for restructuring was submitted to TEA. See www.boardbook.org/apps/bbv2/public/detail_wrapper.cfm?MeetingKey=MjAwMjczNjk%3D (accessed July 14, 2009).

34. See Akins School Report Card for 2006–2007, www.austinisd.org/schools/details.phtml?id=006&lang= (accessed July 10, 2009).

35. Ross, "Moving from 'One Best System,'" pp. 177–178.

36. Ibid., pp. 180–181.

37. Ibid., pp. 185–187.

38. Ibid., pp. 236–238.

39. Ibid., p. 186. The addition of New Tech High as a 9–12 academy means that a program committed to project-based teaching and learning is consistent with the principal's commitment to ambitious teaching. I have visited New Tech Highs in Napa (Calif.) and Mapleton (Colo.).

40. Ibid., pp. 225–226, 178.

41. Ibid., pp. 250–251.

42. Ibid., quote is on p. 253. See Austin School Report Card, www.austinisd.org/schools/details.phtml?id=014&opt=ratings (accessed July 10, 2009).

43. Ross, "Moving from 'One Best System,'" pp. 53–55.

44. Ibid., pp. 254–258.

45. Ibid., pp. 259–260, 261–262.

46. Ibid., pp. 263–264. Teacher quote is on p. 158. Also see Region XIII, "Campus Snapshot: Austin High School, May 2007," in author's possession. Principal quote on p. 15 of report.

47. Ross, "Moving from 'One Best System,'" pp. 264–265. In January 2008, a group of parents upset over the principal's decision to get seniors to pay for pranks that caused damage to school property asked the Board of Trustees to fire Hudson.

The board supported Superintendent Forgione's refusal to do so. See Raven Hill, "Principal Won't Be Dismissed," *Austin American-Statesman,* January 29, 2008. However, in mid-March 2008, Hudson announced that he would be leaving Austin High School in June to take another job. Laura Heinauer, "Austin High School Principal to Leave," *Austin American-Statesman,* www.statesman.com/blogs/content/shared-gen /blogs/austin/education/entries/2008/03/18/austin_high_principal_to_leave .html (accessed July 14, 2009).

48. Theory of action for Disciplinary Literacy, aimed at high school principals and teachers, can be found in Joan Talbert and Jane David, "Evaluation of the Disciplinary Literacy–Professional Learning Community Initiative in Austin Independent School District," Interim Report, August 2007, p. 4.

49. AISD, "Principles of Learning, 2000–2001 Report," Office of Program Evaluation, June 2002, pp. 1–2; *pluribus* and *unum* quotes come from Pascal Forgione Jr., "A District-Wide Approach to High School Conversion: An Urban Superintendent's Perspective," Paper presented at the American Educational Research Association Annual Conference, San Francisco, April 8, 2006.

50. Darlene Westbrook, "Principles of Learning Update," Information item at Board of Trustees meeting, November 10, 2003, pp. 1–5. The theory of action driving IFL's "Principles of Learning" can be found in Janet Quint et al., "Instructional Leadership, Teaching Quality, and Student Achievement," MDRC, December 2007, p. ES-2.

51. The International High School also used DL but was not included in High School Redesign.

52. Talbert and David, "Evaluation."

53. Ibid., pp. 1–15, and p. 2 of appendix on web-based survey.

54. Ibid., p. 19.

55. Ibid., p. 36.

56. Ibid., pp. 21–23.

57. Also in the "deliberate priority" category is Bowie High School. Bowie is rated as consistently high-performing according to district, state, and national standards, garnering award after award (Bowie and Anderson were the only AISD high schools to receive a rating of Recognized in 2002). Kent Ewing, current director of High School Redesign, was Bowie's principal for nearly two decades, and his successor, Stephen Kane, was appointed in 2006. Under Kane, the school has moved

slowly and steadily toward implementing a thirty-minute weekly advisory and planning for a ninth-grade academy and PLCs. Kent Ewing, interview with Larry Cuban, December 5, 2007, and email correspondence January 11, 2008; Parent Teacher School Association, "James Bowie High School Profile," www.bowieptsa.org/profile.html (accessed July 10, 2009); "Principal's Letter to Parents/Guardians," October 2006, www.jbhs.org/principals_corner.htm (accessed July 10, 2009).

58. Sarah Deschenes, David Tyack, Larry Cuban, "Mismatch: Historical Perspectives on Schools and Students Who Don't Fit Them," *Teachers College Record*, 103, no. 4 (2001): 525–547.

59. Ron Edmonds, "Effective Schools for the Urban Poor," *Educational Leadership*, 37 (1979): 10–14; Pamela Bullard and Barbara Taylor, *Making School Reform Happen* (Boston: Allyn and Bacon, 1993).

60. "All children can learn" comes from the Effective Schools movement and the reform rhetoric of its champions. "The soft bigotry of expectations" comes from a campaign speech by Texas governor George W. Bush to the NAACP in 2000. Bush used both phrases in the speech. See www.washingtonpost.com/wp-srv/onpolitics/elections/bushtext071000.htm (accessed July 10, 2009).

61. James Coleman, "Equality of Educational Opportunity," Report OE-38000 (Washington, D.C.: U.S. Office of Education, 1966); Richard Rothstein, *Class and Schools* (New York: Teachers College Press, 2004); Roland Fryer and Steven Levitt, "Understanding the Black-White Test Score Gap in the First Two Years of School," *Review of Economics and Statistics*," 86, no. 2 (2004): 447–464; Douglas Harris, "High-Flying Schools, Student Disadvantage, and the Logic of NCLB," *American Journal of Education*, 113, no. 2 (2007): 367–394. Harris used the U.S. Department of Education's School-Level Achievement Database, which includes three out of four of the nation's public schools enrolling nearly 80 percent of all students for the years 1997–2000. He estimated that low-poverty, low-minority schools (i.e., middle- and upper-middle class largely white students) are eighty-nine times more likely to achieve high performance compared to high-poverty, high-minority schools, such as those found in AISD and other big cities (p. 389). Also see Paul Barton and Richard Coley, "Windows on Achievement and Inequality," Policy Information Report, Educational Testing Service, Princeton, N.J., April 2008; Ronald Ferguson, *Toward Excellence with Equity* (Cambridge, Mass.: Harvard Education Press, 2007).

62. For a persuasive analysis of policy perspectives that inspects the values embedded in each solution to the problem of low-performing schools, see Helen Ladd, "Holding Schools Accountable Revisited," Spencer Foundation Lecture in Educational Policy and Management, Paper presented at the Association for Public Policy Analysis and Management and Spencer Foundation Conference, Washington, D.C., November 8, 2007. My argument draws from the first and third perspectives that Ladd elaborates.

63. The sensitivity of the topic for public airing can be seen in the split within the African American community since the entertainer Bill Cosby began criticizing black middle- and lower-class families for deemphasizing education and neglecting individual responsibility for behavior. Such criticism within the black community has occurred often in the past, but now it is more openly expressed over the role of parents, the absence of fathers in children's lives, and the high percentages of black males in prison. Cosby's criticisms can be seen in the historic debate among academics and policy makers over poverty: some say that poverty persists because the government does not do enough; others say that what the government does has to be done more efficiently and effectively (i.e., welfare programs versus paying cash to poor families in exchange for ensuring that their children attend school, go to health clinics, and so on); others insist that behaviors rooted in cultures of the poor, especially black families, have to change. See, for example, the response to Bill Cosby's "conversations" on black parents who avoid their responsibilities and on how the community can encourage students to work harder in school and to spend less time listening to hip-hop and gangster-praising rap songs. Kevin Merida, "Cos and Effect," *Washington Post*, February 20, 2005, www.washingtonpost.com/wp-dyn/articles/A38675-2005Feb19.html (accessed July 10, 2009); Ta-Nekiso Coates, "This Is How We Lost to the White Man," *Atlantic*, May 2008, pp. 52–62. For a rebuttal to Cosby's argument, see Eric Michael Dyson, *Is Bill Cosby Right? Or Has the Black Middle Class Lost Its Mind?* (New York: Basic Civitas Press, 2006). For an effort to reconcile white and black resentments about the past and aspirations for better schools, health care, and jobs while calling for families to take responsibility for raising their children, see Barack Obama, "A More Perfect Union," speech delivered in Philadelphia, March 18, 2008, www.youtube.com/watch?v=pWe7wTVbLUU (accessed July 10, 2009).

64. Ada Anderson, interview with Larry Cuban, August 29, 2007; Darlene

Westbrook, interview, August 29, 2007; Blanca Garcia, interview, August 29, 2007; Jeff Travillion, interview, August 28, 2007.

65. Meredith Honig, "Complexity and Policy Implementation," in Honig, ed., *New Directions in Education Policy Implementation* (Albany, N.Y.: State University of New York Press, 2006), pp. 1–23.

66. Jeffrey Henig, "Mayoral Control: What We Can and Cannot Learn from Other Cities," in J. Viteritti, ed., *When Mayors Take Charge* (Washington, D.C.: Brookings Institution Press, 2009), p. 21.

67. Quint et al., "The Challenge of Scaling Up." See Michael Fullan, *The New Meaning of Educational Change* (New York: Teachers College Press, 1991).

68. Raven Hill, "High Schools Putting Twist on Tradition," *Austin American-Statesman*, May 17, 2006, p. B1.

4. Assessing Austin Leadership and Reforms

1. Clifton Fadiman, ed., *The Little, Brown Book of Anecdotes* (Boston: Little, Brown, 1985), p. 393.

2. For evidence on charter schools, see Martin Carnoy, Rebecca Jacobsen, Lawrence Mishel, and Richart Rothstein, *The Charter School Dust-Up: Examining the Evidence on Enrollment and Achievement* (Washington, D.C.: Economic Policy Institute, 2005). For different views of evidence on mayoral control, see Kenneth Wong, "Does Mayoral Control Improve Performance in Urban Districts" and Jeffrey Henig, "Mayoral Control: What We Can and Cannot Learn from Other Cities," in J. Viteritti, ed., *When Mayors Take Charge* (Washington, D.C.: Brookings Institution Press, 2009).

3. A recent example of this was evident in Washington, D.C., where chancellor Michelle Rhee, after less than a year in the post, held a press conference on test score gains. Although Rhee spoke proudly of these gains and took credit for them, other factors might have accounted for the rise in scores. See Dion Haynes, "D.C. Students See Big Academic Gains," *Washington Post*, July 10, 2008, p. B01.

4. Nancy Scammacca, "Austin Blueprint Schools Initiative to Leave No Child Behind: Elementary Schools' Three-Year Summary Report," AISD, June 30, 2005; idem, "Austin Blueprint Schools Initiative to Leave No Child Behind: Middle Schools' Three-Year Summary Report," AISD, June 30, 2005.

5. Peter Ross, "Moving from 'One Best System' to a Portfolio: A Study of the

District-Wide High School Redesign Initiative in Austin Independent School District" (diss., Stanford University, 2008), ch. 4 (on changes in the district office).

6. Etienne Wenger, *Communities of Practice: Learning, Meaning, and Identity* (New York: Cambridge University Press, 1998).

7. Mary Stein and Cynthia Coburn, "Architecture for Learning: A Comparative Analysis of Two Urban School Districts," *American Journal of Education*, 114 (August 2008), www.journals.uchicago.edu/doi/full/10.1086/589315 (accessed July 14, 2009).

8. Principal 8, interview with Peter Ross, January 2007.

9. Teacher 6, interview with Peter Ross, February 2007.

10. On First Things First, see James Connell and Adena Klem, "First Things First: A Framework for Successful Secondary School Reform," *New Directions for Youth Development*, 111 (Fall 2006): 53–66. For an analysis of 427 classroom observations during the years 2000–2003 in ten FTF high schools where some changes in teaching practices were noted, see Angela Estacion, Teresa McMahon, and Janet Quint, "Conducting Classroom Observations in 'First Things First' Schools," MDRC (Manpower Demonstration Research Corp.), New York, N.Y., and Oakland, Calif., June 2004, www.mdrc.org/publications/390/full.pdf (accessed July 13, 2009). On Disciplinary Literacy, see Joan Talbert and Jane David, "Evaluation of the Disciplinary Literacy–Professional Learning Community Initiative in Austin Independent School District," Interim Report, August 2007; Final Report, August 2008.

11. A number of researchers have shown that individual teachers respond to new policies by incorporating elements of the new policies that fit their routine practices. For example, see David Cohen, "A Revolution in One Classroom," *Educational Evaluation and Policy Analysis*, 12, no. 3 (1990): 327–345; James Spillane, *Standards Deviations: How Schools Misunderstand Education Policy* (Cambridge, Mass.: Harvard University Press, 2004); Mary Stein and Cynthia Coburn, "Architecture for Learning: A Comparative Analysis of Two Urban School Districts," *American Journal of Education*, 114 (August 2008), www.journals.uchicago.edu/doi/full/10.1086/589315 (accessed July 14, 2009).

12. For a study of elementary school years in which interviews, classroom observations, and surveys were used, see Robert Pianta, Jay Belsky, Renate Houts, and Fred Morrison, "Opportunities to Learn in America's Elementary Classrooms," *Sci-*

ence, 315 (March 30, 2007): 1795–1796; Laura Hamilton et al., "Accountability and Teaching Practices: School Level Actions and Teacher Responses," in B. Fuller, M. Henne, and E. Hannum, eds., *Strong States, Weak Schools: The Benefits and Dilemmas of Centralized Accountability.* For case studies of three elementary schools in a big-city district during the years 2001–2005, see Linda Valli, R. G. Croninger, M. Chambliss, A. O. Graeber, and D. Buese, *Test Driven: High-Stakes Accountability in Elementary Schools* (New York: Teachers College Press, 2008); for a case study of how one Annapolis, Md., elementary school coped with low test scores and the effects of NCLB in 2005–2006, see Linda Perlstein, *Tested: One American School Struggles to Make the Grade* (New York: Henry Holt, 2007). For an extensive survey, see Joseph Pedulla et al., "Perceived Effects of State-Mandated Testing Programs on Teaching and Learning: Findings from a National Survey of Teachers" (Chestnut Hill, Mass.: National Board on Educational Testing and Public Policy, Boston College, 2003), www.bc. edu/nbetpp (accessed July 14, 2009); Sam Dillon, "Schools Cut Back Subjects to Push Reading and Math," *New York Times*, March 26, 2006, www.nytimes. com/2006/03/26/education/26child.html?ex=1301029200&en=0c91b5bd32 dabe2a&ei=5088&partner=rssnyt&emc=rss (accessed July 14, 2009).

13. Joan Talbert and Jane David, "Evaluation of the Disciplinary Literacy–Professional Learning Community Initiative in Austin Independent School District," Interim Report, August 2007, and Final Report, August 2008.

14. District staff spent time in each elementary and secondary school rated Academically Unacceptable in 2008, analyzing test results, classroom teaching, principals' actions, and integration of district support (such as Instructional Planning Guides and various protocols) into schools' daily routines. For example, at Crockett High School, district staff reported to the superintendent and Board of Trustees that "traditional lecture-based teaching . . . [is] utilized by a majority of math teachers." In all four elementary schools rated Unsatisfactory, district staff reported classroom observations showing "inconsistent implementation of best practices in curriculum, instruction, and assessment." See Board of Trustees, "Update on Academically Unacceptable Schools," agenda packet item, October 20, 2008.

15. Direct observation in elementary schools raises serious questions about whether new school structures alter daily teaching practices. See, for example, Robert Pianta and Bridget Hamre, "Conceptualization, Measurement, and Improvement

of Classroom Processes: Standardized Observation Can Leverage Capacity," *Educational Researcher*, 38, no. 2 (2009): 109–119; Richard F. Elmore, Penelope L. Peterson, and Sarah J. McCarthy, *Restructuring in the Classroom: Teaching, Learning, and School Organization* (San Francisco: Jossey-Bass, 1996).

16. For example, studies showing that students who do homework regularly get higher grades are marred by lack of data on other possible explanatory factors. For example, students who get better grades may be more conscientious, or students who do less homework and receive poorer grades may not understand or have any interest in the assignment or subject matter. Without controlling statistically for other factors that might explain the relationship between more homework and better grades, the observed link is not necessarily causal. See Jay Mathews, "How about Some Homework on Correlation vs. Causation," *Washington Post*, March 29, 2007, p. VA13.

17. The Los Angeles Unified District has engaged in institutional reform for decades, altering its governance, district organization, curriculum, and instruction to improve students' academic achievement. New structures have been installed and dismantled; decentralized school-based management, for example, gave way to centralized control of reform. Yet over the decades, the effects of systematic, district-wide reform policies and changes in teaching practices on outcomes such as student learning were rarely assessed. See Charles Kerchner et al., *Learning from L.A.: Institutional Change in American Public Education* (Cambridge, Mass.: Harvard Education Press, 2008). Or consider the San Diego Unified School District (SDUSD) under Alan Bersin and Anthony Alvarado between 1998–2004: in a 2003 superintendent-sponsored conference devoted to the San Diego reforms and institutional changes, not one paper was devoted to actual teaching practices. Most of the papers addressed topics such as new structures that were implemented (new instructional leaders; professional learning communities), the logic of the reform, and leadership aimed at improving students' academic achievement. Officials used test scores as a proxy for student learning. Researchers and SDUSD officials interpreted the rising scores for elementary schools, the leveling-off in those gains, and the low performance of high school students as evidence that reforms were yielding or about to yield desired outcomes—a dubious interpretation. In the 341-page book resulting from that conference, only pages 88–90 were devoted to teaching practice, and even there the evidence was drawn from interviews and surveys of administrators and

teachers, not systematic classroom observations. See Frederick Hess, ed., *Urban School Reform: Lessons from San Diego* (Cambridge, Mass.: Harvard Education Press, 2005).

18. See, for example, AISD, "Austin Insider," Summer 2006, p. 3; AISD, "2005–2006 Annual Report"; AISD, "Strategic Plan, 2005–2010," www.austin.isd.tenet.edu/inside/initiatives/strategic_plan (accessed July 14, 2009).

School-by-school achievement scores within a district can be divided into four equal parts. The three values that divide the four parts are called *quartiles*. The first (or bottom) quartile is the score below which the lowest 25 percent of schools fall. The second quartile (the median) divides the range of scores in the middle, such that 50 percent of the schools fall above that score and 50 percent below it. The third (or top) quartile is the score below which 75 percent of scores fall; the top 25 percent of scores fall above the third-quartile value.

Because school districts vary in their distributions of achievement scores, quartile cutoff-scores will also vary across districts. For example, a high-performing suburban district may have its bottom-quartile score at the same level as the 75th percentile (top-quartile) score in a lower-performing district. That is, the "low-performers" (schools with the lowest bottom-quarter scores) in the high-performing district may actually outscore all but the top 25 percent of schools in a lower-performing district. Since every district has a bottom-quartile score (the cutoff point defining the lowest 25 percent of schools), district quartile scores must be evaluated against some independent standard so that the range in school and district performances can be appreciated.

19. Henig, "Mayoral Control," pp. 35–37.

20. Pat Forgione, interview with Larry Cuban, April 24, 2007; August 29, 2007, and December 3, 2007.

21. Pascal Forgione Jr., "Austin's Trajectory of Progress," talk given to administrators, April 23, 2007; Michael May, "Naked City," *Austin Chronicle*, August 17, 2007.

22. On July 2, 2009, Texas education commissioner Robert Scott informed AISD that Pearce Middle School had received its fifth straight Academically Unacceptable rating, its eighth out of the previous ten years. "This pattern of continuing low performance," he said, "is not acceptable and currently is unmatched by any other campus in the state. I am therefore ordering the closure of the Pearce Middle School effective with the 2009–2010 school year."

The commissioner also informed AISD that Reagan High School had received a rating of Academically Unacceptable, its fourth in a row. Acknowledging the academic progress that the school had made, he ordered the district to take additional actions at Reagan in 2009–2010 to avoid closing the school the following year (letter from Robert Scott to AISD superintendent Meria Carstarphen, July 2, 2009, in AISD press release, July 8, 2009).

In contrast to the situation at Johnston High School, which was closed in 2008 and reopened as Eastside Memorial High School, the options before AISD officials were to provide additional information for a plan submitted earlier aimed at "repurposing" or restructuring the school, or to negotiate other conditions which could extract a reprieve from the commissioner for one more year. See Richard Whittaker, "TEA to Pearce: Drop Dead," *Austin Chronicle*, July 17, 2009, www.austinchronicle.com/gyrobase/Issue/story?oid=810829 (accessed July 17, 2009).

23. One notable exception was the superintendent's decision in 2008 to restore the cuts in elementary school art, music, and physical education staff that had been imposed in 2003–2004 to align with the constricted focus on academics. Pascal Forgione Jr., memo to Larry Cuban, February 13, 2008.

24. Forgione, "Austin's Trajectory of Progress," April 23, 2007; Helen Ladd, "Rethinking the Way We Hold Schools Accountable," *Education Week*, January 23, 2008, pp. 26–27; for empirical evidence, see Fuller, Henne, and Hannum, *Strong States, Weak Schools*, pp. 1–29.

25. See "Austin Independent School District Strategic Plan, 2005–2010, Revised 2007," pp. 5–6, Priority 2: "Provide a quality educational experience that will develop the whole child—intellectually, socially, emotionally, physically, and ethically." Interviews by Larry Cuban with Pascal Forgione Jr., August 29, 2007; Joyce Lynch, August 28, 2007; Jeffrey Travillion, August 28, 2007; Geoff Rips, August 27, 2007; Blanca Garcia, August 29, 2007; Ed Sharpe, August 27, 2007, Darlene Westbrook, August 29, 2007; Glen Nolly, December 5, 2007; Paul Cruz, December 5, 2007.

26. Eighteen elementary schools earned sixty-four ratings of Exemplary in the years 2000–2007. Eight of the eighteen schools were rated Exemplary at least four times in these years. All eight of these schools had very low rates of poverty (less than 10 percent) and had students populations that were two-thirds to four-fifths white. All were west of Route I-35. Author's calculations from AEIS Campus Data,

2000–2007; Raven Hill, "Parents Plan Overnight Vigil to Seek School Transfers," *Austin American-Statesman,* February 2, 2008.

The historical racial divide among schools demarcated by Route I-35 includes, as it did before World War II, businesses and social institutions. Austin's city manager, Marc Ott, the first African American to hold that post, spoke recently to a group interested in increasing economic opportunity in the city. In referring to I-35, he said, "In my twenty-seven years in this business, and in all the places I've been, I've never seen as hard a demographic line." He asked his audience, "Why is East Austin sequestered?" Katherine Gregor, "Ott Tackles Austin's Racial Divide," *Austin Chronicle,* July 3, 2009, www.austinchronicle.com/gyrobase/Issue/print?oid=803456 (accessed July 14, 2009).

5. The Future of Austin Reform and Three-Tiered Schooling

1. See the list of Broad Award past winners: www.broadprize.org/past.shtml (accessed July 15, 2009).

2. Interviews by Larry Cuban with Ed Sharpe, August 24, 2007; Sandy Dolchen, August 24, 2007; Jeff Travillion, August 25, 2007; Joyce Lynch, August 29, 2007.

3. According to Forgione, he had been turned down the first time by AISD when the Board of Trustees offered the superintendency to another candidate in June 1999. That candidate eventually withdrew. In the meantime, Forgione had applied for the job of school chief in Kansas City, Mo., and when offered the post, Forgione decided not to take it. Then the AISD Board of Trustees reopened the search; Forgione was again considered and, in August 1999, chosen. Pascal Forgione Jr., phone interview with Larry Cuban, March 8, 2008.

4. Interviews by Larry Cuban with Pat Forgione, April 24, 2007, August 28, 2007, December 3, 2007; Darlene Westbrook, August 29, 2007; Geoff Rips, August 27, 2007; Paul Cruz, December 4, 2007; Glen Nolly, December 4, 2007. Kent Ewing, interview with Larry Cuban, December 5, 2007. In addition, I observed the superintendent at a Board of Trustees meeting, April 23, 2007, and at a High School Redesign conference at Stanford University, June 19–20, 2007. Forgione has surprised AISD teachers designated "Teacher of the Year" by showing up in their classrooms and presenting them with bouquets of roses and other small gifts. See

Michelle Martinez, "My Teacher Is an Honors Educator, Kids Can Say," *Austin American-Statesman*, April 8, 2004, pp. B1, B4.

5. Douglas Harris, "High-Flying Schools and Student Disadvantage," *American Journal of Education*, 113 (May 2007): 367–394; Angela Valenzuela, *Subtractive Education* (Albany: State University of New York Press, 1999).

6. Andy Alford, "A Dream Deferred," *Austin American-Statesman*, May 16, 2004, p. A7.

7. Pascal Forgione Jr., interview with Larry Cuban, August 27, 2007; Nancy Scammacca, "Austin Blueprint Schools Initiative to Leave No Child Behind: Elementary Schools' Three-Year Summary Report," AISD, June 30, 2005; idem, "Austin Blueprint Schools Initiative to Leave No Child Behind: Middle Schools' Three-Year Summary Report," AISD, June 30, 2005.

8. Quote in Larry Cuban and Michael Usdan, eds., *Powerful Reforms with Shallow Roots* (New York: Teachers College Press, 2003), p. 88. See also Susanne James-Burdumy, Irma Perez-Johnson, and Sonya Vartivarian, "High School Reform in Boston Public Schools, Final Report," June 23, 2008, Mathematica Policy Research, MPR no. 8927-006.

9. Paul Cruz, interview with Larry Cuban, December 5, 2007; AISD, "Middle-Level Education Plan," www.austinisd.org/schools/ms/index,phtml (accessed July 15, 2009).

10. I attended the April 23, 2007, meeting and watched subsequent cablecasts of Board of Trustee meetings. See also the articles cited in Chapter 2, concerning public meetings during the proposed closure of Webb Middle School. Interviews by Larry Cuban with Darlene Westbrook, August 28, 2007; Paul Cruz, December 5, 2007; Ed Sharpe, August 28, 2007.

11. Pascal Forgione Jr., interviews with Larry Cuban, April 24, 2007, August 27, 2007, December 4, 2007.

12. Dale Mezzacappa, "The Vallas Effect," www.hoover.org/publications/ednext/16109997.html (accessed July 15, 2009).

13. American Association of School Administrators, "The State of the American School Superintendency: A Mid-Decade Study," www.districtadministration.com/viewarticle.aspx?articleid=1430 (accessed July 15, 2009). Gary Yee and Larry Cuban, "When Is Tenure Long Enough? A Historical Analysis of Superintendent Turnover and Tenure in Urban School Districts," *Educational Administration Quarterly*, 32, suppl. (1996): 615–641.

14. I draw these three explanations for long-serving superintendents from Larry Cuban, "Turnstile Superintendency?" *Education Week,* 28 (August 27, 2008): 26–27, 29.

15. Ralph Vartabedian, "Giuliani's Poor School Marks," *Los Angeles Times,* September 13, 2007, p. A14.

16. Helen Gao, "S.D. Schools Chief Cohn to Resign at Year's End," *San Diego Union-Tribune,* September 20, 2007, www.signonsandiego.com/uniontrib/20070920/news_1n20cohn.html (accessed July 15, 2009).

17. Amid all of the inflated rhetoric about turning around schools and districts—which often implies that the thousands of schools already in NCLB stage 4 (restructuring the school) or stage 5 (ridding the school of its staff, closing it, and reopening it as a charter school or other alternative) can be transformed into effective schools—a refreshing paper cuts through the hyperbole and calls for more modest claims and hopes: Frederick Hess and Thomas Gift, "School Turnarounds: Resisting the Hype, Giving Them Hope," *Education Outlook* (American Enterprise Institute), February 2009.

18. "Timeline: Rudy Crew," *Miami Herald,* September 10, 2008, www.miamiherald.com/news/more-info/story/680427.html (accessed July 15, 2009).

19. AISD board members, private discussion with Larry Cuban, March 15, 2008; Report on AISD reforms, September 10, 2008.

20. There is no established metric for judging a superintendent's success. The American Association of School Administrators has published standards for evaluating superintendents, but many of these standards are process- rather than outcome-driven. I have included those indicators of success that have appeared in contracts negotiated between superintendents and school boards and that contain performance clauses on student outcomes. I have also included my research on the topic. See Gene Carter and William Cunningham, *The American School Superintendent: Leading in an Age of Pressure* (San Francisco: Jossey-Bass, 1997); Larry Cuban, "Serviceable Myths about the Dilemma-Laden Superintendency," *Teachers College Record,* 100, no. 1 (1998): 181–190. On the correlation between eating pizza and reducing one's risk of cancer, see BBC News, "Eating Pizza 'Cuts Cancer Risk,'" July 22, 2003, news.bbc.co.uk/2/hi/health/3086013.stm (accessed July 15, 2009).

21. Molly Bloom, "Voters Approve AISD Property Tax Increase," *Austin American-Statesman,* November 5, 2008, www.statesman.com/blogs/content/shared-

gen/blogs/austin/election/entries/2008/11/05/voters_approve_aisd_property_
tax_increase.html (accessed July 15, 2009).

22. Joan Talbert and Jane David, "Evaluation of the Disciplinary Literacy–Professional Learning Community Initiative in Austin Independent School District,"
Final Report, August 2008. I observed fourteen classrooms at Reagan High School
over two days in December 2007. See also Molly Bloom, "Austin School Board Ap-
proves Two-school Model for Johnston HS," *Austin American-Statesman,* October 13,
2008; AISD, "Discussion of New Instructional Models for Eastside Memorial
High School," Board of Trustees agenda packet, September 22, 2008.

23. Nelson Hernandez, "Prince George's Superintendent Is Leaving," *Washington
Post,* September 30, 2008, p. B1.

24. "Austin Schools Better Because of Superintendent Pat Forgione" (editorial),
Austin American-Statesman, February 19, 2008, www.statesman.com/blogs/content/
shared-gen/blogs/austin/editorial/entries/2008/02/19/austin_schools_better_
because.html (accessed July 15, 2009); Richard Whittaker, "Forgione's Long Farewell," *Austin Chronicle,* March 21, 2008, www.austinchronicle.com/gyrobase/Issue/
story?oid=oid%3A603823 (accessed July 15, 2009); Raven Hill, "Austin Superintendent to Retire in 2009," *Austin American-Statesman,* February 20, 2008, www
.statesman.com/blogs/content/shared-gen/blogs/austin/education/entries/2008
/02/19/austin_superintendent_to_retir.html (accessed July 15, 2009); Raven L.
Hill, "Parents, Teachers Reflect on Forgione's Legacy," February 21, 2008, ibid.;
AISD, "Austin's Pat Forgione Honored as Nation's Top Educator in 2008," News
release, October 23, 2008.

25. Laura Heinauer, "Board Names Carstarphen as Next Superintendent," *Austin American-Statesman,* March 23, 2009, www.statesman.com/blogs/content/shared-
gen/blogs/austin/education/entries/2009/03/index.html (accessed July 15,
2009).

6. Urban District Reform Strategies

1. "Dean Keppel and the Lions," *New York Times,* March 1, 1990, p. A22.

2. Cities that have concentrated on both "altering governance and bureaucracy" and "disrupting the system" include Chicago, New York City, Philadelphia,
Milwaukee, Washington, and New Orleans. In these places, reliance on charter
schools and external entrepreneurs has created many school options for parents.

3. James Patterson, *Brown v. Board of Education* (New York: Oxford University Press, 2001); Gary Orfield and John Yun, *Resegregation in America* (Cambridge, Mass.: Harvard University Civil Rights Project, 1999); Robert Linn and Kelvin Welner, eds., *Race Conscious Policies for Assigning Students to Schools: Social Science Research and the Supreme Court Cases* (Washington, D.C.: National Academy of Education, 2007); Russell Rumberger and Gregory Palardy, "Does Segregation Still Matter? The Impact of Student Composition on Academic Achievement in High School," *Teachers College Record*, 107, no. 9 (2005): 1999–2045; Richard Kahlenberg, *Using Socioeconomic Diversity to Improve School Outcomes* (New York: Century Foundation, 2007); Richard Kahlenberg, "Socioeconomic Integration and Magnet Schools," www.tcf.org/list. asp?type=NC&pubid=906 (accessed July 21, 2009); Emily Bazelon, "The Next Kind of Integration," *New York Times Magazine*, July 20, 2008, pp. 39–43.

4. New Schools Venture Fund, "2008 Summit: From Innovation to Transformation—Connecting Education Entrepreneurs to Systems Change," May 20, 2008. For a summary of Denver's pay-for-performance plan, see Cynthia Brown and Robin Chait, "A Promising Accord for Denver's ProComp Program," Center for American Progress, September 2, 2008, www.americanprogress.org/issues/2008/09/procomp_denver.html (accessed July 21, 2009).

5. Jim Haviland, "Duties of Area Superintendents Could Be Changed by Forgione," *Oak Hill Gazette*, July 7, 2002, pp. 3, 10.

6. Another whole-school reform, called Accelerated Schools, likewise found a home in AISD. See Walnut Creek Elementary School, 209.85.173.104/ search?q=cache:gHR2jQfVTUcJ:uts.cc.utexas.edu/~swcas/downloads/newsletters/Newsletter-Fall03.pdf+walnut+Creek+Elementary+Accelerated+School+AISD&hl=en&ct=clnk&cd=8&gl=us&client=firefox-a (accessed July 21, 2009). On the Texas High School Initiative, see AISD, "Board Briefs," March 7, 2005.

7. For examples of how fear and shame at doing poorly on state tests can influence some schools' tactics in preparing students for annual tests, see Jennifer Booher-Jennings, "Below the Bubble: 'Educational Triage' and the Texas Accountability System," *American Educational Research Journal*, 42, no. 2 (2005): 231–268; Matthew Springer, "Do Schools Practice Educational Triage?" *Education Next*, 8, no. 1 (2008), www.hoover.org/publications/ednext/10895041.html (accessed July 21, 2009). On the negative impact of state accountability systems on schools, see Linda Perlstein, *Tested* (New York: Henry Holt, 2007); Maria Glod and Daniel de Vise, "Needy Students Closing Test Gap under 'No Child,'" *Washington Post*, October 2,

2008, p. A01. For a more positive study of how schools do better when under accountability pressure, see Cecilia Rouse et al., "Feeling the Florida Heat: How Low-Performing Schools Respond to Vouchers and Accountability Pressure," Working Paper 13681, December 2007 (Cambridge, Mass.: National Bureau of Economic Research).

8. "AISD Reach," www.austin.isd.tenet.edu/inside/initiatives/compensation/index.phtml (accessed July 21, 2009); Laura Heinauer, "Austin School District Rewards Educators at Nine Schools with Bonuses," *Austin Statesman-American*, July 30, 2008, www.statesman.com/news/content/news/stories/local/07/30/0730 compensation.html (accessed July 21, 2009).

9. Kimberly Reeves, "Reagan High Stands Up and Fights," *Austin Chronicle*, October 31, 2008, www.austinchronicle.com/gyrobase/Issue/story?oid=oid%3A696453 (accessed July 21, 2009). TEA commissioner Robert Scott ordered the closure of Pearce Middle School in July 2009.

10. Henry Levin, ed., *Community Control of Schools* (Washington, D.C.: Brookings Institution, 1970); David Tyack, "Restructuring in Historical Perspective," *Teachers College Record*, 92, no. 2 (1990): 170–191; Jane David, "Synthesis of Research on School-Based Management," *Educational Leadership*, 46, no. 8 (May 1989): 45–53.

11. Marshall Smith and Jennifer O'Day, "Systemic School Reform," in S. Fuhrman and B. Malen, eds., *The Politics of Curriculum and Testing* (London: Taylor and Francis, 1991), pp. 233–267; Frederick Hess, ed., *Urban School Reform: Lessons from San Diego* (Cambridge, Mass.: Harvard Education Press, 2005); Dale Mezzacappa, "The Vallas Effect," *Education Next* 8, no. 2 (2008), www.hoover.org/publications/ednext/16109997.html (accessed July 21, 2009).

12. The AISD Board of Trustees has approved the implementation of the New Tech High model for Eastside Memorial High School (formerly Johnston High School) in 2009–2010. Information on the model can be found at www.newtechfoundation.org/initiatives_network.html (accessed July 21, 2009).

13. Joel Klein quotations come from Paul Tough, "How Many Billionaires Does It Take to Fix a School System?" *New York Times Magazine*, March 9, 2008, www.nytimes.com/2008/03/09/magazine/09roundtable-t.html?sq=philanthropists%20education%20March%202008&st=cse&scp=1&pagewanted=all (accessed July 21, 2009).

14. On Seattle, see Gary Yee and Barbara Cloud, "A Vision of Hope: A Case Study of Seattle's Two Non-Traditional Superintendents," in Larry Cuban and Mi-

chael Usdan, eds., *Powerful Reforms with Shallow Roots* (New York: Teachers College Press, 2003), pp. 54–76. On San Diego, see Hess, *Urban School Reform;* San Diego has had two superintendents since Alan Bersin left in 2005. On Philadelphia, see Mezzacappa, "The Vallas Effect."

15. Hess quoted in Tough, "How Many Billionaires Does It Take to Fix a School System?"

16. Frank Levy and Richard Murnane, *Teaching the New Basic Skills: Principles for Educating Children to Thrive in a Changing Economy* (New York: Free Press, 1996).

17. Norton Grubb and Marvin Lazerson, *The Education Gospel* (Cambridge, Mass.: Harvard University Press, 2004); Larry Cuban, *The Blackboard and the Bottom Line: Why Schools Can't Be Businesses* (Cambridge, Mass.: Harvard University Press, 2005).

18. "We sensed around us—in our classes, in the media, in Washington—a host of people who did not know any history to speak of and were unaware of suffering any lack, who thought the world was new and all of its problems fresh . . . and that decisions in the public realm required only reason and emotion." Richard Neustadt and Ernest May, *Thinking in Time: The Uses of History for Decision-Makers* (New York: Free Press, 1986), pp. xi–xii. Neustadt and May, both Harvard professors, are here speaking about Washington top- and mid-level decision makers during the 1970s. My nearly five decades of working with school boards, superintendents, and federal and state policy makers led me to a similar conclusion for educational decision makers. Yet the decision makers that Neustadt and May refer to and the ones I knew used history in their decisions, "at least for advocacy or for comfort, whether they knew any or not."

19. Historian William Reese nicely sums up these multiple and competing goals for public schools: "Schools are expected to feed the hungry, discipline the wayward, identify and encourage the talented, treat everyone alike while not forgetting that everyone is an individual, raise test scores but also feelings of self-worth, ensure winning sports teams without demeaning academics, improve standards but also graduation rates, provide for the different learning styles and capacities of the young while administering common tests, and counter the crass materialism of the larger society while providing the young with the skills and sensibilities to thrive in it as future workers." William Reese, *History, Education, and the Schools* (New York: Palgrave Macmillan, 2007), p. 159.

20. Frederick Hess, *Spinning Wheels: The Politics of Urban School Reform* (Washington,

D.C.: Brookings Institution, 1999); David Tyack and Larry Cuban, *Tinkering toward Utopia* (Cambridge, Mass.: Harvard University Press, 1995).

21. Ann Bradley, "Cobb County, GA, Laptop Plan To Be Probed by Grand Jury," *Education Week*, October 19, 2005, p. 5. For an example of a city undergoing a burst of reform, and the political, economic, and social costs that accrued after the initial funding was spent, see William Boyd and Jolley Christman, "A Tall Order for Philadelphia's New Approach to School Governance: Heal the Political Rifts, Close the Budget Gap, *and* Improve the Schools," in Cuban and Usdan, *Powerful Reforms with Shallow Roots*, pp. 96–124; Gary Dworkin, "Perspectives on Teacher Burnout and School Reform," *International Education Journal*, 2, no. 2 (2001): 69–78.

22. Joan Talbert and Jane David, "Evaluation of the Disciplinary Literacy–Professional Learning Community Initiative in Austin Independent School District," Final Report, August 2008.

23. Meredith Honig, *New Directions in Education Policy Implementation* (Albany: State University of New York Press, 2006).

24. Charles Payne, *So Much Reform, So Little Change* (Cambridge, Mass.: Harvard Education Press, 2008), pp. 186–187, crisply lays out standards for the implementation of an elementary school math program, and argues that these guidelines would help most district officials think through implementing structures and programs.

25. While many people have claimed that professional learning communities produce changes in teaching practices and, subsequently, gains in student achievement, the evidence for these claims is weak, at best. On the kind of research studies that are necessary to demonstrate the effects of professional development on teaching practice and student achievement, see Hilda Borko, "Professional Development and Teacher Learning: Mapping the Terrain," *Educational Researcher* 33, no. 8 (2004): 3–15. On the difficulties that PLCs pose for teachers in urban districts, see Diane Wood, "Teachers' Learning Communities: Catalyst for Change or a New Infrastructure for the Status Quo?" *Teachers College Record*, 109, no. 3 (2007): 699–739.

26. Richard Elmore, Penelope Peterson, and Sarah McCarthey, *Restructuring in the Classroom* (San Francisco: Jossey-Bass, 1996); Audrey Amrein and David Berliner, "High-Stakes Testing, Uncertainty, and Student Learning," *Educational Policy Analysis Archives*, 10, no. 8 (2002), epaa.asu.edu/epaa/v10n18 (accessed July 21, 2009); Jonathan Supovitz, "Developing Communities of Instructional Practice," *Teachers College Record*, 104, no. 8 (2002): 1591–1646.

27. See, for example, AISD "Elementary Level Performance Report," Board of Trustees agenda packet, October 13, 2008.

28. Thomas Ott, "Cleveland Schools CEO Eugene Sanders Thrives amid Challenges," *Cleveland Plain Dealer,* July 27, 2008, blog.cleveland.com/metro/2008/07/cleveland_schools_ceo_eugene_s.html (accessed July 21, 2009); Shannon Mortland, "Executive Chatter with Eugene Sanders," *Crain's Cleveland Business,* November 3, 2008.

29. Marjorie Coeyman, "Troubled Schools Seek Old-Fashioned Hero," *Christian Science Monitor,* September 10, 2002, www.csmonitor.com/2002/0910/p18s01-legn.html (accessed July 21, 2009).

30. Tracy Jan and Marcella Bombardieri, "With Tears, Cheers, Johnson Leaves Memphis," *Boston Globe,* June 19, 2007, www.boston.com/news/education/k_12/articles/2007/06/19/with_tears_cheers_johnson_leaves_memphis (accessed July 21, 2009).

31. Michael Grynbaum, "Greenspan Concedes Error on Regulation," *New York Times,* October 23, 2008, www.nytimes.com/2008/10/24/business/economy/24panel.html?_r=1&hp&oref=slogin (accessed July 21, 2009).

32. Theodore Sizer, *Horace's Compromise* (Boston: Houghton Mifflin, 1984); idem, *Redesigning Horace's School* (Boston: Houghton Mifflin, 1992); Michelle Fine, "Not in Our Name," *Rethinking Schools,* 19, no. 4 (2005), www.rethinkingschools.org/archive/19_04/name194.shtml (accessed July 21, 2009). Statistics come from Erik Robelen, "Gates High Schools Get Mixed Review in Study," *Education Week,* November 16, 2005, pp. 1, 20.

33. Lawrence Bernstein et al., "Implementation Study of Small Learning Communities," U.S. Department of Education Office of Planning and Evaluation, Final Report, 2008; Joe Kahne et al., "Small High Schools on a Large Scale: The Impact of School Conversions in Chicago," *Educational Evaluation and Policy Analysis,* 30, no. 3 (2008): 281–315; Robelen, "Gates High Schools Get Mixed Review in Study," pp. 1, 20.

34. Reeves, "Reagan High Stands Up and Fights." Letter from TEA commissioner Robert Scott to superintendent Meria Carstarphen, July 2, 2009.

35. Deborah Pines, "Thriving in the Zone," *U.S. News and World Report,* October 31, 2005, www.usnews.com/usnews/news/articles/051031/31canada.htm (accessed July 21, 2009). It is rare that instructional practice has been inspected in urban districts after new structures designed to improve student test scores were put

into place. One such study was done in Milwaukee, a district committed to offering parents many school choices for their children. Researcher Ken Montgomery had access to the superintendent, district office staff, principals, and teachers for gathering interview material, conducting surveys, and analyzing documents. See Ken Montgomery, "Building Common Instructional Practice in a Choice-Driven District: What Reform Brought to Milwaukee, 1999–2009" (diss., Stanford University, 2009). Montgomery found that even after structures to change teaching and learning were fully implemented, teachers reported few changes in their daily routines and lessons.

36. An article that underscores this perspective and that has been widely read among urban school board members and superintendents is Stacey Childress, Richard Elmore, and Allen Grossman, "How to Manage Urban School Districts," *Harvard Business Review*, 84, no. 11 (2006): 55–68.

37. AISD Office of Program Evaluation, "Prekindergarten Evaluation, 2001–2002," September 2002, report no. 01.02; Janice Curry, "Prekindergarten Expansion Grant Evaluation Report, 2005–2006," AISD Office of Program Evaluation, October 2006, report no. 05.09, pp. 2, 6–7. Pascal Forgione Jr., memo to Larry Cuban, February 13, 2008.

38. Pascal Forgione Jr., address to the Fourth Annual Summit of "Housing Works," November 10, 2007 (in author's possession).

7. What Can Be Done?

1. "Utopian, banal": Michael Katz, *Improving Poor People* (Princeton: Princeton University Press, 1997), p. 7. Faulkner quote from *Requiem for a Nun* (New York: Random House, 1951), p. 92. A reasonable "School Reformers' Pledge of Good Conduct," as Charles Payne points out, would include such items as "I will not over-promise," "I will not disrespect teachers," and "I will take the time to study the history of reforms similar to mine." See Charles Payne, *So Much Reform, So Little Change* (Cambridge, Mass.: Harvard Education Press, 2008), p. 153.

2. Such waiver-encouraged zones exist in New York, Chicago, Milwaukee, Miami-Dade, and other districts. See New Schools Venture Fund, Summit 2007, p. 12. I also had discussions with Milwaukee participants at a Stanford Redesign Network meeting, June 19–22, 2007. The quote comes from Winnie Hu, "High

Schools Add Electives to Cultivate Interests," *New York Times*, October 26, 2008, p. A21.

3. On New York City, see Deborah Kolben, "Mayor, in Shift, Tries Decentralization," *New York Sun*, June 13, 2006, www.nysun.com/new-york/mayor-in-shift-tries-decentralization/34313. Also see New York City Department of Education on "empowerment schools," schools.nyc.gov/Offices/Empowerment/default.htm. On Milwaukee, see Milwaukee Public Schools, Office of the Superintendent, "FY 07 Superintendent's Budget Overview," www2.milwaukee.k12.wi.us/supt/super/PDFs/budget.pdf. On Boston's seventeen pilot schools and two charters, see www.ccebos.org/pilotschools/bostonpilotschools.html. (All URLs accessed July 22, 2009.)

4. See Andrew Calkins et al., *The Turnaround Challenge* (Boston: Mass Insight Education and Research Institute, 2007); Frederick Hess and Thomas Gift, "School Turnarounds: Resisting the Hype, Giving Them Hope," *Education Outlook* (American Enterprise Institute), February 2009. For a more positive view of school turnarounds, see Daniel Duke, "Turning Schools Around," *Education Week*, February 21, 2007, pp. 35, 37.

5. Of the ten elementary schools rated Academically Unacceptable in the period 2000–2007, five had been Priority Schools from 1987 to 1992 and are located east of I-35. I found only one elementary school that went from the bottom tier in poverty and achievement to a rating of Exemplary; that was Sanchez Elementary School, in 2002. On AISD's Strategic Compensation Initiative, see www.austinisd.org/inside/initiatives/compensation (accessed July 22, 2009).

6. Heinrich Minthrop, "The Limits of Sanctions in Low-Performing Schools: A Study of Maryland and Kentucky Schools on Probation," *Education Policy Analysis Archives*, 11, no. 3 (2003), epaa.asu.edu/epaa/v11n3.html (accessed July 22, 2009); Betty Malen et al., "Reconstituting Schools: 'Testing' the 'Theory of Action,'" *Educational Evaluation and Policy Analysis*, 24, no. 2 (2002): 113–132.

7. Quotation is from Payne, *So Much Reform, So Little Change*, p. 169.

8. Calkins et al., *The Turnaround Challenge*.

9. For the elementary and secondary schools rated Academically Unacceptable in 2008, the interim chief academic officer, Claudia Tousek, presented to the superintendent and the Board of Trustees a detailed analysis of why each school was rated Unacceptable and what staff would do in 2008–2009; see AISD Board Agenda

Packet item, October 20, 2008. Randy Ross, "Is School Success Transferable?" *Education Week,* January 23, 2008, pp. 26–27.

10. AISD and the University of Texas are planning to open an innovative, high-tech middle school in East Austin in 2010. Its goals are to train UT teachers while allowing those parents with children in the UT charter elementary school to continue sending their children into upper grades, if they wish. The proposed middle school is not a charter but will be a partnership between AISD and the university. See Laura Heinauer, "UT, AISD Hook Up on Middle School Plan," *Austin American-Statesman,* April 23, 2009, www.statesman.com/news/content/news/stories/local/04/23/0423utmiddle.html (accessed July 22, 2009).

11. "Austin's Charter Schools," *Austin Chronicle,* April 4, 2003, www.austin chronicle.com/gyrobase/Issue/story?oid%A153361 (accessed July 22, 2009).

12. For evaluations of Career Academies since 1993, see James Kemple, "Career Academies: Long-Term Impacts on Labor Market Outcomes, Educational Attainment, and Transitions to Adulthood," MDRC (Manpower Demonstration Research Corp.), New York, N.Y., and Oakland, Calif., June 2008, www.mdrc.org/publications/482/full.pdf (accessed July 22, 2009).

13. On the Cisco Network Academy, see www.cisco.com/web/learning/netacad/index.html. On Hanover High School, see Ralph Mosher, Robert Kenny Jr., and Andrew Garrod, *Preparing for Citizenship: Teaching Youth to Live Democratically* (Westport, Conn.: Praeger, 1994), pp. 5–21. On Robert F. Kennedy Community High School, see schools.nyc.gov/SchoolPortals/25/Q670/default.htm (accessed July 22, 2009). On the Metropolitan Regional High School, see www.metcenter.org.

14. According to SEED's website, 97 percent of its students have entered college and 85 percent are on track to graduate. See www.seedfoundation.com (accessed July 22, 2009).

15. Dorothy Shipps, "Updating Tradition: Governing the Schools from Chicago's City Hall," New York City Public Advocate, Commission on School Governance, 209.85.173.104/search?q=cache:sK_Tw5g-tgEJ:pubadvocate.nyc.gov/advocacy/schools/documents/csgshippsreformatted.pdf+arne+duncan+dorothy+shipps&hl=en&ct=clnk&cd=11&gl=us&client=firefox-a (accessed July 22, 2009); Thomas Payzant, "The Boston Story: Success and Challenges in Systemic Education Reform," in P. Reville and C. Coggins, eds., *A Decade of Urban School Reform: Persistence and Progress in the Boston Public Schools* (Cambridge, Mass.: Harvard Education

Press, 2007), pp. 243–269; Paul Tough, *Whatever It Takes: Geoffrey Canada's Quest to Change Harlem and America* (New York: Houghton Mifflin, 2008). Also see Jeffrey Henig, "Mayoral Control: What We Can and Cannot Learn from Other Cities," in J. Viteritti, ed., *When Mayors Take Charge* (Washington, D.C.: Brookings Institution Press, 2009), p. 26; John Portz and Robert Schwartz, "Governing the Boston Public Schools: Lessons in Mayoral Control," in Viteritti, *When Mayors Take Charge*, p. 110.

16. See Larry Cuban, *How To Fix It: An Educators' Guide to Solving Problems and Managing Dilemmas* (New York: Teachers College Press, 2001).

17. Pascal Forgione Jr., interview with Larry Cuban, December 3, 2007.

18. Linda McNeil et al., "Avoidable Losses: High-Stakes Accountability and the Dropout Crisis," *Educational Policy Analysis Archives*, 16, no. 3 (2008), epaa.asu.edu/epaa/v16n3 (accessed July 22, 2009).

19. A community activist in the St. John Neighborhood Association—which helped Webb Middle School improve after the superintendent's premature closing announcement—has been involved in planning a twenty-one-point program to keep low-performing Reagan High School from being closed by the Texas Commissioner of Education. Again, district officials turned to the community at a late stage of the high school's saga, rather than collaborating earlier with neighborhoods that send their children to the school. Kimberly Reeves, "Reagan High Stands Up and Fights," *Austin Chronicle*, October 31, 2008, www.austinchronicle.com/gyrobase/Issue/story?oid=oid%3A696453 (accessed July 22, 2009).

20. Richard Whittaker, "Forgione's Long Farewell," *Austin Chronicle*, March 21, 2008, www.austinchronicle.com/gyrobase/Issue/story?oid=oid%3A603823 (accessed July 22, 2009).

21. Dakarai Aarons, "Moving On," *Education Week*, April 29, 2009, p. 28.

Acknowledgments

In writing this book, I received help from many people. First, I thank Professor Linda Darling-Hammond and Director Ray Pecheone of Stanford University's School Redesign Network for asking me to do this study and for making the necessary funds available.

The many people I interviewed in Austin gave graciously of their time; I am indebted to them for the ideas, details, and color they added to the study. In 2007–2008, Cheryl Orth, assistant to the superintendent, scheduled the interviews, arranged space for those conversations, and offered wise counsel. I am grateful for her help.

Other AISD staff members were most obliging, even when I strained their ample patience. Janis Guerrero Thompson, Director of Planning and Community Relations, extended to me the services of her department. Communications Specialist Katherine Anthony secured materials for me that I could not access, and Frances Solis helped me considerably with clipping files. Geoff Rips coordinated the feedback from AISD staff in response to the draft I sent. His comments and that of a half-dozen other administrators, including Superintendent Forgione, helped me to avoid a number of errors. Pat Forgione himself was most generous in allowing me time for many interviews, phone calls, and emails. In 2008, he also arranged for a seminar to be held on this study at the University of Texas. He was forthcoming, thoughtful, and unreservedly enthusiastic about his work in Austin.

I also wish to acknowledge the help of Peter Ross, a graduate student at Stanford University, whose dissertation on High School Redesign in Austin documents changes that occurred in the district office and in three high schools during the initial years of implementation.

Finally, I bow once more to Harvard University Press editor Elizabeth Knoll for her frank advice and unstinting support.

Index